Deportation limbo

Manchester University Press

POLITICAL ETHNOGRAPHY

The Political Ethnography series is an outlet for ethnographic research into politics and administration and builds an interdisciplinary platform for a readership interested in qualitative research in this area. Such work cuts across traditional scholarly boundaries of political science, public administration, anthropology, social policy studies and development studies and facilitates a conversation across disciplines. It will provoke a re-thinking of how researchers can understand politics and administration.

Previously published titles

The absurdity of bureaucracy: How implementation works   Nina Holm Vohnsen

Politics of waiting: Workfare, post-Soviet austerity and the ethics of freedom   Liene Ozoliņa

Diplomacy and lobbying during Turkey's Europeanisation: The private life of politics   Bilge Firat

Dramas at Westminster: Select committees and the quest for accountability   Marc Geddes

When politics meets bureaucracy: Rules, norms, conformity and cheating   Christian Lo

Deportation limbo

State violence and contestations in the Nordics

Annika Lindberg

MANCHESTER UNIVERSITY PRESS

Copyright © Annika Lindberg 2022

The right of Annika Lindberg to be identified as the author of this work has been asserted by them in accordance with the Copyright, Designs and Patents Act 1988.

An electronic version of this book is also available under a Creative Commons (CC BY-NC-ND) licence, thanks to the support of the Swiss National Science Foundation, which permits non-commercial use, distribution and reproduction provided the author(s) and Manchester University Press are fully cited and no modifications or adaptations are made. Details of the licence can be viewed at https://creativecommons.org/licenses/by-nc-nd/4.0/

Published by Manchester University Press
Oxford Road, Manchester M13 9PL

www.manchesteruniversitypress.co.uk

British Library Cataloguing-in-Publication Data

A catalogue record for this book is available from the British Library

Annika Lindberg's inaugural dissertation was submitted in the fulfilment of the requirements for the degree of Doctor rerum socialum at the Faculty of Business, Economics and Social Sciences at the University of Bern. The faculty accepted this work as dissertation on 19 September 2019 at the request of the two advisors Christian Joppke and Shahram Khosravi, without wishing to take a position on the view. The dissertation has been re-written and developed for the purpose of this monograph.

ISBN 978 1 5261 6087 4 hardback

First published 2022

The publisher has no responsibility for the persistence or accuracy of URLs for any external or third-party internet websites referred to in this book, and does not guarantee that any content on such websites is, or will remain, accurate or appropriate.

Typeset
by Deanta Global Publishing Services, Chennai, India

The power relations that characterize any historically embedded society are never as transparently clear as the names we give to them imply. Power can be invisible, it can be fantastic, it can be dull and routine. It can be obvious, it can reach you by the baton of the police, it can speak the language of your thoughts and desires. It can feel like remote control, it can exhilarate like liberation, it can travel through time, and it can drown you in the present. It is dense and superficial, it can cause bodily injury, and it can harm you without seeming ever to touch you. It is systematic and it is particularistic and it is often both at the same time. It causes dreams to live and dreams to die.

(Avery Gordon, *Ghostly Matters*, 2008: 3)

Contents

Series editors' preface	*page* viii
List of figures	x
Acknowledgements	xi
Prologue	1
Introduction: deportation fantasies	4
1 The politics of deportation and the Nordic welfare state	25
2 What you get is a prison: detention in Denmark	43
3 Deporting with care: detention in Sweden	67
4 Politics that kill, slowly: the Danish deportation camps	93
5 The idea is to exhaust them: minimum welfare provisions in Sweden	117
Conclusion: state violence and its effects	140
Epilogue: Abolfazl's death and other afterlives	151
Appendix: on methods	153
References	160
Index	185

Series editors' preface

Ethnography reaches the parts of politics that other methods cannot reach. It captures the lived experience of politics; the everyday life of political elites and street-level bureaucrats. It identifies what we fail to learn, and what we fail to understand, from other approaches. Specifically:

1. It is a source of data not available elsewhere.
2. It is often the only way to identify key individuals and core processes.
3. It identifies 'voices' all too often ignored.
4. By disaggregating organisations, it leads to an understanding of 'the black box', or the internal processes of groups and organisations.
5. It recovers the beliefs and practices of actors.
6. It gets below and behind the surface of official accounts by providing texture, depth and nuance, so our stories have richness as well as context.
7. It lets interviewees explain the meaning of their actions, providing an authenticity that can only come from the main characters involved in the story.
8. It allows us to frame (and reframe, and reframe) research questions in a way that recognises our understandings about how things work around here evolve during the fieldwork.
9. It admits of surprises – of moments of epiphany, serendipity and happenstance – that can open new research agendas.
10. It helps us to see and analyse the symbolic, performative aspects of political action.

Despite this distinct and distinctive contribution, ethnography's potential is rarely realised in political science and related disciplines. It is considered an endangered species or at best a minority sport. This series seeks to promote the use of ethnography in political science, public administration and public policy.

The series has two key aims:

1. To establish an outlet for ethnographic research into politics, public administration and public policy.
2. To build an interdisciplinary platform for a readership interested in qualitative research into politics and administration. We expect such work to cut across the traditional scholarly boundaries of political science, public administration, anthropology, organisation studies, social policy, and development studies.

R. A. W. Rhodes, Professor, University of Southampton
Nina Holm Vohnsen, Associate Professor, Aarhus University

Series editors

Figures

2.1	Illustration by Farhad, Ellebæk	*page* 44
2.2	Photo of Ellebæk detention centre	47
3.1	Evacuation plan of a Swedish detention centre	77
3.2	Notes based on drawing by Lars	84
4.1	Departure centre Sjælsmark	97
5.1	Illustration of the 'return process' by the Swedish Migration Agency	120

Acknowledgements

This book is a piece of collective work, the outcome of so many conversations and exchanges, shared frustrations, and struggles. Rather than an end product, I prefer to see the book as a part of collective thought-work in progress (although responsibility for what is between its covers is solely mine). The book is dedicated to all the remarkable people who have partaken in these collective processes, without whom the book would not have been written. I am thankful to Lisa Borrelli, who ever since we met has been an inspirational force, whose friendship has helped me think and write better, laugh more, and, when necessary, get over myself. Anna Wyss has always provided sharp and healthily sceptical comments on my writing, but has also been there through the difficult conversations on border atrocities and what researching them does to us. Shahram Khosravi was the person whose work motivated me to get into research in the first place. His writing and thinking on borders and deportation regimes, but also on what it means to be in the academic world, and the importance of looking beyond it, remains a great inspiration to me. I am thankful for his mentorship during my doctoral research, and for his encouraging involvement in this manuscript. My warm thanks to Julia Suárez-Krabbe, who has challenged and expanded my understanding of this field and who through our conversations and collaborative work has shown me how research can be done differently. And, to Steve Nwaogu Stanley, for all I have learnt from his brilliant, critical analysis of borders, from our writing, and working together, and from our friendship.

I met Steve in Sjælsmark deportation camp in 2016, and this work is indebted to the sharp analyses and courageous struggles waged by him, Baba, Naser, and the others involved in Castaway Souls to challenge the Danish deportation system. Moreover, to the efforts of Aya Jilani, with her determination to challenge the deportation regime with community and friendship; and to all those movements and communities who tirelessly organise against deportations in the Danish camps, in detention centres, and on the streets in Denmark and Sweden, and throughout Europe. I also wish to thank the state institutions, the non-governmental organisations (NGOs), and the individual frontline officials who agreed to talk to me, share their concerns, and let me hang around in their workplaces. I thank them for enduring my endless questions, and for sharing moments of frustration and disagreement, and I hope that my presence has not deterred them from remaining open to critical research in the future.

I wish to thank Manchester University Press for believing in this manuscript, and for patiently guiding me through the editorial process. Thanks to the anonymous reviewers for investing their time in providing critical feedback that made the book better, and to Ingrid Bobo Lindberg, Katarina Arnold, and Celia Aijmer Rydsjö for proofreading the manuscript and for putting full stops in my never-ending sentences.

This book builds on the intellectual labour of many brilliant scholars, some of whom are cited extensively in the book, while others have contributed in ways that go way beyond citations. These include friends and colleagues who have provided input on the research and manuscript, but even more so, those whose friendship has seen me through the good and bad days of research and writing. The book project began with my dissertation research at the University of Bern, where my appreciation goes out to Vera Truong Dinh, Irina Ciornei, Graham Hill, Tornike Metreveli, Nathalie Bardill, and others at the sociology institute for being superb friends to have as colleagues; and to Tobias Eule and Christian Joppke who supervised the PhD project. I am thankful to all the critical scholars I have met during research visits, at conferences, and during fieldwork: to Ilan Amit, Katarina Rozakou, Ioana Vrăbiescu, Victoria Canning, Francesca Esposito, Nora Stel, Maayan Ravid, Sarah Hughes, Mike Rowe, Barak Kalir, Catherine Besteman, and Mary Bosworth, who have read parts of the book manuscript and provided me with invaluable suggestions and words of encouragement. I especially wish to thank the research team at the Centre for Advanced Migration Studies, University of Copenhagen, and the marvellous friends who helped me get up each morning during the COVID-19 pandemic: Cecilie Odgaard-Jakobsen, Mirjam Wajsberg, Sif Lehman, and Tess Skadegård-Thorsen. I am also grateful for the inspiration and input I have received during conversations with Aino Korvensyrjä, Jukka Könönen, Mahmoud Keshavarz, Melanie Griffiths, Nick Gill, Amanda Schmid-Scott, Patrycja Pinkowska, Livia Johannesson, Daniel Hedlund, Sofia Häythiö, Michala Clante Bendixen, Thomas Elsted, Fedaa Sultan, Anna Lundberg, and Carolina Sanchez Boe; and for the colleagues and friends who I feel privileged to work with at the University of Gothenburg today, including Anja Franck, Sarah Philipsson-Isaac, Joseph Anderson, Avie Azis, Jessie Jern, and Alexandra Bousiou. Many of these people are engaged in the issues discussed in this book in ways that go way beyond the narrow confines of the so-called academic profession. They work within contexts where border and deportation politics are becoming more repressive, where employment is precarious (or non-existing), and where research and social engagements in this field are becoming increasingly – and negatively – politicised. I am thankful for their continuous work to challenge border violence, and for how they demonstrate that other ways of thinking and being in the world are possible.

Above all, I wish to thank my family and friends (categories which I cannot neatly separate). I am eternally grateful to Ida, Jonas, and Max Nilsson Ellemand, who have been my second family and home throughout so much of the research process. For the wit and wisdom of Nakima Ackerhans Schreiber, who always helped me ground myself, and to Andrea Andersson, Amanda Leissner, Julia Flückiger, Sofia Axelsson, Sara Holmberg, Sidsel Stausholm Andersen, Carolina Kihlström, and Emilia Rozsa Fredriksson. To Amin Parsa, for his brilliance, encouragement, and warmth, and for how our conversations have sharpened and expanded my thinking about this research field, about this world we are sharing, and most importantly, for embodying all that is loveable about it. And to my parents, Bobo and Bo Lindberg, for their unrelenting support and for believing in me, always.

Prologue

I first visited Sjælsmark on a pale April morning in 2016. The bus that took me there was empty, as were the streets connecting rows of military barracks lining up behind the camp gates as I arrived. Sjælsmark deportation camp, or departure centre (*udrejsecenter*), as it is officially called, is located in the middle of a military training field in Northern Zealand. A sort of hybrid between an asylum and detention camp, it opened in 2015 as part of the efforts of the Danish government to pressure people whose asylum applications had been rejected to leave Denmark. When it opened, most of its barracks were empty, the streets abandoned, and the fences dividing the camp into distinct zones were half-built and not yet secured. Deportations, and the intolerable policies adopted to enforce them, had yet to enter the centre stage in national debates on borders and migration, and Sjælsmark was yet to become a focal site of enforcement and contestation of the Danish deportation regime.

The absences, anticipations, and not-yets that characterised Sjælsmark at this time were probably among the reasons why the Danish Prison and Probation Service, who oversaw the camp, had agreed to let me conduct fieldwork there as part of my research on deportation enforcement. That first April day, I met the director of the camp to discuss the conditions for my research and plan the fieldwork. The director introduced himself as Niels, a middle-aged, lively Danish man with a long career in the prison service behind him. Once I had reported to the prison officer on duty, he came to greet me at the gates, wearing a full prison officer uniform: a blue shirt, tie, and cap, and a jacket with *Kriminalforsorgen* written across the back. Niels took me on a walk through the camp. The camp was still in a sort of start-up phase, he explained. Fewer residents than expected had arrived, the first couple of barracks along the street were only half full. The camp, which extended beyond our view, was therefore only partly in use, and beyond a temporarily erected fence, there were rows and rows of additional, still-empty buildings.

The camp, Niels explained, was set up to accommodate people whose asylum applications had been rejected but who refused to leave. The political intention, he continued in a matter-of-fact tone, was to make life so uncomfortable that residents would rather return to their countries of presumed origin than remain in Denmark. We passed a resident who was busy rinsing the bushes and planting flowers by the sidewalk of the main road. Niels greeted him with a jolly 'hello my friend', then turned to me:

> We call him the Gardener. He keeps it nice and clean around here, it's all on his own initiative. We would like to encourage that, maybe give him something in return, but we are not allowed to. It is not supposed to look pretty or be nice to live here – if it is, there's no reason for them to return home … but it limits us in terms of what we can do.[1]

The reason why prison officers could not reward the Gardener for his work was the so-called motivation enhancement measures, which prohibited residents from taking up work or education, compelled them to report regularly to authorities in the camp, and obliged them to eat at the camp's cafeteria at specific hours. These measures were, Niels explained, meant to make life as uncomfortable as possible for residents, discourage them from remaining and continuing leading a life in Denmark, and pressure them to cooperate with authorities in their deportation case. This was also the reason why prison officers were not allowed to encourage any activities that could make residents' experience of the camp more pleasant or liveable.

Niels took me to the cafeteria, which was still empty, as it was not yet time for residents to have their lunch. Equipped with a lunch serving consisting of potatoes, beetroot, sauce, and beef, we sat down at one of the canteen tables. Niels asked what I hoped to find out during my fieldwork. I told him that I was interested in how deportation policies were carried out in practice, what the role of the prison service was in the camp (or, as it would later turn out, what it wasn't), and what were the effects of the motivation enhancement measures. Niels nodded sincerely, as if he had been waiting for the right answer to his question, and explained that for himself and his staff, the setup of Sjælsmark was puzzling, even mysterious. As prison officers, they were trained to work with imprisoned people, whom they were supposed to assist in their rehabilitation and eventual reintegration into Danish society. In Sjælsmark, however, they were supposed to neither assist nor care for residents, nor to control them. 'We were given this task for a reason', Niels said, and added with a smirk, 'we are just not quite sure what that reason is … and we still do not know.' As for the effects of the motivation enhancement measures, he maintained that as a public official, he must not voice his opinion on the political measures he was supposed to enforce. But one thing that concerned him was the absence of a long-term plan for what would happen if residents continued to refuse to leave Denmark. The camp with its low standards was supposed to speed up their departure, but if residents kept resisting their deportation order, they could – in practice – remain in the camp indefinitely.

> But politicians haven't realised this implication. At one meeting with the management, I asked them, when do we hire a funeral undertaker in the camp? We will need one for when people start dying here. You see, I'm always the annoying one ... but it's true. Take the man we have here from a Central Asian country who already stayed twelve years in different asylum camps in Denmark. He never makes any trouble, but he has been here for a year now. He obviously thinks this place is better than going back home – so I could only imagine what it is like for him there – it must be something way worse than this.

Niels and I finished our potatoes. I was handed an electronic key that would permit me to move in and out of the buildings in the camp, including the staff building, and we agreed on a time schedule for my fieldwork. As I walked back towards the camp gates, I noticed that the Gardener had finished his work, and a few sprouts were emerging from the bare ground.

The Gardener's name was Abolfazl Salehian. He spent a long time waiting in Sjælsmark, but unlike the scenario that Niels was contemplating, he did not die there. He eventually had his asylum case re-opened and was granted a residence permit in Denmark. A couple of months after that, he died by suicide. The purpose of this book is to investigate the 'mysterious' and indeed, violent implications of states' intensified efforts to force people like Abolfazl to leave, and which sometimes take their lives. In so doing, it aims to understand the normalisation of the state violence that caused his death, and align with the ongoing struggles against it.

Note

1 All interviews were conducted in Danish and Swedish and later translated into English by the author. See more detailed information on the interviews in the Appendix.

Introduction: deportation fantasies

> If deportation is irrational, then perhaps explanations need to examine the fantasies that are made possible through deportation.
>
> *(Coutin, 2015: 667)*

Deportation is the forced physical removal of people from a given territory. A contemporary method of expulsion, it constitutes an extreme form of exclusion, yet has become a normalised part of the operation of states' mobility control regimes. States across the so-called Global North, including Denmark and Sweden, which are the focus of this book, are steadily increasing their investments in deportations and expanding the detention centres, deportation camps, and other control techniques set up to facilitate their enforcement. These investments are made despite the significant empirical evidence that such measures systematically fail to address the 'deportation gap', denoting the mismatch between the number of deportation orders issued and those enforced (Gibney, 2008). They expose non-deported people to a range of coercive and injurious conditions, such as incarceration, destitution, continuous displacement, and protracted uncertainty. Instead of making them leave, these measures circumscribe their freedoms, wear them down, and sometimes, take their lives. Deportation, therefore, is not a rational response to unruly mobility, but a form of state violence, which suspends lives and traps people in indefinite limbo.

If deportations regularly fail to fulfil their declared purpose, they are, as Susan Coutin (2015) argues, productive failures. They are productive of state violence, as manifested in the steady expansion of state-run and private security apparatuses designed to contain and regulate the mobility of primarily poor, racialised travellers in accordance with the interests of wealthy states in the Global North. Deportations create novel global connections, through international agreements and bilateral deals that trade human lives for visas, development aid, and border guard vehicles (Cassarino, 2020). They also create relationships between people who, displaced not only from the place they once came from but also from where they tried to build a new life, make up the global 'deportspora' (Khosravi, 2017a). Deportations are also crucial for politicians to maintain their fantasies that they can control immigration, as illustrated by the Swedish Minister of Immigration's promise to reclaim control over the country's borders by deporting 80,000 people within three years after the 2015 summer of migration. The fantasies materialise in expanding archipelagos of 'mysterious' enforcement sites, such as detention centres and deportation camps, where puzzled, demobilised prison officers like Niels eat their potatoes, and where non-deported people like Abolfazl Salehian are held under liminal, intolerable conditions that render them vulnerable to premature death (Gilmore, 2007).

Deportation limbo is the systemic, violent, yet normalised consequence of states' deportation fantasies and the starting point for this book. The purpose of the book is to critically examine and to comprehend the significant violence mobilised to address the deportation limbo, the functions this violence serves, how it has come to be accepted, and its consequences for the people exposed to it, and for the individuals, institutions, and societies that enforce it. A rich body of literature has documented how violent state measures, which encompass incarceration, formal abandonment, and deportability, are experienced and challenged by those affected by them across a range of contexts (see Boochani, 2018; Coutin, 2010; Djampour, 2018; Khosravi, 2009; Sager, 2011; Wyss, 2019). Building on their insights, this book adds to the comparatively limited body of literature on the institutions and frontline workers, encompassing police officers, migration officials and social workers, humanitarian organisations, and prison officers, who are tasked with enforcing detention and deportations (Bosworth, 2014; Borrelli, 2021; Walters, 2019). Using political ethnography as a method of inquiry, the book draws on fieldwork and interviews with key actors and organisations involved in deportation enforcement. In doing so, the book traces how deportation regimes, and the dehumanisation they are premised on, impact and reconfigure the states, societies, and subjectivities of all those involved in their enforcement and contestation. It demonstrates why these practices must end.

The research has been conducted in a time when deportation emerged as a key focus of the politics of migration in the two countries examined in the book, Denmark and Sweden, as well as in Europe as a whole. The intensification of hostile and criminalising political rhetoric targeting 'undesired' non-citizens, and the subsequent reification of border controls, expansion of detention facilities, and withdrawal of essential welfare for those positioned as rejected, illegalised, and negatively racialised, demarcate the limit and, indeed, constitutive negative of Nordic egalitarianism, liberalism, and welfarism. The deportation limbo renders visible the racial borders of the welfare state and the struggles and contestations they give rise to. It is my hope that this book will add to existing knowledge – derived from research, from lived experiences, and from the struggles against deportations – of how deportation regimes operate, how the violence they rely on has come to be normalised, and what this violence does to the individuals, states, and societies that enact it.

Deportation as the locus and limit of state control

Deportation is the 'compulsory removal of "aliens" from the physical, juridical, and social space of the state' (Peutz and De Genova, 2010: 1). A form of forced displacement, it belongs to a longer history of expulsions, where people have been forcibly displaced as part of colonial conquests and genocides, for the purpose of land appropriations and resource extraction, and as collective or individual punishment (Walters, 2002). Within the growing field of deportation studies, researchers have analysed the driving forces, daily operation, and lived experiences of this now 'standardized instrument of statecraft' (Peutz and De Genova, 2010: 3; see Borrelli, 2021; Coutin, 2015; Drotbohm and Hasselberg, 2015; Khosravi, 2017a, 2019; Peutz, 2006; Walters, 2016). To explain the steady expansion of deportation regimes, especially in the Global North, researchers have analysed how deportations expand and reconfigure state powers in a time when states are presumed to have 'lost control' over cross-border mobility of humans, goods, and capital (Sassen, 1996: 5). Deportation has also been analysed as a nation-building device: as a 'technology of citizenship' (Walters, 2002: 282), it is used to delineate the boundaries of membership in the national community. As such, deportation also forms part of an 'infrastructure of racism' (Khosravi, 2019: 114) that serves to confine or expel people to 'their' assigned place in a hierarchical, racialised global order. Deportation has also become a global industry, which provides employment and profits to punitive and military branches of the state apparatus, private security and technology companies, humanitarian and non-governmental organisations (NGOs), and technocratic experts (Golash-Boza, 2015; Hiemstra, 2020).

These driving forces help explain why we have seen a steady growth in budgets, infrastructures, and sites of detention and deportation in the first two decades of the twenty-first century, in particular in states across the Global North (Besteman, 2020). In the European[1] context, which this book focuses on, the gradual expansion of states' deportation regimes as well as efforts by the European Commission to harmonise deportations among EU member states have been driven by the strategic linking together of notions of 'uncontrolled' migration and issues of crime, terrorism, and threats to the welfare and labour rights of citizens. The development of the

European deportation regime is illustrative of how political deportation fantasies (Coutin, 2015) extend and expand coercive regulatory powers at the expense of migrants' freedoms, rights, and lives.

The expansion, harmonisation, and codification of the deportation capacity of states, in addition to the numerical increase in enforced deportations during the 2000s, prompted scholars to declare a 'deportation turn' (Gibney, 2008: 146) in European migration control regimes. The *Directive 2008/115/EC on common standards and procedures in Member States for returning illegally staying third-country nationals*, or the 2008 Returns Directive, provided a first comprehensive legal framework for the deportation of people lacking legal authorisation to remain in the EU, and set out common standards for the state-sanctioned violence permitted to ensure its enforcement.[2] A renewed deportation turn has arguably taken place since the 2015 long summer of migration. In its proposal for a New Pact on Asylum and Migration, the European Commission (2020) placed 'returns' as 'the main driving force for reform' (Moraru, 2021), and presented measures for strengthening and harmonising member states' capacity to identify, arrest, and deport 'illegally staying third-country nationals'. The proposal contains nothing 'new' but suggests more of the same measures: more coercive measures such as detention and surveillance with reduced legal safeguards, renewed investments in militarised border agencies such as the EU Border and Coast Guard Agency (Frontex), and more neocolonial readmission agreements with countries of deportation (El Qadim, 2014), in which deportable people are traded in return for development aid, trade concessions, and visa facilitation (Cassarino, 2020). As demonstrated in numerous reports by migrant activist networks and research publications, these measures 'fail' to fulfil their ostensible purpose, while causing detrimental harm to deportable people's lives, rights, and freedoms (Freedom of Movements Research Collective, 2018; Statewatch, 2020). Indeed, throughout the 2010s, at the same time as European states have stepped up their deportation capacity, European states have deported around 200,000 people annually (Eurostat, 2019). The numbers encompass deportations from EU member states to so-called third countries as well as 'transfers' between European states in accordance with the Dublin Regulation, which permits signatory states to deport people back to the state where they first entered or sought asylum in Europe.[3] Still, the over two million people deported in the past decade constitute less than half of the close to five million people who received an order to leave EU member states in the same time period (Eurostat, 2020). For deportations to countries outside the EU, the share of 'effective returns' drops below 30 per cent. Those who remain continue to haunt European governments, and the reasons hereto are several.

The people who make up the European 'deportation gap' have ended up with a deportation order for various reasons, ranging from an unauthorised entry, a rejected asylum application or a denied prolongation of protection status, an overstayed visa, or a criminal conviction. Some were illegalised immediately upon entry into Europe; others have switched several times between different legal statuses during their stay. Some are pushed back or deported only after a couple of hours, days, or weeks, while others have defied their deportation orders and remained in Europe for years or decades. Yet others have lived their entire lives without residence permit or citizenship, under threat of forced displacement from the country where they were born. I refer to all of those who have received a deportation order but who cannot or refuse to comply *the non-deported*. They have vastly different trajectories, life histories, and reasons for remaining in Europe, yet share the condition of living under threat of deportation, although their *de facto* deportability is unevenly distributed along the lines of race, class, gender, and national origin (De Genova, 2016). Many have invested significant time and money and risked their lives to reach Europe. Many have also built lives, families, friendships, and communities in the country they risk being deported from, and many fear what would await them post deportation. These people, and the situation they find themselves in, challenge states' deportation efforts in a number of ways.

First, and most importantly, the majority of those who are ordered to leave contest and resist deportations. They may refuse to disclose their identity, destroying or forging documents and signifiers (Keshavarz, 2018); go underground; or move on to another state (Wyss, 2019). They also deploy visible resistance strategies 'in the courts or on the street' (Gibney, 2008: 147), appealing deportation orders and mobilising protests or sit-ins, or physically blocking deportations (Ataç, Rygiel, and Stierl, 2016; Nyers, 2019). A second reason why deportations cannot be enforced is found in international politics: deportations might be halted due to human rights constraints, notably the principle of non-*refoulement*; or, a country may refuse to accept back their citizens or stateless persons (SOU (Statens Offentliga Utredningar) 2017:84). A third set of factors include practical or bureaucratic hurdles to enforcement, such as missing travel documents; slow, protracted bureaucratic processes (Eule et al., 2019); or logistical reasons, such as a lack of travel routes and closed borders – or an ongoing pandemic. Hence, the continued presence of the non-deported challenges the exclusionary efforts of states.

Non-deported people are 'physically present but legally ambiguous' (Coutin, 2010: 201); in legal terms, they 'should not exist' (Heegaard Bausager et al., 2013: 4). Their presence disrupts political fantasies of a linear deportation process and of a world where bodies neatly belong within state borders and are kept in 'their' place within the national order of things (Malkki, 1995). Even as states have an interest in tacitly tolerating their existence – non-deported people often serve as a highly precarious and exploitable labour force (De Genova, 2002) – their 'haunting' presence serves as a reminder of the limits of state control over mobility. This condition exposes them to a range of violent state practices mobilised to enforce their physical, political, and legal disappearance from the territory, including forced expulsion, incarceration, and criminalisation, and indefinite encampment and destitution. To capture the condition that enables and activates these different forms of state violence, I develop the term *deportation limbo*, which encompasses a condition of liminal legality, temporal uncertainty, and physical and social marginalisation. Rather than a mere 'implementation gap', I argue that limbo emerges as a systemic, if not consciously orchestrated, effect of states' deportation fantasies.

Locating the deportation limbo

> This is not heaven, it is not hell. It's torture to keep people here for long when they cannot deport you. People shouldn't stay in a situation like this.

This is how Aya, an activist and resident of Avnstrup deportation camp in Denmark, describes the torturous condition of being stuck in non-deportability, in a state of in-betweenness, of being in limbo. Etymologically, 'limbo' stems from Latin and means 'edge' or 'border'. Limbo is also the first circle of hell in Dante Alighieri's epic poem *Inferno*, the first part of *The Divine Comedy*. Dante's hell encompasses nine circles, each with its own horrors. As the threshold of hell, limbo is inhabited by those who are without guilt but are condemned to live in a lesser form of heaven. Limbo is a condition that does not result from choice but from the lack thereof.

'Limbo' was a term frequently used by people holding different positions in the deportation regime. Some people who, like Aya, lived in a state of non-deportability used limbo to describe the feeling of being physically and existentially stuck, of torturous and meaningless waiting. Somewhat ironically, I also heard frustrated state officials claim to be 'in limbo' when confronted with the non-deportability of people who either resisted deportation, or whose presumed countries of origin refused to accept them. As one migration official told me, 'there are cases where we can't do shit. What politicians and the media don't seem to understand, is that we cannot just simply put people on a plane.' Meanwhile, activists and migrants' rights advocates have used 'limbo' to draw attention to the absurd and adverse consequences of the restrictive interpretations of immigration law that render non-deported people stuck in a condition where they are denied the right to remain but cannot be forced to leave (see Lundberg, 2017). What these different experiences of 'limbo' have in common is a sense of what Ghassan Hage (2009: 97) has termed 'stuckedness', the deprivation of choice or direction, frustration and resignation before 'the system', and experiences of neglect and abandonment. In academic research and reports, limbo has been a term used to capture the 'legal in-betweenness' (Cabot, 2012: 17) characterising the situation for people who are waiting for their asylum applications to be processed, or the lived experience of those who are indefinitely trapped in camps and border zones (Boochani, 2018; Mountz, 2011). Others have used it to describe the condition of protracted (non-) deportability (Clante Bendixen, 2011; De Coulon, 2015). Finally, in legal terms, limbo has been referred to as the particular situation where a person can neither be forcibly deported nor qualify for residence permit (SOU 2017:84). Building on these different yet interconnected captions, I propose a definition that accounts for the torturous and injurious effects of being in limbo, but also for its internal contradictions and contestations.

The conceptualisation of deportation limbo that I propose entails, first, a condition of *liminal legality*, where people lacking fixed status are 'at once no longer classified and not yet classified' (Turner, 1967: 96, cited in Menjívar, 2006: 1007). Legal limbo is systemically produced through restrictive interpretations of immigration and asylum law, but also through contradictions within the legal system. Rather than simply being excluded by law, the condition of liminal legality renders people 'simultaneously accountable to the law but also excludes them from legal protections or rights' (Menjívar and Abrego, 2012: 1385). As this book will demonstrate, liminal legality is not constructed through exceptionality, but through an intricate web of laws that render people's entire lives into objects of regulation, discipline, and criminalisation. Hence, limbo is a condition that marginalises: non-deported people generally have limited or no access to jobs, housing, education, and healthcare. It is a condition that disciplines, as it keeps people vulnerable to the unpredictable violence of detention, destitution, and deportation. It is economically and politically generative, since non-deported people can be used to fuel the border industrial complex and as exploitable labour (De Genova, 2002), or be instrumentalised as scapegoats in racist political discourse (Elsrud, 2020). Second, the deportation limbo materialises in certain *spatial* configurations: as a bordering process, deportation not only delineates an inside and outside of a territory but also produces liminal spaces in between. Geographer Alison Mountz (2020: 23) has suggested that the border 'as a site of crossing has been replaced by "revolving door" and legal limbo'. This shift is manifested in the expanding archipelago of detention camps and other confinement-like sites (see

Bosworth, 2014; Gill, 2016; Turner et al., 2022), but the 'revolving doors' can also be found in the waiting halls of bureaucratic offices, police stations, and homelessness shelters (Schmid-Scott, 2018). These sites are interconnected as non-deported people are pushed back and forth between them as a 'floating population of exiles' (Sanchez Boe, forthcoming). This brings us to the third dimension of the deportation limbo, which is its *temporal* indeterminacy. Non-deportability implies a state of suspended, even permanent impermanence (Bendixsen and Eriksen, 2018; Brun, 2015), which might last for a few days or go on for decades. In this process, people's time is stolen (Khosravi, 2019) and weaponised to wear them down into compliance by trapping them in a protracted state of waiting, or by pushing them into incessant circulation through repeated cycles of deportation and re-migration (Canning and Bhatia, 2021). Nevertheless, law, space, and time can also be appropriated as sites and means of struggle, as non-deported people contest deportation orders, keep on living their lives, and 'wait out' the state (Hage, 2009). Deportation limbo is therefore a site where we can observe the violent efforts by state authorities to retain control over unruly mobility, and to produce and enforce distinctions between those whose lives are valuable, and which ones are disposable. Yet these are also sites where we encounter the limits of these control efforts, and the fissures and gaps between state fantasies of effective enforcement, and the messy, violent realities they generate.

Deportation and the COVID-19 pandemic

At the time of writing, in 2022, the COVID-19 pandemic is still ongoing. It has drastically affected the conditions of mobility within and across state borders worldwide. At the onset of the pandemic, containing human mobility was among the first, almost automated, reactions by governments trying to address the uncontrolled spread of the virus (Anderson, 2020). In European countries, the virus was framed as an exterior threat, as were cross-border travellers (as well as minoritised citizens, who were politically stigmatised and blamed for their disproportionate exposure to illness), leading to increases in the use of pushbacks and confinement directly at state borders under the pretext of protecting public health (see Ghezelbash and Tan, 2021). Next to border closures, the pandemic sparked a proliferation of confinement practices such as mandatory quarantines, ostensibly for the protection of citizens and border crossers alike, although confinement often turned out to be 'anything but protective' (Tazzioli and Stierl, 2021: 78), instead exposing people to heightened risks of contagion and other harms to their health.

The health hazard resulting from migration-related confinement led the European Commissioner for Human Rights (2020) and the United Nations High Commissioner for Human Rights (2020) to call on states to release incarcerated migrants from facilities where it was impossible to maintain physical distancing. For a brief period, some European governments, such as Spain, followed the recommendations, and released people from detention; and in Portugal, non-deported people were formally granted access to welfare services (although access remained limited in practice). Several countries temporarily suspended deportations within Europe, as air traffic nearly came to a halt. Yet, they soon resumed. Overall, the very limited regard that governments paid to the health of non-deported people and others with precarious legal status has led researchers to suggest that the pandemic has supplemented the 'global mobility apartheid' (Balibar, 2004: 9) with a 'sanitary apartheid' (Heller, 2021: 113), in which mobility control regimes are used as measures to differentiate between people whose lives are worth safeguarding from the virus, COVID-19, and lives that can be put at risk. Sanitary mobility apartheid does not only endanger the health of the people who are contained, confined, or deported, but also captures the disregard for how deportations spread the virus to their countries of presumed origin (ECRE, 2020). The Afghan government pleaded to European countries to halt all deportations during the pandemic, as the country was already struggling to provide care for citizens returning from neighbouring countries. Their demands went unheard.

The Nordic countries are cases in point here. During the pandemic, I have been engaged in efforts initiated by migrants' advocacy groups to investigate conditions of detained and deportable people in Denmark and Sweden (see Ellebæk contact network, 2020; Häythiö et al., 2020). In Denmark, we initially saw the number of detained people drop between March and June 2020. Denmark also suspended Dublin deportations to prevent further transmission within Europe. However, Danish authorities continued trying to carry out deportations to countries outside Europe, and no initiative was taken to release detained people who, due to international travel restrictions, were non-deportable. Meanwhile, in Denmark's crammed detention and deportation camps, authorities introduced further restrictions to people's freedoms, adding to the lack of safety and sense of uncertainty already experienced by many detained people (Stokholm et al., 2021).

In Sweden, authorities declared at the onset of the pandemic that they would continue detaining and deporting people as usual. In April 2020, the Swedish Network of Asylum and Refugee Support (FARR) conducted a survey among detained people to investigate how far authorities had followed their own regulations for how to protect detained people from the virus. I partook in the analysis of the survey, which demonstrated significant shortcomings in authorities' implementation of rules and guidelines for how to prevent the virus from spreading inside detention facilities (Häythiö et al., 2020). We found that no measures were taken to facilitate access to healthcare, shelter, food, or sanitary facilities for homeless migrants at risk of deportation (Lindberg et al., 2020). Hence, the pandemic has, if anything, exposed states' continuous prioritisation of migration enforcement over non-deported people's health. The fact that deportations have continued to operate with 'tick-tock regularity' (Mountz, 2020: 13) during this time demonstrates that the global health 'crisis' has only reified the uneven distribution of vulnerability and access to mobility along the lines of race and class on a global scale. If anything, it makes the study of the state violence that maintains these structures even more pertinent.

A continuum of state violence: defining the stakes and the state

Annika: Could you tell me what a deportation process looks like?

Henrik: The best-case scenario is when a deportation proceeds without us having to pacify the deportee; that is, when we don't need to use force. I also have to say, that if we have a layover in a country, I try to have a look around as it will usually be a country that I would not have visited privately. I can get some insights into the local conditions there.

Annika: And what kind of scenarios do you find particularly challenging?

Henrik: The most challenging cases are when there are children around, and when they have to watch as we pacify their mother, their father or both, because they are making trouble and try to resist the deportation. And more generally, it can be incredibly challenging if the deportee resists all the way, if they make a number two into the diaper that we put on them. If we suspect that a deportee might shit themselves during the deportation, we put a diaper on them before we get them in the car from the detention centre to the airport. This way, we prevent such accidents from happening.

Henrik is a Danish border police officer whose primary job is to enforce deportations. Our conversation took place in 2017 at the border police headquarters, which used to be the site – until the so-called Danish Return Agency (*Hjemrejsestyrelsen*) took over in 2020 – where deportations from Denmark were scheduled, identity documents checked, flight tickets booked, and the act of deportation meticulously planned by the police. Henrik describes a successful deportation as a smooth operation entailing minimal use of 'pacification' measures, which he uses as a code word for physical force. His ideal scenario is that the person in question 'voluntarily' cooperates in the deportation process – and Henrik gets the opportunity to explore a novel travel destination. In Henrik's account, we can discern two parallel realities: one in which deportation is a professionalised procedure of calculated, routinised, and 'strangely technical choreography of "non-lethal" force' (Makaremi, 2018), and where the deportation itself is an event, and an opportunity for an explorative journey. In the parallel reality, the 'event' of corporal removal is but one stage in a protracted deportation process, which might already have plagued and disrupted the deportable person's life and social relations for years (Drotbohm and Hasselberg, 2016). For the person who is deported, the 'event' of deportation, as Henrik readily admits, is likely to be experienced as turbulent, traumatising, violent, and degrading.

Henrik's account of deportation enforcement only captures a fraction of the deportation process and represents only one extreme end of a *continuum* of state violence mobilised to govern the deportation limbo. My understanding of this violent continuum, and of the context-specific politics of naming it as 'violence', emerged through conversations with people holding very different positions in the deportation regime. From state officials like Henrik, I learnt about the various discursive and material techniques – from codified language to manuals and the technification of force – they used to obscure the violent nature of deportation, and how this violence run through them. Meanwhile, resident activists in the Danish deportation camps taught me about the other end of the continuum: namely, the 'slow' violence of imposed isolation, and the structural violence of poverty and formal abandonment.

The violence of the deportation limbo comes in multiple forms and mobilises a range of state and non-state actors. Studying the operation of this violence offers a lens for understanding the actors, processes, and practices that constitute 'the state' at the border. Following Trouillot (2001: 127), I understand 'the state' not as a unitary apparatus but as a 'set of processes' and practices, which constantly produce new spaces for the deployment of power. This book builds on anthropological and sociological scholarship looking at how 'the state' materialises through the enactment of violence, which can be direct and coercive (Fassin, 2014; Sutton and Vigneswaran, 2011), indirect and structural (Gupta, 2012; Povinelli, 2011), symbolic and stupefying (Graeber, 2012), magical (Taussig, 1997), and always, affective (Aretxaga, 2000; Laszczkowski and Reeves, 2017; Stoler, 2004). More specifically, the book traces the expansion and reconfiguration of state powers taking place through the deployment of a *continuum of violence*, mobilised to govern the non-deported. I borrow the notion of a violent continuum from Scheper-Hughes and Bourgeois (2003:1), who include in this concept direct acts of physical violence; structural violence, including exposure to 'poverty, hunger, social exclusion and humiliation'; and symbolic violence, which reconfigures the subjectivities of those affected, as continuous and complementary forms of violence. Translated into the context of deportation regimes, we can identify direct forms of violence in the forced deportation proceeding described by Henrik, and in the violent pushbacks taking place at the EU's external borders (Border Violence Monitoring Network, 2020). We also find it in the routine incarceration of non-deported people in prison-like detention camps, where they are routinely exposed to degrading treatment, physical and verbal abuse, and arbitrary deprivations of rights and liberties (Arbogast, 2016). The use of direct, corporal violence, and the significant efforts made to mask, redress, and legitimise it and its harmful effects, are discussed in Chapters 2 and 3.

Of equal importance to understanding how states govern the deportation limbo are the structural forms of violence (Galtung, 1969), which include protracted exposure to impoverishment, degradation and isolation, absence of healthcare, and everyday exclusion. In contrast to the spectacularised violence of coercive control, structural violence is enforced through the removal of possibilities to sustain a liveable life; through encampment (Davies, Isakjee, and Dhesi, 2017), impoverishment (Mayblin, Wake, and Kazemi, 2019), and formal abandonment (Kalir and van Schendel, 2017). These forms of violence often go unrecognised, since the harms they inflict are not immediately visible: they are expressions of 'slow' violence, which kills by 'letting die' (Povinelli, 2011) or, in the words of activists in the Danish deportation camps, which 'kills you, slowly' (Castaway Souls, 2016). The notion of 'slow' violence also highlights how time is weaponised as a technique of control and discipline (Khosravi, 2019), and how it causes protracted harms that may last longer than the violence itself. Slow violence helps us to capture the haunting relation between the lasting violence of the deportation limbo and the premature death of Abolfazl Salehian. This connection is explored in Chapters 4 and 5.

Understanding state violence as a continuum challenges the notion that violence is exceptional, manifested only in instances of (extra-legal) abuse or rights violations. The prevalence of extra-legal violence in deportation processes has been extensively documented in research reports by human rights organisations, and migrants' advocacy groups (Asylum Commission, n.d.; Danish Institute for Human Rights, 2016; Freedom of Movements Research Collective, 2018; Arbogast, 2016; Statewatch, 2020). There are also examples of such violations here. However, the systemic forms of violence detailed here – from the routine, administrative incarceration of people for 'motivational' purposes and forced testing for COVID-19 for the purpose of deportation enforcement, to the denial of access to food, shelter, and medical treatment – are all, as Menjívar and Abrego (2012, 1387) argue, 'embedded in legal practices, sanctioned, actively implemented through formal procedures, and legitimated – and consequently seen as "normal" and natural because it "is the law"'. Re-politicising these practices as violence is a step towards denaturalising them and calling into question the artificial distinctions between 'violence' and 'force', and between 'voluntary' and 'forced' deportations. Indeed, tracing the continuum of state violence mobilised to govern non-deported people not only enables a comprehensive documentation of the human costs at stake in the increasingly restrictive, deportation-oriented European politics of migration. It also enables an exploration of the systemic, and, indeed, constitutive function of this specific form of border violence for 'the state' as such.

Borders produce categories of citizens and non-citizens, and assign them hierarchies of value, rights, and freedoms. Borders are 'infrastructures' of racism (Khosravi, 2019: 421), which generate group-specific vulnerabilities, including physical, social, and psychological injuries, and cause deaths (Gilmore, 2007) that are either intentional or foreseeable. Postcolonial and abolitionist scholars have underscored the colonial roots of border regimes (Davis and Dent, 2000; Mongia, 2018; Samaddar, 2020), and how the racially hierarchical worldviews that emerged during this era continue to characterise borders in the present (Mayblin et al., 2019; Sharma, 2021). Borders rely on a hierarchical division of humanity, which devalues a large proportion of the world's population to the status of non-human (Grosfoguel et al., 2015), denying them access to mobility freedom, resources, and a liveable life. Borders' inherently racial logic and the coloniality of the mechanisms used for their enforcement have led scholars to describe the global mobility regime as a system of apartheid (Balibar, 2004; Besteman, 2020). Indeed, even as racial categorisations have vanished from the official vocabulary of border and immigration law, this legal regime perpetuates a hierarchical conception of humanity founded on racial matrices. We see 'race' re-appear in the political discourses that portray racialised[4] travellers as a threat to the culture, values, and security of their nations; and in the uneven exposure to border violence, including policing, detention, and deportation. Racism, then, is what normalises the state-sanctioned production and exploitation of racialised border crossers' vulnerability to premature death (Gilmore, 2007: 28).

Addressing the foundational role of racism in states' border-making projects is important to understand how the state-sanctioned violence detailed in this book, including incarceration, deportation, destitution, and dehumanisation of non-deported people, becomes publicly accepted as part of the normal operation of 'migration enforcement'. It also enables us to deconstruct and move beyond the often-cited 'paradox' that the Nordic states, which proclaim their commitment to values such as humanitarianism, egalitarianism, and universal welfare, simultaneously engage in violent exclusion of those conceived as others (cf. Barker, 2013; Franko, 2020). Approaching race as a systemic and structuring feature of border and deportation regimes also takes discussions on racism beyond individual or group attitudes circulating among those propagating and enforcing deportations, including frontline officials and the broader public. It permits us to see how the violence that deportation mobilises comes to be perceived as acceptable, even necessary, and possible to enforce with 'the best intentions'.

A political ethnography of deportation enforcement

This book centres on the institutions and actors enforcing violence at the border. They are at once involved in the dehumanisation of non-deported people and, as I will argue, dehumanised and brutalised through this very same process. My interest in 'studying up' (Nader, 1972) the structures and actors of deportation enforcement departed from my personal experience of working as an asylum caseworker at the Swedish Migration Agency between 2012 and 2013. My role was to process asylum applications, conduct asylum interviews, and write decisions on residence permits, but also detention and deportation orders. I was unsettled by the speed at which we were expected to conduct asylum interviews, by the default suspicion inscribed in the procedure, by the abrupt silencing – of grief, of anger, and of the messiness of lived realities – that characterised the formulaic re-ordering of people's asylum narratives as they were recorded and routinely copy-pasted into asylum decisions. I learnt that 'refugeeness' was a label that was granted or rejected depending on which decision maker I consulted, on the universalising and inferiorising stereotypes they held about certain national groups, on their mood of the day – or on what they had for lunch. I felt how the bureaucratic stupidity described by David Graeber (2012), and the social indifference outlined by Michael Herzfeld (1992), dehumanised the people behind the case files, and reduced me as a caseworker to a function of red tape and an almost fictional role in a performance of due process. I also noticed how we as asylum caseworkers were remarkably disconnected from the implications of the decisions we made: as a fellow caseworker once noted, we had never been asked whether we knew or told what a detention or deportation order implied before we started issuing them.

None of these observations would surprise the people who have been through an asylum procedure, or the lawyers and advocates who support them – or the bureaucratic officials working within the system of migration control. Yet the experiences informed the questions I asked in this research, and the people I asked them to. Accordingly, this research has focused on how state violence translates into everyday practice, and how the actors tasked with enforcing it interpret, perform, justify, or refute their role in these violent arrangements. As anthropologist Laura Nader (1972: 284) argued, 'studying up' permits us to critically examine the 'processes whereby power and responsibility are exercised', and, I would add, how power and (ir)responsibility operates on those who are enacting it. In taking a political ethnographic approach as a method for studying these processes, this book adds to the work of critical migration and border scholars who have used political ethnography to analyse external and internal bordering practices (Eule et al., 2019; Hiemstra, 2020; Kapoor and Narkowicz, 2019), decision making in visa procedures (Infantino, 2021), asylum decision making (Cabot, 2012; Johannesson, 2017), migration-related detention (Bosworth, 2014; Gill, 2016; Hall, 2010), and deportation processes (Borrelli, 2021; Sutton and Vigneswaran, 2011). This body of research has demonstrated how 'street-level bureaucrats' (Lipsky, 1980), who interact directly with border crossers in their everyday work and make decisions that impact their lives, play an important role in making and reconfiguring border regimes 'on the ground'. In this book, I use a similar approach, while also expanding the common definition of street-level officials to encompass professionals working for NGOs in close collaboration with state authorities or even on state contracts. As previous research has discussed, their role as gatekeepers of rights and benefits, and their position vis-à-vis non-deported people, is often similar to that of state officials (see Kalir and Wissink, 2016; Lindberg, 2020b). I therefore understand all these actors as *frontline workers* (see Borrelli and Trasciani, 2019) who are 'petty empowered ... the dominated segment of the dominant' (Marcus, 2000: 3); at once complicit in and subjected to the control and discipline they are enacting.

Here, the crucial questions must be asked of whether centring state agents does not entail a risk that the voices and perspectives of the dominant are amplified at the expense of those oppressed in the deportation regime. While the ethics and politics of this research are discussed in further length in the Appendix, I want to reflect on the ethical-political question posed by Tuck and Yang (2014: 223): 'How do we develop an ethics for research that differentiates between power – which deserves a denuding, indeed petrifying scrutiny – and people?'. In their article on ethnographic refusals, Tuck and Yang (2014; see also Simpson, 2008) take issue with the common assumption that research is always the intervention that is required, and necessarily an act of good. They criticise the routine extraction and commodification of oppressed people's stories of pain and suffering and highlight the symbolic and epistemic violence that characterise much of academic practice. Border and migration research is not spared from such criticism but has been problematised as a research industry that with its obsession with border crossers, naturalises and reifies the state-centric order it should be calling into question (Cabot, 2019). Moreover, the field has been called out for extracting and profiting from the stories of and about 'others' without ever acknowledging these others as knowledgeable subjects (Khosravi, 2020; for a discussion on the uneven distribution of power and labour and coloniality of knowledge in 'migration studies', see Cabot, 2019; Fiddian-Qasmiyeh, 2020). The border and migration research field as practised in the European context also tends to reproduce hegemonic, Northern- and state-centric, sedentary perspectives (Bejarano et al., 2019), where border crossers are produced as anomalies to the national order of things, and ahistorically posited as 'outsiders' of nation states (Malkki, 1995). Meanwhile, what is obscured in such accounts are the historical and ongoing global processes of colonialism, violent dispossession, and exploitation that have shaped 'the state' and produced the figure of 'the migrant' in the first place.

This research is embedded in and part of these problematic structures of academic knowledge production. Yet it is my hope that, by turning the lens towards the structures and actors that generate and perpetuate the conditions that cause suffering, illegalisation, and dehumanisation, rather than towards the people targeted by these practices, the book will contribute to the 'denuding' (Tuck and Yang, 2014) of power. Relatedly, if research on state actors runs the risk of reifying ideas of 'the state' as a unitary, bounded, and fixed object of analysis (Abrams, 1988), I maintain that the risk of essentialising and naturalising 'the state' as a container of political and social analysis is even greater if we do not critically scrutinise the ideas and violent practices through which it materialises. The potential of political ethnography to challenge the bordered order that deportation fantasies are meant to perform lies in its ability not only to uncover but to contextualise and re-politicise the often messy, violent, and contested processes that seek to naturalise the national order as the natural order of things.

The research: patchworks of ethnographic observations and engagements

State control of non-deported people is carried out in migration offices and police stations, in migration-related detention and deportation camps, in social welfare offices – and on the streets. Many of these sites are remote, securitised, and inaccessible places, obscured from public view (Mountz, 2020). To some extent, this invisibility is orchestrated and serves distinctive political ends, with implications for how far, and under what conditions, they can be researched (Bosworth and Kellezi, 2016; Kalir et al., 2019). The detention and deportation camps where non-deported people are held in Denmark are embedded in the security branch of the state apparatus; in Sweden, they form part of a highly politicised bureaucratic field. In both contexts, 'the field' of deportation enforcement is messy and ever-changing, the sites of enforcement constantly reconfigured through political and legislative amendments and bureaucratic re-organisation. As a result, the trajectory of my research was messy, too. It was contingent upon uneven and partial access to detention and deportation camps, which I was granted through a piecemeal process: partly because of luck, and partly due to gendered prejudice and white privilege.

Research access is one of the processes where the racialised, gendered, and classed division of labour within academic research is manifested (see Vanyoro, Hadj-Abdou, and Dempster, 2019). In this case, whiteness, understood a structural position of social privilege, led research participants to ascribe me a position of shared belonging with the 'state' and 'nations' they worked for vis-à-vis the deportable 'others'. As such, I was perceived as harmless, which enabled my access to securitised state institutions. The formal access that I was eventually granted remained partial and time limited. The research project is therefore better described as a 'patchwork ethnography', which Günel, Varma, and Watanabe (2020) describe as a method combining 'short-term field visits, using fragmentary yet rigorous data', with 'long-term commitments, and contextual knowledge', yet which also acknowledges the changing nature both of the field and of the living and working conditions that structure how and under what conditions we conduct our research. My research consisted of several shorter stints of fieldwork combined with long-term relational engagements, and therefore differs from 'traditional' ethnographic research projects (the standard against which my research, and the research of other precariously employed junior scholars, is regularly measured). The research encompassed several month-long periods of fieldwork, including observation studies inside locked migration detention centres in both Denmark and Sweden, in a Danish deportation camp, and in migration offices and departure housing units in Sweden. These observations were complemented by interviews with police officers, lawyers, social workers, and representatives of NGOs and migrants' advocacy groups in both countries; a full list of sites of observation and interviews is provided in the Appendix.

The fieldwork in detention and deportation camps focused on the frontline workers involved in enforcing deportations and included participant observation and interviews. My fieldwork schedule usually followed the shifts of officers, and I followed frontline workers in their everyday work, observing their interactions with each other and with detained or deportable people. As I spent time with staff while they were undertaking their daily tasks (which, among other things, included monitoring surveillance cameras, escorting detained people around the premises, or registering information in their case files), and had endless cups of coffee on the couches or armchairs in staff offices, I became familiar with what officials did, and what they did not do; what they saw, and what they chose not to see; what they said, and what they did not bother to talk about. During research inside detention – arguably among the most ethically and politically fraught among the research sites – being a white woman of relatively young age fixed my position in the racial, gendered, sexual, and classed order of the detention regimes. I stopped counting the times I was told, 'we don't mind some additional female company' and 'you don't look so dangerous to me'. As a woman and junior researcher, I was also variably sexualised by research participants (in particular by white men) or ascribed the position of a vulnerable object of care and protection, especially in the hypermasculinised Danish deportation prison. It also allowed me to benefit from what Zachary Whyte has suggested we call 'mansplaining as method', as officials regularly sought to re-educate me and challenge my 'leftist and politically correct' opinion on matters of migration, crime, and state violence. Through our conversations, then, I learnt of their perceptions of their roles, how they practised them, and the consequences of the policies they were enforcing. The interviews with police officers, lawyers, social workers, and representatives of NGOs and migrants' support groups provided complementary perspectives on the ways in which deportations are enforced and contested, on the positioning of the different 'arms' of the state in relation to one another. They enabled me to trace how authorities sought to control, regulate, and make disappear non-deported people beyond the sites of confinement, and how they balanced the intertwined logics of care and repression in their everyday work.

Next to my research on the agents of enforcement of states' deportation regimes, the book is informed by the ongoing struggles against deportations organised by and in support of non-deported people in Denmark and Sweden. The testimonies from non-deported people cited in this book come mostly from people involved in these struggles. Their analyses of deportation regimes, stemming from their lived and situated knowledge of state violence, have informed this book to a great extent: from how Castaway Souls named the 'slow violence' of the Danish deportation camps, to the insights about the ambivalent positioning of humanitarian actors within the deportation regime. The extracts from conversations with people living the deportation limbo have taken place in Danish deportation camps, at demonstrations and sit-in protests in Stockholm and Copenhagen, and on walks through Paris. Together, these different perspectives make up a patchwork of observations of the mundane enforcement and 'asymmetrical negotiations' (Eule et al., 2019: 5) in the deportation regime.

When we enumerate our research participants, I believe that we do not emphasise often enough the conversations and engagements with colleagues and friends and how they help us articulate and refine our analyses. This book has come about through such collaborations and ongoing dialogues. Some friends have been present throughout the research process, while others have been with me as imaginative conversation partners also in the lonely moments of writing. As a way of acknowledging the inherently collaborative – and ongoing – nature of the thought processes behind this book, I have included extracts from conversations and exchanges with four people who have been immensely important for this research as well as for my learning process: Lisa Borrelli, Shahram Khosravi, Steve Nwaogu Stanley, and Julia Suárez-Krabbe. While writing this manuscript, I asked each of them to reflect on selected quotations or ethnographic vignettes that appear in the book and which illustrate experiences we share, or issues that I have come to understand better through our dialogues. With their consent, I have included extracts of our conversations in different parts of the book.

Chapter guidance

In the prologue, the reader was introduced to Sjælsmark deportation camp, and to Niels and Abolfazl. The purpose of this book is to investigate the state violence mobilised to enforce deportations, the role and positioning of Niels and his colleagues who are tasked with enacting it, and how it produces the premature death of Abolfazl and others stuck in the deportation limbo. The point is not to identify and point out individual perpetrators of this violence, but to analyse its systemic nature, and how it comes to be perceived as a normal and, indeed, necessary part of border and migration politics. It is my hope that the book will contribute to challenging the normalisation of the conditions that permit non-deported people like Abolfazl to live and end their life 'intolerably'.

Chapter 1 provides an overview of the politics of deportation in Denmark and Sweden and contextualises the expansion of the countries' respective deportation regimes since 2015. While Denmark and Sweden have been discussed as radically different in terms of their approaches to migration, instead I highlight the continuities between them. They include, first, the social imaginaries of Nordic 'exceptionalism', which encompass a denial of complicity in racist global histories and structures, and imaginations of social, cultural, and racial homogeneity. Second are the bureaucratised welfare state apparatuses, ostensibly designed to foster and protect the lives of the population, but which are also mobilised to render the lives of those excluded from the welfare state, including non-deported people, unliveable. The chapter sets the scene for the empirical investigations that follow.

The empirical chapters are structured in accordance with the violent continuum that I argue organises deportation regimes. Chapters 2 and 3 focus on direct violence and coercive control and consist of ethnographic investigations of migration-related detention in Denmark and Sweden, respectively. Here, the protagonists are people like Henrik, whose job is to incarcerate and enforce deportation orders, variably using criminalisation and symbolic punishment (in Denmark) and discourses of benevolence and care (in Sweden) as techniques of discipline and control. The next two chapters discuss the indirect forms of violence mobilised to pressure non-deported people to leave by making their lives unliveable. Chapter 4 returns to Sjælsmark deportation camp, the site of Niels and Abolfazl's interaction, and describes the 'mysterious' conditions of semi-confinement that Niels and his colleagues were supposed to enforce, and the 'slow violence' experienced by those confined in the deportation camps. Chapter 5 traces the technique of formal abandonment and derecording of non-deported people in Sweden. It details the narratives of responsibilisation that migration officials draw on to enforce so-called voluntary deportations, while withdrawing the latter's access to minimum welfare provisions. Whereas the first three chapters focus on the structures and agents of deportation enforcement, Chapters 4 and 5 also consider how non-deported people navigate and struggle against the deportation regime, by staying put, refusing to disappear, or moving on.

Together, these policies form the framework within which the asymmetric struggles over the deportation limbo take place. The concluding chapter revisits the main empirical and analytical arguments of the book, and discusses how deportation regimes, and the continuum of state violence they mobilise, extend transnationally as part of the global apartheid regime, and internally, as one of the mechanisms through which racialised state borders are produced and maintained within societies. It also considers how state violence colonises the identity not only of those who are exposed to it, but also those who partake in enforcing it. Finally, I turn the lens to academic research and discuss what kind of knowledge is or can be useful for documenting and challenging border and deportation regimes, and the violence which sustains them.

Notes

1 By 'Europe' and the 'European' deportation regime, I am here referring to the states that have signed the Schengen and Dublin Agreements. These states also form part of the historical and *political* project of 'Europe'. The continuous

assertion of the geographical, discursive, and judicial boundaries of 'European' space is instrumentalised in order to reify an image of a peaceful, coherent Europe in relation to 'third countries' and 'their' crises, problems, and conflicts (see Casas-Cortes et al., 2015).

2 The Directive establishes that it is the *duty* of member states to issue deportation orders to all persons remaining unauthorised in a member state, while also emphasising that deportees must be treated 'with full respect for their fundamental rights and dignity' (*Directive 2008/115/EC*, Article 2–6), which includes respecting the prohibition against *refoulement* (in accordance with Article 33 of the 1951 Geneva Convention, and the protection against torture and inhuman treatment safeguarded by the Convention against Torture and the European Convention of Human Rights (ECHR)). In addition, the Convention on the Rights of the Child obliges signatory states to consider the best interest of the child in immigration cases, including in deportation procedures. This does not preclude the deportation of children but can influence decisions on residence permit/deportation. Article 8 of the ECHR, which outlines the right to respect for private and family life, can also be actualised in deportation processes.

3 According to the European Commission, 'third-country national' refers to 'any person who is not a citizen of the European Union within the meaning of Article 17(1) of the Treaty establishing the European Community (TEC) and who is not a person enjoying the Community right of free movement, as defined in Article 2(5) of the Schengen Borders Code' (Heegaard Bausager et al., 2013: 7). The Dublin Regulation, which provides different criteria for determining which signatory state is competent for processing an asylum claim or unauthorised entry, also establishes states' right to transfer (i.e. deport) asylum seekers to the member state responsible for processing or enforcing their asylum case (Kasparek, 2016).

4 The term 'racialisation' refers to the marking of bodies according to racial logics, which posits some as superior, and others as inferior. Hierarchies of racial superiority/inferiority can be marked by skin colour or be constructed by ethnic, cultural, or religious markers – or nationality. These delineations are neither static nor universal, but produced through ongoing processes that are embedded in specific relations of power (Grosfoguel et al., 2015).

1

The politics of deportation and the Nordic welfare state

Maybe you stay in one place for a few years, then you leave to a new place, you have to change places and then come back again ... and from what I understand that's what people do. They get frustrated in one place, they try their luck in another place. But when you are already in the position of being rejected here, it's not the same as in Greece, Italy, or Spain ... there, you are allowed to walk around freely without documents, because they cannot afford or organise your deportation. But in Sweden, Denmark, Germany, it's more difficult ... The system is made to protect you but can also control you. That's why, when the economic situation was good, it was actually ok to be a refugee in Greece, Spain, Italy ... that's why it's so difficult to live underground or as rejected here. Then you are basically wasting your time, you will never fit in. All is regulated.

Issa was a man in his thirties who was forced to move to Sjælsmark deportation camp when his asylum application was rejected by the Danish immigration authorities. Denmark had been the first country in Europe where he had sought asylum, but prior to his arrival, he had also lived as undocumented in Greece and France. One day, on the bus on our way from Sjælsmark, Issa and I discussed how the conditions for non-deported people differ across European states. Issa explained that Southern European countries are more lenient towards people lacking legal authorisation to remain, but at the same time, they only offer very limited welfare services. Still, he found it easier to get by in Greece or France than in Northern Europe, where the expansive bureaucratic system put in place to ensure welfare protections for its members was turned into an intricate web of exclusion for those who, like him, are rejected. Issa's observation is in agreement with the bulk of comparative research on welfare and migration control regimes across Europe, which has highlighted the significant variations in terms of access to welfare, labour market regulations, and experiences of policing and control for people living with precarious legal status or as non-deported (Ataç, 2019; Floros and Jørgensen, 2020; Heegaard Bausager et al., 2013; Leerkes and van Houte, 2020; Triandafyllidou and Ambrosini, 2011). Issa's reflection also points to the argument made by scholars that bureaucratised welfare states, which pay lip service to egalitarianism and inclusion, and which devote substantial resources to distributing welfare among its population, also practise radical forms of exclusion when it comes to people positioned as 'non-members', including rejected migrants (Abdelhady, Gren, and Joormann, 2020; Khosravi, 2010; Sager, 2011).

Issa's remark serves as a starting point for critically interrogating Northern European deportation regimes. The Nordic countries are often heralded – in politics and in much scholarship – for their supposed humanitarianism, egalitarianism, and 'exceptionalism' from the global history of colonialism, slavery, and imperial warfare, yet their deportation regimes serve as entry points for analysing the radical exclusion of racialised (non)citizens and historically marginalised groups, which are and always have been inherent to the welfare state project (Keskinen et al., 2009; Leets Hansen and Suárez-Krabbe, 2019). Hence, notwithstanding their different policies on border and asylum issues, which are often centred in comparative research on migration in the Nordics (Brochmann and Dørvik, 2018; Schierup and Ålund, 2011), Denmark and Sweden expose important similarities in terms of how the welfare state becomes a vehicle for radical exclusion of 'others'. The mapping out of the Danish and Swedish deportation regimes presented in this chapter should not be understood as a strictly comparative research endeavour. Instead, by putting emphasis on continuities, I employ what Theo Goldberg (2009: 1274) calls a 'relational analysis', which traces the 'constitutive condition of the relational components' and their various manifestations. Accordingly, and while I account for different politics and policies of deportation, I will in this chapter also describe the constitutive connections in terms of how violent exclusion operates in the bureaucratised, Nordic welfare states.

The deportation turn in the Nordics

'Sweden has been too naïve when it comes to immigration. They took in too many and look at what's happening there now.' This was an almost standard conversation opener during my fieldwork with prison officers in Denmark's detention and deportation camps. The conversation would then evolve along the following lines: the prison officer would begin enumerating the social problems that, in their view, were direct results of immigration to Sweden, such as rising crime rates, rape cases, and urban unrest. As sources, they would cite a Facebook account of a Swedish police officer, a blog entry, or a Danish newspaper article. When I questioned these sources, they would add that 'Swedish newspapers don't dare to write about this' due to their political correctness. The same political correctness was what prevented me from seeing this reality, they claimed. We would continue quarrelling until we eventually changed conversation topics. On the other side of the border, Swedish detention officials would rhetorically ask me, 'at least, the conditions here must be better than in Denmark, right?'. They awaited my confirmation that they were more benevolent than their Danish counterparts (a confirmation that I could not offer them since in my view, this was only superficially true), and they expressed surprise that people resisted Dublin deportations back to Sweden – because surely, 'here' must be better than elsewhere.

Such oppositional portrayals of the Danish and Swedish approach to migration – one being repressive and protective, the other one naïvely benevolent – are in line with most representations in media, and with what we find in much mainstream migration research, which tends to highlight differences between the two countries' immigration policy regimes. However, these accounts tend to understate the continuities in policy as well as practice between the two countries, some of which have evolved historically, others which have been accentuated since Sweden joined the European 'race to the bottom' in asylum and migration policy following the 2015 long summer of migration (Slominski and Trauner, 2018). Sweden and Denmark have held similar positions on issues of borders and migration also prior to this partial convergence: both countries are part of the European migration and border regime, which ever since the 1990s has pushed states towards harmonisation of migration policies across EU member states and fuelled the criminalisation and securitisation of migration from the Global South and from Eastern Europe (Besteman, 2020). Sweden and Denmark are both members of the EU and of the Schengen Area (signed in 1996, the Schengen Regulation came into effect in both countries in 2001), and as a result, their border checks are externalised while proliferating internally (Balibar, 2004). They are both signatories of the Dublin Regulation since 1997, and Sweden is also signatory of asylum reception- and deportation-related EU regulations, while Denmark has a parallel arrangement that allows them to opt in and out of EU legislation within the field of migration policy, including the Return Directive.

Moreover, as two wealthy and resourceful states located in Northern Europe, Sweden and Denmark have to a large extent been able to steer migration remotely, by co-financing the expanding security apparatuses designed to deter, monitor, filter, and prevent undesired mobility into Europe through its Southern and Eastern borderlands (Bigo, 2014; Statewatch, 2020). This means that Sweden and Denmark have been able to buy themselves out of responsibility for the reception of people seeking protection or better life opportunities in Europe. Even in 2015, when Sweden claimed to have taken 'exceptional' responsibilities for refugee reception, the number of people who arrived in Sweden remains small compared to arrivals in Southern European countries such as Greece and Italy at the time. In politics and in research, the Nordic countries have thus largely evaded critique of malfunctioning bureaucracies, inadequate reception conditions, illegal pushbacks, and violent enforcement measures regularly directed against the EU's externalised borders (Border Violence Monitoring Network, 2020). This is not to say that the Nordic countries are engaging in such practices to an equal extent as countries geographically located at the EU's external borders, but that there are problematic bordering practices taking place in the Nordics, which due to geographical – and geopolitical – biases have remained relatively understudied, leaving intact the perceptions that the Nordic countries are overall characterised by well-functioning, effective bureaucracies and humanitarian ideals. There are, moreover, significant differences between Danish and Swedish migration politics and practices of policy implementation. In what follows, I try to account for structural similarities as well as variations between the two deportation regimes under scrutiny.

Denmark's deportation-oriented migration regime

In April 2021, Denmark appeared on the front pages of international news media as the first EU country to withdraw protection status and revoke residence permits for Syrian nationals who had fled the decade-long war in the country. The decision targeted people originating from the Damascus and Rif areas where, according to Danish immigration authorities' own, much-criticised reports (see ECRE, 2021), the security situation had improved to the extent that those who were granted subsidiary protection based on the ongoing war could now 'safely' return. The decisions on revocations were expected to encompass around 4,500 Syrian nationals and Palestinians who had lived in Syria. The first round of revocations has disproportionately affected women, people of older age, and those who had arrived in Denmark as children, sparing men who risk forced conscription to the military (Clante Bendixen, 2021).[1] Commenting on why the security situation in Syria was no longer sufficient to qualify people for protection, the Social Democratic parliamentary spokesperson on immigration issues said, 'it makes a big difference if the regime has a personal issue with you, or if you have fled because there's a general situation of war. There might be a risk that a bomb will fall on your house. That doesn't necessarily mean there is anything personal between you and the government' (Stoklund, cited in Hørkilde, 2021, author's translation). Syrian refugees in Denmark begged to differ, and in May 2021, the Syrian Association in Denmark staged a month-long sit-in protest in front of the Danish Parliament, demanding that Danish authorities acknowledged their well-founded fear of returning to a country still ruled by the regime they had fled from, of indiscriminate bombing and widespread poverty, and of the risk of arrest and disappearances that returning refugees were reportedly exposed to. A protester told the newspaper *AlJazeera* (Bjerkestrand, 2021), 'The Syrian people were killed by bombs in Syria. Here in Denmark, we are dying from fear that the government will deport us.' Since Denmark had no readmission agreement with the Assad government in Syria, they knew they could not be deported by force. Therefore, if they did not leave 'voluntarily', they risked forced relocation to Danish deportation camps, where they could be held indefinitely.

Formally responsible for the decisions to revoke the protection status of Syrian nationals are the Danish Immigration Service and the Refugee Appeals Board. However, the revocations have only become possible through the gradual shifts in the Danish asylum and migration control regime that have taken place since 2015: from restrictive asylum policies and an assimilationist integration regime (Rytter, 2018) towards the articulation of deportation as the explicit aim of Denmark's asylum immigration policy. The case of the Syrian refugees is paradigmatic of this policy regime, which balances at the very edge of human rights conventions, and which extends the condition of deportability (De Genova, 2002) to people who are recognised refugees and their families. It is a regime where, in the words of legal scholar Jessica Schultz (2020: 172), 'the "future returnee" is the new refugee'.

The restrictive developments in Danish asylum and migration policy towards a deportation-oriented asylum regime have taken place over several decades but culminated after 2015. Denmark's modern-day Aliens Act dates to 1983. At the time, it was considered ground-breaking both in terms of its strong human rights protections and in its 'humane' approach, where responsibility for people seeking asylum was transferred from the police to civil migration authorities. Yet already in 1986, Denmark adopted more restrictive asylum laws with a view towards rendering Denmark unattractive for those referred to as spontaneous asylum seekers (Gammeltoft-Hansen and Whyte, 2011), by imposing more restrictive conditions on those who were already present on the territory. In the early 1990s, Denmark saw increasing arrivals of people seeking protection from the war in former Yugoslavia. This, and the rise of the right-wing populist Danish People's Party, which pushed a racist, anti-Muslim, and anti-immigrant political agenda, fuelled a politicisation of matters of asylum, integration, and deportation, and popularised the notion that Muslim migrants in particular were 'unwanted' and 'threatening' due to their presumed cultural and religious difference (Meret and Gregersen, 2019).

A series of restrictive policy changes were adopted in consecutive years by conservative-led and Social Democratic governments and with wide support from parties across the political spectrum (Whyte et al., 2020). In their historical overview of the evolvement of Danish immigration and integration laws, Gammeltoft-Hansen and Whyte (2011) estimate that laws in these fields changed on average once a month between 2001 and 2009. Changes include restrictions in admission policies in the fields of asylum and family reunification (Brochmann and Hagelund, 2011; Vedsted-Hansen, 2017), and the institutionalisation of asylum camps, which worked as a means to regulate, contain, and isolate people seeking asylum from the surrounding society while their applications were being processed (Syppli-Kohl, 2015; Whyte, 2011; Whyte et al., 2018). Restrictions were also introduced in terms of access to welfare, including social benefits and labour rights (Floros and Jørgensen, 2020; Rytter and Ghandchi, 2019), and in the rigorous so-called integration programmes, which authorised far-reaching state interventions into the lives and habits of migrants. The racialised social imaginary underpinning these laws portrayed migrants, and Muslim migrants in particular, as religiously or culturally archaic, unhealthy, and patriarchal, and as such, inherently 'un-Danish' (Rytter, 2018: 683).

Critical border and migration scholars have described how the Danish migration and so-called integration policy regime thus emerged 'as a site for racial and racist discourse, and as a site of conjuncture between the welfare state and its citizens' (Gullestad, 2002: 45). Danish state racism is manifested and continuously reproduced and reconfigured through this intrinsic web of external and internal bordering practices, which produces degrees of differential inclusion, precarity, and vulnerability in accordance with racialised, gendered, and classed rationales (Arce and Suárez-Krabbe, 2019; Eika et al., 2019; Suárez-Krabbe and Lindberg, 2019). While language of race is absent from Danish migration and integration regimes, the people disproportionately targeted for policing, surveillance, social control, detention, and deportation are primarily people racialised as non-white, or 'non-Western'. The term 'non-Western' was invented by Denmark's central authority on Danish Statistics. It is used in population registries as well as in political rhetoric, and encompasses migrants originating from countries outside Europe, Australia, New Zealand, and the United States and their (Danish-born) descendants. In practice, however, 'non-Western' is used as a euphemism for Muslims (see Zhang, 2020). The language of Western/non-Western is illustrative of how racism in Denmark has morphed into a language of presumed cultural superiority/inferiority, where people's rights to inclusion and participation are measured based on their perceived difference from the Danish/white/Christian norm (Eika et al., 2019). The presumed difference of the 'non-Western' in turn fuels the idea that 'egalitarian' welfarism presupposes ethnic, religious, cultural, and racial 'sameness' (Rytter, 2018: 693);[2] and since people with non-Western backgrounds cannot become 'the same', they can be legitimately and radically excluded or expelled.

In 2015, Denmark, like many other EU member states, declared a 'crisis' of its asylum reception system, even though Denmark received relatively few asylum applications compared to other member states, since around 80 per cent to 90 per cent of those who passed through Denmark during the long summer of migration were heading towards Sweden (see Whyte et al., 2018). Yet, the crisis politics provided justification to introduce further restrictions in Denmark's asylum and immigration policy regime, and between 2015 and 2021, the policies moved further towards absolute minimum human rights standards. The conservative Danish government (a coalition between Venstre, the Liberal Alliance, and the Conservative People's Party, ruling with parliamentary support of the far-right Danish People's Party) made it into a numbers game: during their years in power between 2015 and 2019, they counted – and celebrated – a total of 146 restrictions (*stramninger*) in the field of immigration and asylum. These included restrictions on family reunification, reduced material standards in asylum camps for the sake of deterrence, expanded legal grounds for detaining foreign nationals, and the criminalisation of a range of migration-related offences. In 2019, the same government declared a 'paradigm change' in the country's asylum law (L 140, adopted 21 February 2019) 'from integration to temporariness and repatriation' (Danish Government, 2018: 5). The law was supposed to 'send a clear sign that refugees' stay in Denmark is temporary', and that 'Denmark is both willing and able to act swiftly and effectively, when the grounds for protection have ceased' (Danish Ministry of Immigration and Integration, 2019). It introduced automated reassessments of refugee status holders' need for protection; the integration programmes were exchanged for 'return programmes' and social benefits for 'repatriation and self-sustenance benefits', to remind temporary protection holders that their future lay elsewhere than in Denmark.

The Social Democratic government coalition that assumed power in 2019 maintained the restrictive, deportation-oriented approach. Although a record low number of 1,547 people applied for asylum in Denmark in 2020, the government declared its aim to reduce new arrivals to zero, launching a novel 'Return Agency' (*Hjemrejsestyrelsen*), whose job is to 'assist foreigners without legal right to remain in seeing the opportunities in returning' (Return Agency, n.d.) and to render deportations more effective. They adopted Denmark's first deportation law, which legalises authorities to use more surveillance, coercive measures, and incentives to pressure non-deported people to leave. They also announced their controversial plans to externalise asylum processing to a third country. The case of the Syrian nationals finding themselves at threat of deportation to a country in ongoing war is therefore illustrative of the Danish government's fantasies of stopping unwanted immigration altogether, expelling those already present from the country, and outsourcing their responsibility for human rights protections, which they remain bound to by international law (Brekke, Vedsted-Hansen, and Stern, 2020). The stakes are high, and the human costs of Denmark's increasingly repressive, deportation-oriented migration regime are significant. Research has demonstrated how people holding temporary protection status are exposed to growing poverty (Egaa Jørgensen and Schapiro, 2019), precarity, and exploitation in the labour market (Floros and Jørgensen, 2020; Rytter and Ghandchi, 2019). Moreover, families risk being torn apart by restrictive entry laws or deportation. The 'paradigm change' with its protracted deportability disproportionately affects women, people with disabilities, and those of older age, who often hold subsidiary protection status and who are not valued as exploited labour (Clante Bendixen, 2021).

The bureaucratic structures that enforce these policies encompass the immigration service, which assesses asylum applications; the Refugee Appeals Board, which reviews their decisions; and the Danish Return Agency, the police, the prison service, the municipalities, and the Red Cross, who enforce deportations and run asylum, detention, and deportation camps. While these are formally independent of political influence, they are all affected by the restrictive shifts: the restrictive approach is reflected in the low accommodation standards in asylum and deportation camps, which are supposed to serve as infrastructures of deterrence (Whyte et al., 2018); it manifests in the asylum procedures, where decisions are made in an environment ridden by institutionalised suspicion and rules set up to reject, rather than support, people seeking protection (Clante Bendixen, 2020). It affects the politics that takes place behind the scenes, in the secret so-called readmission agreements with countries like Somalia and Iraq, which enable Danish authorities to deport people under conditions that are obscure even to the lawyers of those who are to be deported. Finally, it materialises in the rules and regulations set up to make the lives of non-deported people so intolerable that they will leave Denmark. As of 2020, the number of people who were in a 'departure position' after their asylum cases had been rejected or their protection status withdrawn, amounted to 1,900, compared to around 1,200 in previous years (Danish Refugee Council, 2020). These people, who are in 'deportation limbo', are the main targets of the intensified deportation efforts of the Danish state, although they extend to encompass temporary protection holders and their families, who are or risk becoming deportable.

Sweden: a 'U-turn' of the humanitarians?

In 2016, a stern-faced Social Democratic prime minister and a crying deputy prime minister of the Green Party announced that Sweden needed a 'breathing space' (*andrum*) from the arrival of people seeking protection (Swedish Government, 2015). The government officials inhaled deeply and adopted the Law 'on temporary restrictions in the possibility to obtain residency in Sweden' (Lagen, 2016: 752) *om tillfälliga begränsningar i möjligheten att få uppehållstillstånd i Sverige*), which rendered conditions for people seeking protection and their families among the most restrictive in Europe. In a second breath, they promised to expand the state's capacity to deport those who had been rejected. The government was criticised for the hasty preparation of what came to be known as the temporary law, the disregard they showed for the concerns voiced by consultative bodies (many of which, including municipalities and the Swedish Migration Agency, questioned the need for a 'breathing space' in the first place; see Skodo, 2020), and for the law's actual content (Lundberg, 2017). Among the most drastic changes were the introduction of temporary rather than permanent residence permits for protection status holders, severe limitations on their right to family reunification, and the withdrawing of welfare support for people who received a deportation order. In addition, steps were taken towards a merging of asylum and labour migration policy, when the prospect to remain and earn one's right to family reunification was made contingent on labour market participation (Sager and Öberg, 2017). In 2021, the temporary law, which was temporarily extended in 2019, was made permanent. To create a migration policy that was going to be 'sustainable in the long term', they figured, they needed to permanently make life more precarious for people seeking protection.

When it was first adopted, the temporary law (and its temporary extension) was portrayed as a U-turn (Parusel, 2016) away from Sweden's relatively generous asylum policy regime and an integration policy granting expansive rights to people who arrived to settle in Sweden (Brochmann and Hagelund, 2011). However, researchers have since underlined how the latest round of restrictive measures follows an established pattern: in the past, Swedish governments have regularly sought to reduce unwanted immigration in times of increased arrivals, while simultaneously seeking to retain Sweden's high profile on human rights issues (Stern, 2014; 2017). This balancing act captures how Sweden has consistently sought to combine an expansive rights regime for those conceived as members with interventionist and exclusionary treatment of those conceived as 'others'. This duality is important for understanding the continuities in Sweden's restrictive, regulatory migration control regime. Khosravi (2018) has highlighted that the very first codified Swedish Aliens Act, the 'Act regarding the prohibition of certain foreigners to stay in the country' (Lagen (1914: 196) *angående förbud för visa utlänningar att här i riket vistas*) was a deportation law. It did not contain regulations on admission, passport requirements, or other conditions for controlling entry, but it codified the possibility to deport 'unwanted foreigners' who were variably perceived as competitors for jobs, security threats, or potential burdens to the state due to their poverty, illness, or old age (Hammar, 1964). The same law made possible the administrative detention of foreigners (Jansson-Keshavarz, 2016). Not only foreign nationals, but also other groups of mobile poor and historically marginalised groups have been exposed to spatial and social regulation and forced assimilation as part of the ongoing process of constructing the Swedish citizen and 'anti-citizen', respectively (Khosravi, 2009). Much like in Denmark, the Social Democratic ideology of the welfare state as the 'people's home' (*folkhemmet*) has been premised on ideas of racial and social homogeneity; ideas which were also supported and promoted by the Swedish academy (as illustrated by the work of the State Institute for Race Biology (1922–1958)). The expansion of the welfare state has taken place in parallel with the dispossession, displacement, and oppression of the indigenous Sami, Tornedalfinns, and Finns, and historically marginalised groups including Jews and Roma (Mulinari and Neergaard, 2017). However, there has long been a laudable silence around the constitutive role of racism and race inequality in the formation of the Swedish welfare state. Instead, racial inequality is conceived as something that 'arrived' with racialised migrants and the 'multicultural' society (Mulinari and Keskinen, 2020). Accordingly, migrants and historically marginalised groups have come to be framed as threats to the welfare state and its supposed egalitarianism, democracy, and tolerance – by virtue of their very exclusion from these principles.

It is in this context that the Swedish 'humanitarian' approach to immigration needs to be read. Sweden's history of immigration control after the Second World War was shaped by its demand for foreign labour, and the arrival of guest workers and their families, which came to a halt with an economic crisis in the early 1970s. The 1976 Aliens Act laid the foundation for a migration and asylum policy that combined relatively generous rules within the realms of asylum and family reunification as well as inclusive welfare rights. The act lent Sweden its reputation as a safe haven for people fleeing persecution (Hammar, 1999). However, following an increase in asylum applications in the late 1980s, with the so-called Lucia decision in 1989, the Swedish Social Democratic government adopted drastic restrictions in their asylum laws and expanded the grounds for detention of foreign nationals for the purpose of rendering them identifiable and deportable (Johansson, 2005). The decision was justified by the invocation of a 'crisis' of asylum reception, and by a convoluted understanding of humanitarianism, according to which the rights of all must be compromised and saved for 'those who need it the most' (Johansson, 2005: 90f). The Lucia decision has been cited as a precedent to the 2016 shift in Sweden's asylum policy and illustrates how its humanitarian values have always been conditioned on relatively limited immigration (Jansson-Keshavarz, 2016). It also exemplifies how restrictive measures are justified in the name of benevolence and care for those deemed the most 'deserving'.

The 1990s saw a steady expansion of Sweden's detention and deportation apparatus. This was also a time of increased politicisation of asylum and immigration, and of a proliferation of political imaginaries where immigration was presented as a threat to Swedish national identity, its presumed racial homogeneity, 'progressive' humanitarian values – which were supposedly at odds with the presumed inferior, archaic culture of immigrants – and expansive welfare state (Mulinari and Neergaard, 2017). This was also a time when 'voluntary return migration' emerged as a main policy goal of migration policy, alongside a relatively generous and rights-based regime for those classified to be in need of protection. In the 2010s, several initiatives were taken to reinforce internal border controls and to enhance the effectiveness of deportations (among them the much-debated REVA project), and the budget for deportation enforcement gradually expanded: between 2011 and 2020, it grew by 49 per cent (Prop. 2010/11: 1; Prop. 2017/18). This legal and political 'displacement' of asylum and migration law towards a more restrictive, deportation-oriented regime, has been accompanied by a harsher political rhetoric (Elsrud, Gruber, and Lundberg, 2021), which has been fuelled by – but can by no means be attributed solely to – the growth of the far-right Sweden Democrats, a party with roots in the Neo-Nazi movement, and the mainstreaming of racist rhetoric among political parties both on the right and on the left of politics (see Mulinari and Neergaard, 2017).

An important insight from this overview is that migration control in Sweden has always balanced between political rhetoric praising humanitarianism and human rights ideals on the one hand, and an expansive capacity for exclusion, containment, and deportation, on the other (see Weber et al., 2019). It has shaped the organisation, politicisation, and operation of the migration control apparatus, and generated heated political debates over enforcement practices considered too harsh or unfairly targeting people who, in the eyes of the public, were deemed particularly 'deserving' (for instance, the cases of children suffering from resignation syndrome; or children classified as unaccompanied minors). On the other, it has solidified public perceptions – which, as I will show, are also prevalent within bureaucracy – that the Swedish migration control regime is morally superior and its bureaucracy practically infallible. The bureaucratic authority in charge of most migration-related processes is the Swedish Migration Agency, a civil authority that both registers applications for visa, asylum, and other residence permits; operates reception facilities and processes asylum applications; and is also responsible for 'return migration', encompassing 'voluntary' return processes, detention, and deportation. The latter part of the process is also supported by the Swedish police, who conduct internal Schengen border controls and may take decisions on the detainment of foreign nationals. The police also assist in carrying out deportations, with support from the transportation unit of the Prison and Probation Service acting as deportation escorts. For the pandemic year 2020, the Swedish Migration Agency (Migrationsverket 2021) reported 28,258 open deportation cases, which had not yet or could not be enforced, compared to 16,271 in 2018. All authorities, including those mandated to use coercive force, operate within discourses of 'humane, voluntary', and 'discrete' migration enforcement (see DeBono et al., 2015); indeed, an escort from the prison service whom I interviewed assured me that their job was to make deportation a 'pleasant travel experience'. Some scholars have argued that the 'humane' face of Sweden's migration enforcement regime, with its emphasis on rule of law and migrants' dignity, leads to 'goal conflicts' and impedes the effectiveness of enforcement (Leerkes and van Houte, 2020; Malm Lindberg, 2020). In contrast, I will argue that there are forms of state violence enabled not despite but *through* such beliefs in the inherently humane or humanitarian nature of the state.

From racial exceptionalism to racial welfare state

The above overview exposes significant differences, but also continuities in the evolution of the Swedish and Danish deportation regimes. The continuities that I wish to emphasise entail, first, the shared history and founding ideology of the Nordic welfare states, which rely on the exclusion of historically marginalised and racialised groups, who have all – in different ways and at different times – been portrayed as the 'others' challenging the imagined homogeneity and cohesion of the welfare state and nation (see Keskinen et al., 2019; Loftsdóttir and Jensen, 2012). These shifting and continuously evolving racial social imaginaries have legitimated the expansion of state powers to govern 'anti-citizens' (Khosravi, 2009), ranging from coercive control and surveillance to formal abandonment, which are also used to regulate non-deported people. Secondly, and relatedly, the countries share a generalised belief in the 'good state' and a welfare state apparatus characterised by a high level of bureaucratisation, which enhances the lives of 'members', but which also holds significant capacity to enact radical exclusion of 'others'.

'"Race"', argues Gloria Wekker (2021: 2–3), 'is a silent but powerful organizing principle in the way that we have organized society, our knowledge and ourselves [...] however much it is denied and disavowed.' Her argument, which discusses racial inequality in the Netherlands, applies well to the Nordic context. Public and political debates on issues of migration, 'integration', and racial inequality in the Nordic countries are characterised by a myth of 'racial exceptionalism' (Goldberg, 2006: 353). According to this myth, these countries, which include Denmark and Sweden, are excepted from the history of colonialism, slavery, and repression of historically marginalised groups, and instead marked by their presumed racial homogeneity and 'humane', progressive values (Leets Hansen and Suárez-Krabbe, 2019; Loftsdóttir and Jensen, 2012). The myth obscures the 'colonial complicities' of Nordic welfare states (Vuorela, 2009), and the processes whereby '(post) colonial imaginaries, practices and products' are incorporated as part of the 'national' cultural project of the Nordic states (Keskinen et al., 2009: 17). It makes possible the claim that racism does not exist in the Nordic countries and that they are excepted from global processes that uphold racial inequality, even though they invest in and profit from white supremacist mythologies and the militarised border regime that sustains global mobility apartheid (Arce and Suárez-Krabbe, 2019). The myth of Nordic innocence also silences the erosion of livelihoods and inferiorisation of Sami and Inuit peoples, and the racist policing and interventionist social regulation of Roma, much of which has also taken place under the guise of humanitarianism, solidarity, and welfarism (Keskinen et al., 2019).

In public and political discourse on issues of racism and racial inequality in the Nordic countries (and for a long time, also in academia), 'racism' has been narrowly understood as acts and attitudes of discrimination based on beliefs in biological difference. Racism has been perceived as an exterior problem, existing only in the past (see Goldberg, 2006), far away (manifested in the routine dismissal of e.g., racist policing as an 'American' problem), or confined to the 'fringes' of far-right politics (Danbolt and Myong, 2018). This narrow definition hides the fact that racial hierarchisation and exclusion have been 'core organizing principles' in the evolvement of the modern Nordic welfare state, and how ideas of racial superiority/inferiority continue to inform practices of inclusion and exclusion, even as the reference points have shifted from 'race' to 'ethnicity', 'cultural values', 'traditions', and so on (Mulinari and Keskinen, 2020: 2; see also Loftsdóttir and Jensen, 2012; Keskinen et al., 2009). Notably, in the twenty-first century, the 'difference' around which racism has been organised is embedded in the figure of the migrant.

From the above overview of the politics of immigration in Denmark and Sweden, we learn how immigration has historically been constituted as an *exterior* threat to the presumably homogeneous, egalitarian welfare societies. Indeed, national myths of homogeneity portray racial difference as something that 'arrived' in the Nordic countries with immigration from 'non-Western countries' (Keskinen et al., 2009). This 'migratisation' of racial inequality (Tudor, 2017: 1057) externalises problems of racism, and sustains the notion that immigration (rather than the differential treatment of people positioned as migrants) destabilises the egalitarianism of the welfare state. This trope has been used to legitimise restrictive policies that reinforce and sustain racial inequalities under the guise of 'protecting' the welfare state against the imagined threat posed by racialised migrants. Indeed, such rhetoric was behind the restrictive asylum laws adopted by the Swedish government in 2015 (Mulinari and Neergaard, 2017), and have justified welfare chauvinist policies that exclude non-citizens from social safety nets (Finnsdottir and Hallgrimsdotter, 2019). They have also been instrumentalised to promote the Danish 'integration' measures targeting people of so-called non-Western backgrounds for their 'archaic' and inferior cultural practices (Rytter, 2018: 683), while portraying the people exposed to such measures as responsible for their own exclusion. The structural racism underpinning Sweden's and Denmark's approaches to immigration has been documented and problematised in research detailing racialised migrants' experiences of encounters with the bordered welfare state (Tervonen, Pellander, and Yuval-Davis, 2018). This literature has captured people's experiences of racial profiling (Borrelli and Lindberg, 2020; Mulinari and Keskinen, 2020), racial exploitation (Sager and Öberg, 2017), and incarceration and deportation (Arce and Suárez-Krabbe, 2019; Khosravi, 2010). I draw on this body of literature when I investigate the deportation limbo as a site where the structural racism of Nordic welfare states manifests itself.

Bureaucratic exclusion 'where all is regulated'

The Nordic welfare states were long known for their high social expenditures and relative social equality, with the state primarily manifesting itself in people's lives via 'soft' regulations, such as bureaucratic inscription and public service provisions. However, scholars have debunked the myth of Nordic 'exceptionalism', highlighting how the welfare state apparatus also exercises coercive forms of social control (Schierup and Ålund, 2011: 45), and how they, too, have undergone neoliberal restructuring, notably since the 1990s (Baeten et al., 2015). Moreover, scholars of borders and social policy have demonstrated how certain groups of foreign nationals have consistently been denied participation and access to the rights afforded to citizens (Tervonen et al., 2018). Nevertheless, remnants of the idea of welfare exceptionalism and belief in the 'good state' prevail within the bureaucratic state apparatus in both Denmark and Sweden. A Red Cross employee who worked in a Danish asylum camp told me, 'I could never work as part of the system in, say, Hungary, but in Denmark, we have a humane system' (Lindberg, 2020b: 220). It is worth noting that my interview with this Red Cross worker was focusing on the Red Cross's participation in operating the Danish deportation camps, which the Minister of Immigration and Integration in office at the time had promised to make as intolerable as possible for the non-deported people living there.

The welfare state ideology with its high level of trust in government institutions is sustained by the above-mentioned colour-blindness, and by a belief in Nordic democracies as inherently progressive, humane, and protective of human rights. Accordingly, when violence or injustices are generated within the bureaucratic state apparatus, these are portrayed as aberrations or deficiencies, *external* to the welfare state project itself.[3] As a reformist project, the welfare state finds answers to any external critique within its own procedures. This has implications for how frontline officials working for state authorities (or NGOs operating on state contract) understood and practised their work, and for the form and content of the critique articulated from 'within' the system.

The Danish and Swedish welfare states are also characterised by high levels of bureaucratisation, which together with the widespread public belief in the 'good' of the state, has implications for deportable people and others who are excluded from welfare state services. For migrants lacking legal authorisation to remain, the welfare state's 'generalised mechanism of enrolment' (Hörnqvist, 2018: para. 7) has exclusionary implications. The requirement of bureaucratic inscription renders access to the healthcare system, to housing and social benefits, to work, and to leisure activities – from libraries to football clubs – difficult to access for those lacking appropriate documentation (Khosravi, 2010; Tervonen et al., 2018). As Khosravi (2010) has argued, non-deported people are subjected to a form of 'inclusive exclusion': they are excluded from welfare services and labour rights, yet may remain included as taxpayers, and as cheap, exploitable labour in the informal labour market. They have legal protections but are vulnerable to intensive law enforcement, and to access minimum welfare, they must produce bureaucratic evidence of their exclusion: to give one example, in Sweden, an NGO working to support non-deported people with legal advice, healthcare, and social benefits explained that to access support, people had to provide documents from authorities proving that they lacked appropriate documentation. As proof, they might have to present a rejected asylum application, or a deportation order.

These strong internal bordering mechanisms and 'gatekeeping' were some of the challenges that Issa referred to in our conversation, and which he argued set the Nordic countries apart from, for instance, Southern European countries, where control mechanisms were relatively more relaxed (see Triandafyllidou and Ambrosini, 2011). Hence, if the mechanisms for formal welfare provisions are more rigorous, exclusion is also more orchestrated and, indeed, institutionalised (Floros and Jørgensen, 2020; Rytter and Ghandchi, 2019; Sager and Öberg, 2017). This has implications for how we can understand the forms of structural violence enforced *through* well-regulated welfare bureaucracies. Davies, Isakjee, and Dhesi (2017: 1269) argue,

> Advanced states such as those in northern Europe have ample resources with which to ensure those within its borders are protected from hunger, provided with shelter and given the security required to live without constant fear. Welfare systems are relatively well funded; but just as power can be activated by such states through distribution of provision, exclusionary power can be exerted through its withdrawal.

In Chapters 4 and 5, I discuss the withdrawal and denial of access to welfare for non-deported people as a form of structural violence. At the same time, the withdrawal of rights and services causes tensions among the regulatory welfare state authorities, and the continued presence of non-deported people, and their participation in social, political, and economic life, thus challenges the welfare states' bureaucratised boundaries of inscription and its capacity for violent exclusion.

Concluding remarks

This chapter has contextualised the politics of deportation in Denmark and Sweden, two Nordic welfare states traditionally known for their generous welfare provisions for members, but also for their strong bureaucratic 'gatekeeping' (Triandafyllidou and Ambrosini, 2011: 251) and capacity to regulate, control, and enforce the exclusion of different groups of 'anti-citizens' (Khosravi, 2009: 40). This capacity was what made exclusion tangibly felt by non-deported people like Issa. In addition, and as postcolonial and critical border scholars have emphasised, the exclusion of racialised migrants – and historically marginalised groups – is facilitated through the myths of Nordic exceptionalism, and beliefs in a benevolent and indeed, infallible state. While denying that 'race' and racism are inherent to Nordic welfarism and egalitarianism, the Nordic countries rely on and profit from notions of racial superiority/inferiority

(Wekker, 2016). Their egalitarianism and welfarism, then, are not opposed to racial inequality but presuppose it (Mulinari and Neergaard, 2017). For the purpose of this book, it is important to emphasise how ideas of 'the state' as colour-blind and, indeed, 'good' lend normative coverage for the state-sanctioned violence, enacted through strong, regulatory bureaucratic structures, which makes racialised border crossers vulnerable to premature death (Gilmore, 2007; Leets Hansen and Suárez-Krabbe, 2019). It is also important to underline that border and immigration control is far from the only policy field where the 'racial formation' (Mulinari and Keskinen, 2020: 378) of the Nordic welfare states takes place; indeed, as noted by Tudor (2017), there is a risk that research tracing racism in the field of migration reproduces the idea that racism is something external and indeed, exceptional; something that only applies to people positioned as 'migrants'. Deportation is but one manifestation of a border regime that on the one hand is part of global processes of racial hierarchisation (Leets-Hansen and Suárez-Krabbe, 2019), and, on the other hand, operates (and always has operated) internally to produce and govern 'difference' within the Nordic countries (Tervonen et al., 2018). Therefore, while this book focuses on transnational expulsions and the coercive regulation of international mobility, these practices should also be considered in relation to internal bordering practices that encompass the regulation, assimilation, and expulsion of indigenous and historically marginalised groups. I return to this matter in the concluding chapter.

In this chapter, I have emphasised the similarities and continuities between the ideological and bureaucratic formation of the Danish and Swedish deportation regimes. Needless to say, and as the policy overview also demonstrates, there are also important differences between them. However, in placing emphasis on relations and continuities, I seek to avoid a conventional, 'comparativist' account (Goldberg, 2009: 1274), which risks overlooking the ways in which global structures and practices, which are manifested and reconfigured differently across different localities, nevertheless remain interconnected (see also Leets-Hansen and Suárez-Krabbe, 2019). Tracing continuities in the logics and techniques used to govern cross-border mobility enables us to overcome the trap of methodological nationalism (Wimmer and Glick Schiller, 2002) and of reproducing ahistorical notions of nation states as natural, bounded, and fixed entities. Indeed, deportation regimes produce and reconfigure state borders – and connect them. Deportation regimes are at once globally structured and configured, and locally and intimately felt in their effects (Hiemstra, 2020). Therefore, following Issa's lead, this account of deportation regimes 'where all is regulated' is but a localised starting point for a systemic critique of deportation regimes in their abhorrent ordinariness.

Notes

1 This is possible because of a novel form of subsidiary protection introduced in Danish immigration law in 2015, which lowers the bar for when changes in the security situation in a protection holder's presumed country of origin are considered 'sustained' enough to warrant cessation of protection.
2 It is important to note that not only migrants, but also long-term residents and citizens of so-called non-Western background, are targeted by racist policies that circumscribe their access to welfare and criminalise their cultural practices. The most notable manifestation of this is perhaps the laws on so-called parallel societies (formerly 'ghetto laws'), which single out socio-economically deprived residential areas with more than 50 per cent 'non-Western' population for interventionist government programmes of intensified policing, a parallel set of penal codes, and social interventions in children's upbringing (see Almend modstand, n.d.). As a result of the forced redevelopment plans of the Danish government, 11,000 people were as of 2022 facing the threat of forced eviction and redevelopment based on the racial composition of their neighborhood. The laws on parallel societies demonstrate the complementary ways in which racist laws in Denmark discriminate, stigmatise, and criminalise racialised residents, creating hierarchies between groups that transcend citizenship, and effectuating a system of apartheid (Suárez-Krabbe and Lindberg, 2019).
3 Critiques of discriminatory and harmful practices by authorities are either refuted or generate strong political backlashes. This is illustrated by the political dismissal of critique against e.g. police authorities voiced by researchers (Nefstad and Parsa, 2020), and by the political attacks on 'activist researchers' within the fields of migration studies, gender studies, and critical race theory, and scholars working with abolitionist and decolonial approaches in Denmark and in Sweden (see Danbolt and Myong, 2018; Schmidt, 2021; Suárez-Krabbe, 2022).

2

What you get is a prison: detention in Denmark

'We don't want detention to be a black box, so we try to show all the things we do in here. Like the production room, or the workshop where they can do handicraft. We have some people here who are very talented.' The director of Ellebæk, Martin, who is giving me an introduction to the detention centre during my first day of fieldwork, picks up a postcard painted by a man who was detained there some time ago.

> There's the sunset over the sea, and look how the fence is turned into birds flying off, it's really nice, isn't it? We really liked it so we printed it as one of our official postcards of the Danish Prison and Probation Service (Kriminalforsorgen), and he got to put his signature on it. Farhad.

I ask, 'What happened to Farhad – did he fly off, too?' 'Well, yes', Martin responds, 'then he flew back to Afghanistan.'

On my first day of fieldwork in Ellebæk deportation prison, Martin took me into his office, located right at the entrance of the prison, to give me a formal introduction. He talked me through a PowerPoint presentation he had prepared for the upcoming scheduled visit of the Schengen Evaluation and Monitoring Mechanism the week after, which contained information on Ellebæk's institutional setup, some statistics, and a list of the activities offered to the people detained. Visits by monitoring bodies were routine in the prison system. After finishing his presentation, Martin looked around among the objects on his desk and picked up this postcard, painted by a man who had been detained in Ellebæk while awaiting deportation to Afghanistan. Martin told me the story of the postcard and its painter with great enthusiasm: to him, the postcard represented a counter-image to the common, negative representations of the deportation prison, a proof that this space of confinement could also be a place for creativity. Looking at the picture, Martin saw beauty and freedom in the birds freely flying over the fence towards the sunset. I never met Farhad and could not hear his

Figure 2.1 Illustration by Farhad, Ellebæk

own interpretation of the picture, but I suspect that the flight he embarked on was of a different kind than that of the birds on the postcard. I am also not sure if Martin was aware that the motif of the fence disintegrating into flying birds is an image that holds a different symbolic meaning among No Borders activists.[1] Still, Martin's enthusiasm over the postcard said something about him, and about Ellebæk. His insistence on finding a positively loaded purpose of the deportation prison, which was informed by his own background as a lawyer and prison director interested in prison reform, explained the ambivalence with which he approached his job at an institution that had as its sole purpose the symbolic criminalisation and expulsion of people like Farhad. His ambivalent feelings became even clearer to me as I gradually got to know Ellebæk as a place fraught with racism, insecurity, and violence.

The official purpose of Ellebæk, Denmark's only purely migration-related detention centre, is to keep people available for deportation, and to pressure non-deported people to cooperate in the deportation process. The comprehensive body of research on migration-related detention has time and again demonstrated that confinement is an ineffective, costly, and harmful technique of deportation enforcement (see e.g., Bosworth, 2014; Hiemstra, 2020). Researchers have argued that rather than facilitating control, detention centres – or deportation prisons, which I will henceforth call them – are primarily designed to serve a number of other functions. Like prisons, they serve to contain the mobility of citizens or non-citizens (Davis and Dent, 2001), who are regarded as 'not belonging' to the state and nation (Sharma, 2021: 184). As such, they serve as mechanisms of social sorting and control that limit the freedoms and economic, social, and political power of subordinated groups in the interest of nationalist projects – and of global capital, both of which profit from investing in coercive state powers. Indeed, strong cases have been made for why we should focus on the continuities, rather than differences, between the logics and effects of 'regular' prisons and deportation prisons (see Sharma, 2021: 185). Bearing these continuities in mind, their seeming separation serves to legitimise both immigration control and prison regimes. Some of these functions will be described in this chapter. If prisons punish 'deviant' behaviours and shape notions of the 'failed citizen' (Anderson, 2013: 28), deportation prisons criminalise and symbolically punish non-citizens 'for being who they are: foreign' (Bosworth, 2018: 3). Accordingly, their official aim is not to discipline and 'resocialise' deviant citizens, but to punish, contain, and expel undesired 'others' from the territory altogether (Bigo, 2006). This process builds upon and necessitates dehumanisation, which is achieved by breaking incarcerated persons down mentally, physically, and existentially (Boochani, 2018), hence reducing them to expellable bodies (Khosravi, 2010). What is more, it produces the dehumanisation of those enacting it.

Ellebæk: from *hyggested* to banoptic prison

Udlæningecenter Ellebæk (Foreigners' Centre Ellebæk) was inaugurated in October 1989 as Denmark's first and only prison devoted to the incarceration of non-deported migrants. The Danish government had received domestic and international criticism for detaining people who had sought asylum in police custody together with people held for criminal charges and was under pressure to come up with an alternative. Ellebæk, a former military facility in the Northern Zealand Region, became the government's solution for separating people detained on migration-related grounds from 'ordinary criminals'.[2] Ellebæk is located in an active military training zone, where the sounds of shooting exercises echo across the fields, and military tanks regularly pass by. The regional branch of the Prison and Probation Service runs the prison. In an essay detailing the initial setup of Ellebæk, Freddy Frederiksen (2009: 10), a prison officer who worked there since its inauguration in 1989, explains how Ellebæk had initially been a 'small and cosy place' (*hyggested*) with 'well-behaved detainees' who were detained under 'relatively good conditions' while authorities were trying to investigate and fixate their identity. Much like Freddy, the prison officers I met who had worked in the prison since the 1990s talked nostalgically about the relatively relaxed atmosphere of the early days. Back then, and despite the militarised nature of the prison facilities, they had not experienced it as an overtly securitised environment: control mechanisms were lax, officers wore jogging clothes, and the old, malfunctioning surveillance system made it relatively easy for detained people to escape, without anyone making too big a fuss about it. However, as Denmark saw a steady increase in the number of people arriving to seek protection in the 1990s, the prison was gradually filled up with people whose asylum claims had been rejected and who were awaiting deportation. With this development, the atmosphere in the prison changed. Karsten, a senior prison officer who had worked in Ellebæk since its inauguration, explained to me how this change in the clientele had heightened officers' awareness of the harmful design of the deportation prison.

> Early on, we had Yugoslavians here who were supposed to return when the war was over. They had bullet wounds, shrapnel still in their arms ... they really went through war. The wounds were not fresh, but they still carried the scars. And then they were shooting all around here. That was strange.

If Ellebæk was allegedly supposed to improve conditions for detained foreign nationals compared to the prison where they had been detained earlier, Karsten's reflection illustrates the lack of preparedness among officers to handle people who carried traumas of war and displacement, and who were awaiting deportation to the place they had once fled from. For Karsten, this insight was 'strange'. As the years went by, and as border controls became increasingly politicised and securitised in Denmark, Ellebæk kept developing in a more restrictive and punitive direction. The prison expanded, additional layers of secure fences were erected, and CCTVs were installed around the compound. Prison officers exchanged their jogging clothes for full prison uniforms with *Kriminalforsorgen* written across their backs. Ellebæk deportation prison developed into a spectacular manifestation of Denmark's restrictive deportation regime.

In 2020, Ellebæk had the capacity to incarcerate 136 people in cells shared by up to four people (after ongoing renovations, its capacity is expected to increase to 200 people). Statistics on those incarcerated are difficult to come by, since Danish authorities do not keep public records on the number of foreign nationals detained annually. The Prison and Probation Service recorded that 2,180 people were incarcerated on migration-related grounds

Figure 2.2 Photo of Ellebæk detention centre

in 2016: the majority of the people detained were identified or identifying as men. People identifying as women made up around 10 per cent, and at the time of my fieldwork, they were held in a separate building. Those incarcerated in Ellebæk are people whose asylum cases have been rejected, people apprehended at the border without authorisation to enter or remain in Denmark, visa overstayers, and people who have been found working without authorisation. Some of them are sex workers, many of whom have been arrested in the heavily policed Copenhagen neighbourhood *Vesterbro*; others were arrested in police raids on restaurants or construction sites. Statistically, the absolute majority of those detained in Ellebæk are eventually deported from Denmark (Herschend, 2019), but Danish immigration authorities also used incarceration as a so-called motivating measure to pressure people to comply with a deportation order against their will. Therefore, whereas most people pass through Ellebæk quickly – in 2018, the average length of stay was thirty-two days (Global Detention Project, 2018) – there are some who are released after they resisted deportation, only to be detained again at a later point; and yet others who are held in Ellebæk up to the maximum eighteen-month time limit. The routine prolongation of detention orders in Ellebæk has repeatedly drawn critique from detained people as well as detention visiting groups (see Ellebæk Contact Network, 2020), who found that even people who wished to leave Denmark as soon as possible, and whose incarceration therefore did not serve any practical function, have reportedly been held for extended time periods. During the COVID-19 pandemic, the number of incarcerated individuals dropped only temporarily (between March and June 2020) and then increased again, according to the Danish Immigration Agency (2020). Hence, the pandemic did not cause any major disruptions to the routine incarceration of foreign nationals, even during a time when authorities had limited prospects of deporting them due to global travel restrictions.

If Ellebæk formally operates as a deportation prison, it also holds symbolic and disciplinary functions. It subjects non-deported people to arbitrary and often protracted confinement under very poor material conditions that many referred to as 'worse than prison'. Even though incarcerated people were – legally, and in theory – imprisoned on administrative rather than punitive grounds, they were governed by rules identical to those in locked prisons. Cell phones were prohibited, and detained people had no access to the internet; at the time of my fieldwork, the internet café was closed, allegedly because officers were uncertain of which webpages should be accessible. Those detained were served the same meals with identical portions, and activities followed the same schedule as in regular prisons. Officers regularly referred to detained people as *fanger* (inmates), the same term they would use for 'ordinary' prisoners. Yannick, one of the officers, once told me bluntly, 'Of course it's a prison. It actually doesn't make a difference if you violated the Aliens Act or Penal Code, it's a crime nonetheless and they get you into jail.' Martin, the director, also contended,

> We often hear that it resembles a prison – and it does. If you put prison officers from a prison in charge of running the place, what you get is a prison. That's just how it is. Politically, they wish to keep conditions at a minimum. It's supposed to be strict. And people only stay here for four weeks on average. So, it's like a student corridor, right? You know, people only stay there for short periods of time and you see it on the facilities, no one makes it their home and they get worn down ... it's a bit like that here. And if it's already worn down you don't get motivated to keep it clean. Look, somebody scribbled down the alphabet here ... and over here it says 'fuck Denmark', 'fuck the system', 'prison'.

A student corridor might seem like a misplaced metaphor for a facility surrounded by three layers of fences several metres tall, topped with barbed wire, and with gates and windows covered with metal bars. A person who tried to escape would first have to climb a metal fence; then a taller fence topped with barbed wire; and lastly, a wooden, opaque fence, which also served to obscure the inside of the prison from an outsider's view. It was not uncommon, I was told, that those who attempted escapes ended up severely hurt by the razor-sharp blades of the fences. While the external fences of Ellebæk were deliberately designed to harm potential transgressors as part of its spectacular penal performance (see Pugliese, 2008), inside the prison wings, any means that could be used by detained people to self-harm had been removed. The walls were unevenly painted and covered with scribbles and drawings. Next to names, tags, and numbers, I noticed a piece of paper glued onto the wall with the text 'kidnapped by the Danish police', and a house with a Danish flag, under which it was written, 'a home in Denmark is different from this'. Prison officers told me that there used to be couches and a TV in the common area in the corridor, where they would sometimes sit down together with the detained people, but these had been removed, nobody really knowing why. Conditions were slightly better in the women's wing: according to Martin, it had been renovated following critique by the Parliamentary Ombudsman, who found it problematic that women were placed in a corridor adjacent to the men's department. According to the prison janitor, a civilian staff member, such cosmetic renovations were regularly conducted to please external monitoring bodies. However, and as he also concluded, they were not enough to prevent or appease the severe criticism that Ellebæk has repeatedly received for its prison-like environment, deplorable material conditions, inadequate health provisions, degrading treatment of incarcerated people, and excessive use of punitive measures (see Amnesty International, n.d.; Ellebæk Contact Network, 2020; Council of Europe's Committee for the Prevention of Torture, 2019).[3]

I was told that this harmful and punitive setup of Ellebæk was intentional. Martin maintained that the low material standards were the result of a political decision to keep conditions strict. 'And that's a dilemma for us', Martin explained, 'on the one hand, we have the public opinion, which is very restrictive and wants tougher control measures. On the other hand, we must treat each individual humanely ... that's our dilemma. And it's difficult to build relations with detainees, as they only stay for a short time, and they think this place is shit.' When we discussed the poor material standards and the rundown facilities, several prison officers acknowledged that they 'would never allow such conditions for Danish prisoners'. Hence, Ellebæk, with its neglectful and directly harmful architecture, was a material manifestation of a strategic use of symbolic criminalisation for the purpose of mobility control, but also of how sharp, racialised distinctions are deliberately constructed between incarcerated citizens and deportable others, which obscure the continuities between their respective conditions (see Sharma, 2021). The remainder of the chapter demonstrates how this hierarchical difference was sustained and reproduced in the everyday interactions between the Danish officers and incarcerated people at Ellebæk.

Prison officers turned border guards

'We are not criminals … they make us into criminals.' Andrew, who was incarcerated in Ellebæk for a total of twelve months, rightly notes that Ellebæk effectively served to make people into migrants and to equate migrants with criminals. At the same time, it made prison officers into reluctant border guards. Ellebæk was an unpopular workplace, and officers jokingly refer to it as the 'trash bin of the prison system'. Martin, who had become the director of Ellebæk because of an organisational reform, admitted, 'when I got the job, my colleagues even said to me, should I say congratulations? I think that says a lot about how this place is perceived.' Like Martin, most prison officers in Ellebæk had not actively chosen to work there – nor in the Prison and Probation Service, for that matter. While they had all undergone the three-year training to become a prison officer, several of them told me that they had ended up doing so simply because they could not find any other job. There were some exceptions: John, for instance, a man in his forties who had previously worked for the Danish military, said that the reason why he had joined the Prison and Probation Service was 'the adrenaline. There's constantly something happening here, and that makes it exciting. On the other hand … compared to the military, it might not be worth the risk to get stabbed for DKK 24,000 a month.'[4] Prior to his arrival at Ellebæk, John had also worked in a high-security unit in a Danish prison, and his colleagues regularly joked about how well he fitted into that environment with his shaved head, tribal tattoos, and pumped biceps. Yet, John was now getting tired of his job, which, like many of the other prison officers, he considered to be underpaid, undervalued, and associated with threats and violence. To make ends meet and to get a break from the violent prison environment, John – and others with him – worked two jobs in parallel. Next to being prison officers, they worked as supply teachers, personal assistants to young people with disabilities, foresters, or electricians. This was not only to top up their salary but also to create a lifeworld outside detention (see also Bosworth, 2018), where they worked in a more positive atmosphere, and felt they were 'able to help people'. The people they wanted to help were not the ones incarcerated in Ellebæk.

Compared to regular prisons, officers had fewer responsibilities and interactions with the people incarcerated in Ellebæk. Very few among the officers spoke any other language than Danish and poor English. None of them had received any training in immigration law, and they had little or no insight into detained people's cases. Some of the senior officers also told me that they used to try to educate themselves about the deportation process and to read the case files of those incarcerated, but nowadays, few were willing to make time for such additional engagements. What officers knew about the people detained was therefore limited to the first page of their case files, which only listed a case number, name, physical characteristics (height, eye colour, body type, hair colour and type), and grounds for detention (categorised either as '§ 36', 'other Aliens Act', or 'asylum shopper'). To some extent, their disassociation from the deportation regime enabled prison officers to share their critical views on what they perceived as an ineffective, even absurd spectacle of law enforcement. Moreover, and even though most people detained in Ellebæk were eventually deported (in 2018, 87 per cent of detention orders ended in deportation, and in 2020, the figure was 74 per cent, according to numbers retrieved from the Danish Return Agency), stories of deportation 'failures' circulated among officers. One recurrent story shared by several prison officers was of detained people who 'had fallen asleep on the train from Sweden and woken up in Copenhagen by mistake'. These people would be apprehended by authorities and subsequently incarcerated in Ellebæk, sometimes for several weeks, while awaiting deportation back to Sweden according to the Dublin Regulation. Prison officers found it hard to see why, since the matter would have been more easily resolved if the person had simply been put on a returning train back across the bridge. One man, I was told, had been in and out of Ellebæk seven or eight times, always stating the same reason for his reappearance. As we were discussing the seeming absurdity of deportations, Arash, one of the prison officers, told me a more fantastic story:

> I don't know if it was just a rumour – it's a story about two Swedish police officers who were going to escort a deportee to Iran. At the airport in Tehran the police were locked into a room and nobody told them what was going on. After a while, the Iranian police came and told them that they just got on their shift and had no idea who these Swedish police officers were or what they were doing there – and on top of this, they had no valid visas in their passports! – so the Iranian police felt obliged to deport them to Sweden immediately. They put hand cuffs on the Swedish police officers and asked the Iranian deportee to please escort the police officers back home to Sweden.

The truth behind Arash's story is difficult to assess. But the tales of the sleepy cross-border commuters and spectacularly failing deportations are examples of the chaotic operation of deportation enforcement and how it generates cyclic mobilities, time traps, and sometimes absurd outcomes (see Eule et al., 2019; Hiemstra, 2020). Prison officers also remarked on how the court proceedings for detained foreign nationals were Kafkaesque compared to 'real' (criminal) court cases. Mikkel once told me about a colleague of his who, while auditing the court hearing of a detained man, had stood up in the courtroom and exclaimed, 'But all detention orders are just the same!' For this, he had been scolded by the management. It was, after all, not the prison officers' job to question court orders[5] – although, the unintelligibility of court hearings regarding detention orders was also in agreement with detained people's experiences (see Ellebæk Contact Network, 2020). Yet, the illegibility and seemingly arbitrary operation of the detention and deportation apparatus reinforced prison officers' perception that Ellebæk, the people imprisoned there – and, by extension, the officers themselves – were neglected.

While working in Danish prisons, officers had been responsible for ensuring imprisoned people's access to education, vocational training, civil rights, and psychosocial support. Yet, none of these schemes was available in Ellebæk, even though there were, like in all other prisons, 'opportunities' offered to those incarcerated to undertake prison labour, and/or partake in daily activities in exchange for a small amount of money (less than EUR 2 per hour or EUR 35 per week; see Canning, 2019b), for which they could buy snacks and cigarettes, or phone cards, which were their only means of communicating with the outside world. As prison labour, they would clean the detention wings, cook, or distribute food. They could also work in the so-called production room, a large warehouse adjacent to the main prison building, where those imprisoned spent five hours a day, Monday through Friday, sorting red plastic strips into boxes of 1,000 each, placing stickers on low-price products, or putting recycling stickers on San Pellegrino bottles. These products, I was told, were shipped from China via Rotterdam, and eventually ended up in low-price stores in Denmark. 'It gives inmates something to do and keeps their minds off other things', Yannick explained to me: 'we don't give them any advanced tasks, this is more like something you put handicapped people to do. But they earn good money here, some of them get more than they would earn in their home countries.' A teacher was also hired in Ellebæk to offer English classes, held in a separate building, which according to the teacher allowed participants to 'get out of their rooms, make some coffee, and relax for a while'. Finally, detained people could partake in a workshop for handicrafts, such as sewing and drawing. This was where Farhad had drawn the postcard of the prison fences disintegrating into birds, and Martin, the director, spoke warmly about these different 'activation offers'. He was particularly proud of a recent initiative, where workshop participants had been asked to paint a memory game with the flags representing the countries they had passed through on their way to Denmark. Martin explained,

> These people often passed many different countries, so this is a way for them to make use of their story. And then they can choose to put their signature on

them and we save them and can give them to visitors, or to children. It really motivates them that they are offered the opportunity to give something to children. This way, they leave a piece of remembrance of themselves here. Also, we see that they bring experiences, that they also have 'hearts and minds' and aren't just an anonymous mass.

The activation schemes were presented as ways of rendering incarcerated people's time productive, if not profitable. Like elsewhere, such prison labour was considered an ethical and 'restorative' intervention (see Sliva and Samimi, 2018), where incarcerated people were offered a chance not only to demonstrate their productivity, but as Martin's comment suggested, to restore their humanity. Implicitly, then, they were considered less than human in the first place. Reflecting on how this differed from how officers approached incarcerated citizens, Mikkel, a senior prison officer who was approaching his retirement, explained, 'It's a bit different from Danish prisons, because there the aim is to make prisoners become better people. And that's not our aim here. We're just warehousing them […] we don't have an aim with them.' He continued with a shrug, 'we lack a proper work description. Politicians find it convenient just to hide people here. The conditions are shit … sometimes, I feel ashamed. But that's how the system is, it's just because they are asylum seekers that they can treat them like that. After a while, you get used to it.'

To get used to and to make sense of the dehumanisation of incarcerated people ostensibly based on their legal status, prison officers relied on racial matrices. Race, alongside gender, sexuality, and class, functioned as axes of differentiation that officers drew on to position themselves in relation to the people detained and to structure interactions in Ellebæk. The vast majority of prison officers were white men with Danish working-class or lower middle-class backgrounds. Many officers came from rural areas in Denmark and frowned at my mention of living in the Nørrebro area in Copenhagen, which they associated with social problems of delinquency, poverty, and insecurity – issues which in their imaginary had 'arrived' in Denmark with people of 'non-Western origin'. The racialised, classed sense of togetherness that brought prison officers together was more intensely felt by some: Karsten, for instance, jokingly referred to Ellebæk as 'a refuge for weirdos', amiably recounting the story of a colleague who had temporarily moved into a cell in an empty prison wing for a few weeks following his recent divorce, until he found a new place to live. Yet, prison officers' sense of togetherness was constituted through depicting detained people as 'others'; stripped of their social and rehabilitative functions, and operating in an environment that they perceived as a poor replication of the prison system, prison officers drew on racial imaginaries to make up for and to make sense of their role as border guards.

Racial matrices and the production of difference

It is dinner time. Two detained men who are working in the kitchen are distributing the food in each detention wing, accompanied by three prison officers. People in the wings approach the gates one by one, receiving their portion of rice and stew and complimentary pieces of bread. One man walks up to the officers and asks if he can make a phone call (phones are installed in each corridor but he would need money to use them) but it is unclear whether the officers understand him. One of the officers, Yannick, cuts him off: 'Tomorrow! Tomorrow!' And the man gives up. Yannick turns to another man who is just about to pick up his food, 'You look just like another guy who had the same name as you. He stayed here for a year!' The man looks startled. 'Me – one year?' 'No no, another guy, smaller than you', Yannick tries to assure him; the man is still confused. Yannick turns to me: 'I am just making conversation with them to check the atmosphere. Just to see how they react.' The incarcerated men who are distributing food finish their work and we move on with the food cart to the next wing. Two people initially do not show up to collect their dinner, which makes Yannick irritated. When they arrive, he snorts, 'Are you from Somalia or what? Are you stupid? Dinner is served at the same time every day. How can you miss it? Next time we are not giving you any.' He jokingly nods towards the men working in the kitchen: 'They will beat you with a loaf of bread if you are late next time.' A younger detained man, whom I have been chatting with in the past few days, stops us to ask the officers something. He offers us some dried dates. I take one, Yannick refuses. 'It looks like camel shit', he snorts, 'I never accept anything from the inmates.' Before we leave the wing, another man comes up to us with a piece of paper, which he points at while asking Yannick, 'Does it say I get out of here?' Seemingly stressed by the sudden question, Yannick quickly responds, 'No', and continues, seemingly in an attempt of a joke, 'we can take away your freedom, but we can't take away your dreams!' Once we have left the detention wing and shut the door behind us, Yannick is told off by Mikkel, who overheard the last interaction. 'I don't know what these decisions mean and therefore I never read them out to them, so I don't give them the wrong information.'[6]

The interactions I observed between prison officers and the people detained in Ellebæk usually played out along the lines of the encounters exemplified above. Officers' main tasks consisted in escorting detained people between different appointments, including inscription and discharge, and meetings with lawyers and visitors. They also conducted the daily headcounts and distributed meals and medicine (many of those incarcerated were prescribed anti-depressive medication, sleeping pills, or painkillers). Interactions were brief and limited by language barriers, and by officers' impatience to get done with their task, which regularly created misunderstandings. Officers used offensive jokes and racial slurs to 'test' the atmosphere, and discipline and degradation to assert their authority. When they were not occupied with overseeing the daily routines in the prison, officers would spend most of their work shifts in their offices, from where they could hear but not see the people detained. This was also where I spent the main part of my fieldwork. Especially on weekends and during night shifts, after the evening headcount, the prison officers' job did not entail much else than staying awake, watching TV, and chitchatting to each other – or with me. Our conversations ranged from forestry, officers' plans for vacation or life after retirement, and comparisons between the cartoon-like characters of the Swedish and Danish royal families, to stories from a hardened prison world, discussions over the alleged threat of mass immigration, and relatedly, the racialised threat that officers ascribed to the people detained.

I'm in the office of detention wing 17 with Mia and Markus, who are among the junior officers. Not much is happening. I usually get restless from sitting down there so I stand up, clutching today's fifth cup of coffee. Arash enters the office, panting. He has played football with some of the detained men in the sport hall, and Mia asks how it went. 'We won', he says, triumphantly, 'but there was a North African who started a fight. I don't get why they always have to fight; they haven't even lived through war themselves. If you have then I understand you get aggressive, but with these boys …', Arash turns to me, 'You know, North Africans are thieves and tricksters who cheat on the system. I promise you, Muslims stand for 90 per cent of all crimes in the Nordic countries. I'm not racist but I'm telling you like it is.' Arash often engages in lengthy rants over incarcerated people with North African backgrounds in particular, making some of his colleagues roll their eyes, and me bite my tongue. I ask how that makes him feel about working here, given his irritation with the people he works with. 'You get an identity crisis! It breaks my heart when we are separating families or sending Afghans and Iranians back to war and persecution, but we let North Africans and others, who are just here to trick the system, stay. You want to help those who are in need but you end up doing something else.' Arash leaves to change from his sportswear back into his prison uniform. The other officers in the room laugh quietly, exchanging some jokes on Arash's behalf. Some of them would not express it as bluntly as he does, but they agree with what he says. Mia emphasises that stereotypes are an important source of knowledge for prison officers, as it helps them anticipate the behaviour of inmates. Hans agrees and goes on listing another couple of racist stereotypes. 'Somalis are proud, Russians are calm as many of them are criminals and are used to being imprisoned. And Nigerians fight hard. You would rather have ten North Africans against you than one Nigerian. Not the women, the African women are loud, but I can tolerate that. Just not threats. But', Hans mutters, *'don't call me racist, that makes me irritated. I'm not racist. I'm equally mean to everyone.'*

Conversations such as these demonstrated officers' reliance on racist, gendered stereotypes to fixate the identity of incarcerated people. Arash was among the very few prison officers with a migrant background. It was the irony of fate, he told me, that he, who had once been imprisoned, was now imprisoning others who had fled persecution. On the other hand, he insisted, this had taught him to distinguish between 'real war survivors' and 'tricksters' who, in his view, sought to manipulate the Danish system. In the eyes of his colleagues, Arash's racialised identity as migrant from a 'non-Western country' lent his rants – while often outrageous – an air of legitimacy; his anti-Muslim statements did not seem to count as such, since other officers considered him to be 'one of them'. Moreover, Arash's white colleagues often repeated similar statements, insisting that their 'gut feelings', trained in the prison system, made them able to read and know the people detained (see also Hall, 2010, 2016).

Aretxaga (2000: 404) has argued that the state strives to produce 'legibility' of the bodies it produces as non-normative or alien. Therefore, 'the official gaze constantly scans these bodies for signs (of the criminal, the terrorist, the immigrant, the undocumented), in an attempt to [...] extricate the secret opacity of its uncanny familiarity'. In their efforts to render detained people legible, officers insisted that their racist gut feelings provided them with a reliable source of knowledge. The matrices that officers drew on to identify their 'uncanny familiarity' consisted of colonial and racist tropes, which transformed detained people into tricksters and criminals, imbued with dangerous, predatory masculinity, or which reduced them to filthy, sly 'tricksters'. The fear, anxiety, and hatred that officers felt when encountering detained people were what Bonilla-Silva (2019: 1) has called 'racial emotions', which serve to sustain 'the distinctions between citizen and other [...] in the minutiae of everyday life' (Hall, 2010: 883). Moreover, by racialising the people incarcerated, prison officers also racialised themselves, and 'the state' they represented. Some of them explicitly saw their role as defending Danish/Nordic whiteness; a whiteness which also encompassed me as a white woman. I would often get into heated arguments with Hans, who during one of our conversations told me that I must make sure to 'marry white' or I would 'soon be a racial minority in my own country'. Such conspiracist fantasies of 'foreignisation' – understood as a fear of loss of imagined racial and cultural homogeneity (Rodríguez, 2018: 18) – were regularly circulated among officers in Ellebæk. In these conversations, I was positioned either as a prospective victim of this process, or as a potential racial traitor (Andreassen and Myong, 2017); for officers, my 'naïve' political views and 'political correctness' made my ascribed part in their white supremacist project fraught and ambivalent. Hans was the officer who seemed the most concerned with this ambivalence. While he was explicitly critical of my political positioning (and reproductive responsibility), he was also careful not to argue with me for too long. In the midst of a heated debate, he would switch topics from whom I should marry to another issue where we might agree – be it Doc Martens shoes (which we were both wearing), or my opinion on his wife's Chinese crested dog. When I got tired of arguing, I would silently agree to end the discussion, and ask about his own feelings for his wife's preferred dog type.

While officers relied on racial tropes and used racial slurs as techniques of dehumanisation in their everyday work, they also firmly and consistently denied being racist. The plentiful testimonies by detained people who have experienced racist and degrading treatment from staff (see Ellebæk Contact Network, 2020) have also routinely been dismissed by the prison management. Like Hans, several officers stated that they 'would not tolerate being called racist'; how could they be racist, they pondered, when they treated *all* incarcerated migrants equally badly? On a different occasion, I spent the day with Yannick in the detained women's wing and witnessed an argument between him and an incarcerated woman, who at some point during their discussion called him racist. The situation immediately escalated, with Yannick pushing her up against the wall, twisting her arm, and escorting her to solitary confinement. Afterwards, Yannick was self-conscious that I had witnessed the incident, and asked me if it had 'made me feel uncomfortable', well aware that it had. I asked why he had taken her to solitary confinement. 'This is not the first time she has called me racist', Yannick replied, 'you have got to show them who's in charge. But she will just stay there until she calms down.' Shielding themselves from allegations of racism by punishing its utterances enabled officers (and the prison management) to claim that their practices were 'innocent' and indeed, 'colourblind' (see Wekker, 2016: 4), even as racism was a structural and structuring logic of the deportation prison. Racist attitudes were after all only the most superficial expressions of the racism structurally embedded and reproduced in Ellebæk.

The everyday violence of confinement

> My husband is always worried when I go to work. I do understand him because we have quite a lot of incidents here. When I started, we had eight

suicide attempts within the first three weeks and I'm like – thank you very much, this is my welcome. Only one of them completed it, though. We have been exposed to everything here, I've been bitten, beaten, kicked … but you can't think about what could happen all the time because then you can't work.

Violence was omnipresent in Ellebæk. You could feel it in the carceral materiality of the prison; it circulated in the racist, degrading language of prison officers, and it manifested in the tools available to officers to discipline and punish those incarcerated. In the quotation above, the prison officer Mia explains how violence was present not only in her own mind – although she actively tried to shut it out – but also spilled over into the concerns of her partner. In everyday life inside Ellebæk, violence was also present as anticipation. Stories of violent incidents, like the one above, circulated among prison officers: during the hours I spent with them in the armchairs, they would often share stories from eventful work shifts and dramatic situations, when detained people had resisted detention by staging escape attempts and riots, harming themselves, or physically confronting officers. The stories served as a reminder that violence, and the threat thereof, was omnipresent, even though most of the time, nothing happened. I was regularly told, when I left the detention centre after a shift, 'You were lucky – today was a calm day.' These comments made me wonder whether I was missing out on something; if the prison was such an insecure environment, and violent interactions between staff and detained people as common as prison officers' stories suggested, these events seemed to evade me, and I them.

Violence and its anticipation are inscribed into the very nature of confinement (Drake, Earle, and Sloan, 2016), as is its uneven distribution over time. Research on asylum camps, prisons, and migration-related detention has documented the temporal violence of incarceration, where those confined are forced to endure oceans of 'sticky', protracted time (Griffiths, 2013; 2017) spent waiting, experiencing boredom (Torbenfeldt Bengtsson, 2012; Wagner and Finkielsztein, 2021), but also anxiety, as the stillness can at any point be pierced by disruptive events. In deportation prisons, waiting is overshadowed by the anticipation of expulsion (Borrelli, 2021). The anticipation of violence and the uncertainty it brings has a high toll on detained people, causing stress, sleep deprivation, frustration, and depression (see Boochani, 2018; Bosworth, 2014; Esposito et al., 2020), and sometimes, premature death. In Ellebæk, six suicide attempts were recorded and two people killed themselves between 2012 and 2018 (Folketingets Ombudsmand, 2019), but it is not clear whether suicide attempts such as the one described by Mia as routine, almost mundane occurrences, were included in these statistics. What remains uncounted is also the long-lasting, traumatising effects of incarceration that people continue to experience long after they are released from deportation prisons like Ellebæk.

Hence, violence is integral to incarceration. To return to its manifestations inside Ellebæk, I found that the sticky time, boredom, and anxiety also operated on officials, leading them to provoke confrontations that, like self-fulfilling prophecies, reaffirmed their violent anticipations. Similar dynamics have been described by Didier Fassin (2017) in his ethnography of urban policing in the banlieues of Paris, where officers, in the absence of tangible work tasks and action that they had anticipated, provoked confrontations with residents of the suburbs in order to fulfil their own expectations of what police work should entail. The officers' perceptions of the suburbs as 'savage' neighbourhoods were informed by racist tropes, and a glorification of violence, fear fostered through political and media discourse, and officers' own lack of familiarity with and comprehension of the neighbourhoods they were policing. However, their prejudices stood in sharp contrast to the everyday realities of police work, where they spent most of their shifts idly waiting for alarm calls that rarely came or patrolling quiet neighbourhoods in search of criminal activity that did not occur. Fassin observes how an 'illusion of action' was nevertheless maintained by officers: by recounting spectacular events that had taken place during previous shifts, they maintained the impression that violence, delinquency, and disorder were around the corner 'despite all evidence on the contrary' (Fassin, 2017: 291). These illusions led officers to step up their proactive policing efforts, principally consisting of harassing *sans-papiers* and racialised young people with unwarranted stops and frisks and responding to any misdemeanour with disproportionate violence. Consequently, the relations between the police force and neighbourhood residents kept aggravating, largely because of police officers' futile efforts to fill their work hours.

Fassin's observations are useful for understanding how the anticipation of violence among frontline workers makes them resort to pre-emptive and disproportionate use of force in their encounters with racialised (non)citizens. The latter are in turn framed as those responsible for danger and disorder. In a similar way, the circulation of racist tropes, chauvinist attitudes, and violent anticipations among Ellebæk's prison officers led them to use force pre-emptively as a way of affirming their authority – and of confirming their racist suspicions that incarcerated individuals were imbued with danger and violence. This way, the structural violence of detention was reproduced in everyday life. The following vignette offers an example of this dynamic.

I am spending the evening in detention wing 18. John, Alex, and Markus, who used to work together in a high-security prison, are finishing up dinner in their office. Their food consists of fried bacon, which they have carefully arranged on their plates and topped with fried eggs. They offer me a huge glass of Pepsi Light, which I decline. We talk about how working in the prison impacts them. Alex says, 'You do get a bit crazy here … you must not bring work home. You must shut down, don't feel sorry for them. Some do – but they don't last here for long. You have to protect yourself.' I ask about their exposure to violence. Markus joins the conversation:

> You get used to it. You can't think about that every time you go to work, that would make you crazy. Personally, I can see how incidents where I have used force sort of become blurred, I can't separate them. Like on New Year's Eve, when three inmates cut themselves, they cut deep and there was blood everywhere, but neither the police nor the healthcare personnel had time because it was New Year's Eve and just after midnight, so we had to take care of it. We did what we could, but one of them took off the bandage in the isolation cell and there was blood all over again and we had to redo it … Afterwards one of them got sixty stitches. And at the same time, two people tried to escape through the roof! I was exhausted that morning when we had the debriefing and diffusing and whatever it's called … but then, the next day I was at work, I used force three times. These incidents become blurred, you get used to it.

Markus now notices that the Pepsi bottle is still on the table. It should be in the fridge, he grunts, because he prefers it cold. 'It's just because we were so distracted by the female presence!' They all laugh. I blurt, 'You're all quite macho here, huh?'[7] Markus replies,

> No, this is nothing, believe me. They act differently when you or some other woman is around. When you are here it's much calmer than usual. Boys be boys, you know, we are loud and joke around with each other, that's just the way we are. And, maybe you have noticed, we have a very dark humour. It's necessary to deal with all of this, people think we are harsh, but it's our jargon.

We are interrupted by the news that the police are on their way with four people who have been stopped at the border in Padborg. The prison officers get up and go off to conduct the evening headcount and lock down the wings to prepare for the new arrivals. The police soon arrive with the four men, three of whom are escorted to a waiting room, while the fourth is called in for registration. The prison officers exchange some cordial jokes with the police, whom they seem to know, wave them off, and get to work. 'He has got a lot of luggage', John remarks, as he searches through the man's confiscated bags. Wearing plastic gloves, John picks out prohibited items such as liquids, consumable goods, and sharp objects, and puts them in sealed plastic bags. The man asks in English whether he can keep his own shampoo. Alex, who is standing behind the computer desk and enters the man's personal details into a digital file, remarks, 'This is not a hotel, this is a prison.' 'But I'm not a criminal', the man protests. 'Yes', says Alex, fixing his eyes on him, 'yes you are. You are illegal here in Denmark and therefore you are a criminal. It's criminal for you to be here.' The man doesn't answer this time. Instead, he asks if the officers can please give him back some papers that John is just about to put into a plastic bag. Markus, who's standing by, now approaches the man, measuring him. John replies with a firm 'No. The police need to check these papers, we don't know what they are for, so they will have to check them and then you can have them.' The man protests, 'but the police said I could have them back!' He now stands up, but Markus takes him by the collar of his sweater, pushes him towards the wall and then down onto the chair. 'You sit down. You calm down', he says in a firm, loud voice. The man is visibly upset but does not fight. 'Listen. No papers now. You calm down!' Markus and John order the man to stand up and then escort him to the solitary confinement cell,[8] where they tell me he will be staying until he 'calms down'. He is released into one of the wings one hour later once the other new arrivals have been registered.

The officers call the next man to registration. Alex takes his photo and measurements; the man is taller than Alex, which makes the other officers laugh. The man has a rucksack, in which John finds a bag of makeup. 'This yours?' John asks, visibly amused, as he examines its contents: mascara, lip gloss, and rouge. 'You like makeup?' He turns to the others: 'Should we put him in the ladies' department, perhaps?' The man does not speak English, only some German, but he gets the message, and points to the bag. 'Frau, Frau.' 'You stole it?' John asserts, 'He stole this, I'm sure.' Here, I object. I'm unsure of what the implications will be if the officers keep insisting that the man has stolen the bag, and I believe I understand what the man tries to say. 'He says the bag belongs to his wife', I tell them. 'Whatever', John snorts; he has found a sanitary pad in the bag and is now even more amused. 'This? You need this? You bleed?' The three prison officers laugh. The man chooses not to react. Once the prison officers have unpacked all his belongings before his eyes, he receives his bed linen and is led down into one of the wings. Once they have left, Alex turns to me and explains:

> Arabs – they are usually troublemakers. Africans are very proud – like you could see with that man who we brought to solitary confinement – but this was nothing. Sometimes we are down fighting them on the floor. They are frustrated when they arrive here and it's better to show them straight away who's in charge. But if it gets uncomfortable for you, you just leave, ok?

I assure Alex that I am fine, although I am boiling. I watch Markus bringing the next detained man into the room for registration, while John jokingly smacks Alex on the bum with his plastic glove.

This evening shift was significantly more eventful than most other nights I spent in Ellebæk. Yet, the incident is instructive for understanding how the violence endemic to the prison was reproduced in everyday life and materialised in prison officers' degrading language and arbitrary use of force. In the situation described above, the prison officers – much like Fassin's police officers – used provocations and so-called pre-emptive force in order to prevent detained people from challenging their authority, even though they gave no signs of intending to do so. Humiliating, racist, emasculating, and homophobic jokes were made for no reason other than provocation, and punitive measures – including solitary confinement – were used lightly and arbitrarily. However, officers did not consider any of the above to amount to 'violence', since their actions all fell inside the purview of the law; 'force' was the word they preferred to describe their own acts of legalised infliction of social, psychological, and physical harm.

Official statistics suggest that such expansive uses of 'force' were not exceptional. In 2019, there were thirty-nine reports of uses of 'force' by prison officers in Ellebæk, two of which included the use of pepper spray, and reported incidents of violence or threat of violence (Herschend, 2019). In the same year, solitary confinement was reportedly used forty-one times (eighteen people were held for more than fifteen days; see Dignity and Amnesty International, 2021). Solitary confinement – or the 'special room', as it was commonly referred to – entailed further intrusive and degrading measures, since those confined people were stripped of their clothes, allegedly as a suicide-preventive measure (see Stokholm et al., 2021). I do not know whether incidents such as the ones I witnessed, where it was clearly prison officers' behaviour that provoked the physical confrontation, were included in any of these reports, and I doubt that their provocations were reported. What I do know is that the everyday violence in Ellebæk had effects on the minds and bodies of the people incarcerated. Philip, who was part of the healthcare team in Ellebæk, said, 'You can observe how someone enters here and is 100 per cent human. But after some rounds in and out of solitary confinement and after having been subjected to force, there's maybe 15 per cent left of that person. It's like there's a light that goes out.' Philip, and the uniformed prison officers in Ellebæk, were well aware that the routinised exposure to physical force and degradation, and inadequate healthcare provisions, combined with the stress and anxiety induced by the unintelligible judicial proceedings that characterised Denmark's restrictive deportation regime, had a detrimental impact on the people incarcerated. In addition, prison officers actively partook in breaking detained people down spiritually (through the protracted uncertainty, amounting to mental torture; and through degrading and dehumanising treatment) and physically (through physical force and violent anticipation). This dehumanisation performed important legitimation work for the deportation regime.

Without downplaying officers' responsibility or excusing their participation in maintaining a racist and violent system, and without comparing their experiences to the conditions of those detained, I want to linger for a moment on how the dehumanisation of detained and deportable people operated on the subjectivities of prison officers. In the vignette above, just before entering the registration room and beginning the ritual of degradation and violence against the newly arrived men, Markus and Alex reflected on how they had become desensitised to the types of violence they witnessed and participated in inside Ellebæk. On the one hand, they saw violence (or 'force') as a necessity to maintain order in the prison because, according to Markus, incarcerated people 'could only speak the language of violence'. On the other, they were well aware that this violence caused harm and also profoundly affected them. On a different occasion, I spoke to Markus about how he had changed as a prison officer, to which he answered 'well you saw what happened in the Stanford experiment. How the guards couldn't handle the power. It's like that.'[9] Scholars writing on bureaucratic violence (Arendt, 1963; Bauman, 2013; Gupta, 2012; Herzfeld, 1992) have highlighted how the division of responsibilities, de-individualisation, and routinisation of force enable state officials to remain morally and emotionally indifferent to the violence they inflict upon others. This way, violence which would otherwise have been perceived as exceptional or morally repulsive becomes normalised. Affective disengagement did indeed help some prison officers cope with the violence they were enacting; John once told me, 'you can't get too engaged ... so you put a filter on instead. You focus on the daily routines, distributing rice, giving them an extra apple. I think that's a survival instinct. Otherwise, it becomes overwhelming.' And Mikkel explained, 'Many of us have burnouts. Either you become too hard, some have this approach but that will eventually break you, it's not sustainable. Others are too soft, and they get sort of filled up. Others just quit.' However, the violence presented in this chapter is not primarily enabled through indifference (cf. Herzfeld, 1992) but through the construction and reproduction of racial *difference*. The neglect of detained people's health and lives, and the affective 'hardening' of prison officers, are part of the operation of systemic racism, here disguised under 'race-indifferent' classifications of citizenship and (non)belonging (see Armenta, 2017: 83). The dehumanisation and violent treatment of racialised others were neither aberrant nor exceptional; it was constitutive of the political identity that officers were invested with as border guards of an imaginative white Danish nation.

Concluding remarks

Ellebæk is a place that, in the words of Weil (1939), reduces 'a still human being into a thing'; an expellable and disposable thing. The state violence embedded in Ellebæk deportation prison operates through corporal control and everyday violence and degradation. These practices make incarcerated people disappear: existentially, as they are deprived of their humanity; and corporally, through their eventual expulsion. Central to this project is the racialisation of incarcerated and non-deported people, which takes place through the spectacular criminalisation, symbolic punishment, and routinised dehumanisation of foreign nationals racialised as 'illegal' criminalised migrants. In this chapter, I have shown how race operates as a fundamental and not-so-well hidden 'organising grammar' (Wekker, 2021), which reverberates in – but is by no means limited to – prison officers' racial slurs and violent treatment of those incarcerated in Ellebæk, in the neglectful institutional setup, which prison officers readily admitted would be 'unacceptable' if those incarcerated were Danish citizens, and in the racist political discourse in Denmark which works to gradually deprive non-deported people of their rights and their humanity.

If race was an organising principle in the prison, it was also persistently denied by the prison officers, for whom racial matrices were perceived as a neutral way of 'knowing' those imprisoned and anticipating their actions. This way, racism was at once hyper-visible and depoliticised; similarly, the violence – structural, and interpersonal – used to control incarcerated people is codified as 'force' to lend it an air of legitimacy and proportionality. Prison officers were at once using this force and were subjected to it, with some of them readily admitting how it dehumanised not only those incarcerated but affected them, too. In this realisation of how violence shaped their subjectivities, we also see a shift away from the view of violence as 'exceptional' and 'extra-legal', which the codified language of 'force' suggests, towards a realisation of its systemic character. This does not remove the responsibility of staff for their violent and degrading behaviours but helps us understand how it has come to be, and how it has come to be acceptable, even legitimate. The systemic, racialised violence that underpins and is implemented in Ellebæk deportation prison needs to be situated within a global context, where deportation prisons are already embedded in what Khosravi (2019: 114) has called a global 'infrastructure of racism' that ascribes differential value to the lives of racialised border crossers. This is the way we can grasp how institutions such as Ellebæk, and the harms they cause, have come to be perceived as a normalised, if not necessary part of the national order of things.

Notes

1 For example, the image is used on activist merchandise: www.no-gods-no-masters.com/section-zip-hoodie/revolution-anarchy-communist-zip-hoodies-C65348/?p=2 (accessed 9 August 2022).

2   The Aliens Act stipulates an initial time limit of detention to six months, with the possibility for the court to extend it to a total of eighteen months (§ 37(8)). Decisions on detention are taken by the police, who are in charge of deportation processes (since 2020 in collaboration with the Home Travel Agency), and must normally be reviewed by a court within seventy-two hours. The Danish Aliens Act (§ 36) justifies detention on the following bases: If a person who has applied for residence permit refuses to stay in the location designated by authorities (§ 36(1)), fails to appear before the immigration service or police for interrogation (§ 36(2)) or fails to 'comply' during an asylum process, for instance by refusing to clarify their identity, nationality, or travel route (§ 36(4)); or if they do not cooperate with the police in their deportation process (§ 36(5–8)). Danish immigration law allows for the detention of children. However, following critique from the European Committee for the Prevention of Torture (CPT), who deemed Ellebæk unsuitable for children, detention of children is extremely rare. Instead of detaining, for example, an entire family, authorities incarcerate one parent while the children are held in the adjacent Sandholm asylum camp or in a deportation camp together with the other parent. People who are held for immigration-related purposes but who also have a criminal conviction are detained in police custody (§ 35).

3   In their 2019 report, the CPT concluded that the conditions in Ellebæk were 'unacceptable', criticising, among other things, the overcrowding, inadequate access to medical screenings for detained persons, and excessive use of punitive measures such as solitary confinement. In their response to this criticism, authorities blamed the 'large turnover of detainees (with short stays) who commit substantial vandalism at the centre' for having caused the standards in the prison to deteriorate (Danish Government, 2020: 3).

4   Roughly EUR 2,700 (EBT).

5   The officer's remark repeats previous criticism that Denmark has received regarding automated detention orders and faltering legal procedures; see Council of Europe's Committee for the Prevention of Torture and Inhuman or Degrading Treatment or Punishment, 2019; Ellebæk Contact Network, 2020).

6   The last part of this fieldnote also appears in Eule et al. (2019: 124).

7   The 'macho culture' was but one manifestation of how the togetherness among prison officers was gendered, which has also been documented elsewhere in research on 'regular' Danish prisons (see Andersen, 2017). This culture endorsed a 'hard' attitude towards incarcerated persons, manifested in offensive humour, and a readiness to use force (*magt*). Women officers were by default perceived to be 'soft' (*bløde*) and physically weak, and as such, perceived as a threat to the safety and security in the prison. This was a tension they were constantly forced to navigate (see Lindberg, 2022).

8   Ellebæk has three solitary confinement cells, which can be used up to twenty-eight days in case a detained person is perceived as 'problematic or non-compliant with the centre regimes' (cf. Canning, 2019b: 38). The rooms contain nothing but a bed pinned to the floor. Sharp edges are removed in order to prevent instances of self-harm. From the solitary confinement cell, detainees have to call on prison officers to go to the bathroom or go out for a cigarette.

9 Markus referred to the infamous prison simulation experiment that took place at Stanford University in 1971, which explored the psychological effects of authority by letting students act as prison guards and prisoners, respectively. The experiment was abandoned only after a few days, as students allegedly quickly began abusing their power. Not only the ethics but also the validity of the experiment and its research design have recently been called into question. Yet I interpreted Markus's comment as a reflection on how state violence affects those who enforce it.

3

Deporting with care: detention in Sweden

Dear Swedish King and Prime Minister,

I am an eleven-year-old boy and I am very sad because my parents, my four-year-old sister and I are in a prison. In the weekend we were in a guesthouse where we saw the police coming. We were very afraid when we saw them, there were many policemen, and we didn't know what to do […] they took us in a car and my sister asked on the way where are we going with the police. […] Here there is only me and my sister no other children. I cry at night because I don't want my sister and parents to see it and get sad. Please release us from here and don't send us back to my country. I love my country but I'm afraid something bad will happen. If your children had been in my place, what would you have done, you would have fought like a parent. […] I know you and everyone else who comes from Sweden are nice and kind and I know you love children. Please don't send us back to my country.
(Letter to the Swedish king and prime minister, published in Magnusson and Mikkelsen, 2017, author's translation)

On 25 August 2017, the Swedish border police raided a weekend leisure camp organised by the Swedish church for families who lived under threat of deportation. The incident attracted significant media attention, since the police had breached the informal principle of church asylum; a principle that, with few exceptions, has historically been respected by the Swedish police.[1] Several among the apprehended families had open deportation cases, and one of the families was brought to the deportation prison where I was conducting fieldwork. One of the children, a young boy, wrote the letter to the Swedish king and the prime minister quoted above. He pleaded for the family's release and for their deportations to be suspended, since his father feared for the family's safety in the country they had fled from. The family had also appealed the deportation order, claiming there were new circumstances in their asylum case that had not been taken into consideration (in accordance with the Aliens Act, chapter 12, § 18–19). When I arrived at the deportation prison one morning, detention staff had just learnt that the family's appeal had been dismissed. The police were already on their way to pick up the family for deportation. They would be there within ten minutes.

In the common room, the atmosphere is tense. I stay there with two detention officials while two others go to wake up the family, staying in the section for women and families. The family appears a few minutes later. The father is on the phone, unsuccessfully trying to reach their lawyer. The young boy starts making breakfast sandwiches for himself and his younger sister, carefully buttering the pieces of tin loaf bread, to save for their journey. The mother hugs some of the other incarcerated women who have stood up to say goodbye. Staff are quietly standing by. They are notified that the police have arrived, and the family is escorted to pick up their luggage and retrieve their personal belongings, which had been confiscated when they were incarcerated. When they leave, they will exit through the back door and enter directly into the police car, which is parked in an enclosed hangar attached to the building. From there, they will be escorted to the airport. Back in the common room, the staff slowly resume their routine tasks of filling up the coffee thermoses for breakfast and inspecting the detention premises. I stay with two senior detention officials, Greta and Livia, who are discussing what just happened.

> Livia: They submitted a demand to suspend the deportation last night. It's a dirty trick – they do it in the last minute because they know that the deportation will be suspended until their application has been reviewed. And – did you read that letter in the newspaper? They are exploiting the children! You might feel sorry for them but they shouldn't use their kids like that, imagine the responsibility that puts on the kids.

> Greta: Yes, and when you opened the newspaper this weekend you would read on one page that the police are horrible people who raid church camps and deport families. And on the next page, you read that the police are too lenient and criticised for not deporting more people. It's crazy, what are people supposed to believe ... no matter what they do, people think it's wrong!

I follow Zita, another detention official, as she goes to clean out the family's room. Sheets, towels, and cups with the family members' names on stickers are collected to be washed up. The name tags are removed, and plastic dinosaurs are put back into the box of toys that was brought in for the children. Zita tells me that this was a particularly difficult case. Not only did it involve children, which for her is always upsetting, but it was also mediatised because of the police raid in the church and the young boy's letter in the newspaper. Detention staff who spoke to the family had also got the impression that the father's fear of returning was genuine. Zita explains that she often finds deportation emotionally strenuous, 'It's hard to know how to react when they leave. Shall we wave goodbye and smile? Not really. Or look sad? No, you know, we must keep our act together.' This time, it was hard. But, Zita concedes, as we carry the box of toys back to the storage room, her opinion doesn't really matter. The outcome of the asylum case is not in her power to decide.

The incident, which took place at the beginning of my fieldwork, illustrates the contestations over deportation that take place within and beyond the walls of the deportation prison. The vignette exemplifies some of the strategies that people threatened by deportation may use in their struggle to remain, the suspicion that resistance evokes among state officials (who called the uses of legal and public appeals 'dirty tricks'), and how deportation is always a matter of (highly asymmetrical) contestations until the very last minute of enforcement. It also shows the ambivalence with which detention staff move between serving coffee in personalised coffee mugs, 'waving goodbye' to people bound for deportation, and partaking in the enforcement of this turbulent process. This ambivalence encapsulates the oxymoron of a 'humane and dignified' detention regime (DeBono et al., 2015: 19), where welfarist care and compassion are mobilised to justify and smoothen incarceration and deportation enforcement.

If Ellebæk deportation prison was a spectacularly punitive institution, ridden by orchestrated neglect and violent anticipation, the Swedish detention regime exemplifies a rather different governing logic. In Swedish deportation prisons, care and compassion are mobilised for the purpose of facilitating 'smooth' and 'humane' deportations, and significant efforts are made to downplay the inherent violence of the deportation process. As critical researchers on detention and deportation enforcement have shown, sensitivity and care are 'perfectly compatible with brutal systems of control' (Gill, 2016: 17). The chapter describes a detention regime where state violence is meticulously calculated, codified, and performed under the guise of humanitarianism, for the supposed good of the people who are about to be deported. In the final section, I reflect on the continuities and the differences between the Danish and Swedish deportation prisons, and what they have to say about 'the state' and its performances of punishment and control.

A 'humane and dignified' detention regime?

When I tell people I work in detention (*förvaret*) they ask, what are you warehousing there? Tomatoes, gherkins, furniture? I say no, it's the Swedish Migration Agency detention centre, but the term is just wrong. These are people we are dealing with, not chairs.

Shahram Khosravi (2009: 41) has argued that the Swedish term *förvar*, which literally translates as 'warehouse', well captures the impersonal infrastructure set up not 'to tend or to treat' but to *keep* incarcerated people *available* for investigation or deportation. Yasmin, the official quoted above, agreed that the term had dehumanising connotations. Yasmin, who was in her mid-twenties and was working part-time in detention while finishing her master's degree in human rights, was uncomfortable with the official name of her workplace. When friends asked her about her job, she told me, she would usually just tell them that she worked for the Swedish Migration Agency, or simply, 'for the state'. Yet with all its uneasy connotations, the terminology is illustrative of the rationalising and depoliticising approach to deportations that prevails in Sweden. We can understand *förvar* as an 'alibi term', a political artefact (Lecadet, 2018), which encloses the paradoxes of a 'humane' and 'dignified' deportation regime.

The notion of a 'humane' deportation apparatus dates back to 1997, when the Swedish Migration Agency took over responsibility for running deportation prisons from the police. Prior to this, people detained on administrative grounds in accordance with the Aliens Act were held in police custody, supervised by private security firms. Following reports of violent incidents and degrading treatment by staff, responsibility for the operation of pre-deportation detention was subsequently handed over to the civil migration authorities (see Khosravi, 2010). In the preparatory works of the new law on detention (Prop. 1996/97: 147), it was underlined that the deportation prisons should henceforth retain a *civil* character and should 'remain as close as possible to reception centres' (Prop. 1996/97: 2), while any resemblance to prisons should be minimised. The vision of a civil detention apparatus was later codified in the 2006 Aliens Act, which stipulates that the prisons should be run in a 'humane and dignified' manner. This principle has been codified and inscribed into institutional practice. It is manifested in the setup of deportation prisons, which are low security facilities with relatively high material standards, and in the strong emphasis and preference that authorities place on voluntary over forced deportations (DeBono et al., 2015). In contrast to Ellebæk prison, Swedish deportation prisons are designed to *de*criminalise detained people, and ascribe staff a considerably more proactive role in their detention and deportation cases.

The use of deportation prisons for the purpose of controlling 'illegal immigration' has continuously expanded since the mid-2000s (Jansson-Keshavarz, 2016),[2] and the number of people incarcerated annually has been on a steady rise (from 1,645 in 2008 to 3,200 in 2014 and to 4,295 in 2019).[3] The maximum length of stay is twelve months, while the average time of detention was fifty-five days in 2020 (Migrationsverket, 2020). In spring 2021, there were six operating deportation prisons with a holding capacity of 519 people, and there are plans to build a seventh prison in Northern Sweden. The deportation prison where I conducted fieldwork was inaugurated in 2011. At the time of my research, it had the capacity to incarcerate eighty people in two separate departments, with a separate section for women and families. A renovated warehouse building, half of which still served as storage for an electronic utility service provider, the prison was located next to the highway outside a de-industrialised small town. Its architecture reflected the political ambition to retain a civil-oriented detention regime: for unknowing passers-by, there was little revealing that it was a site of incarceration, unless they happened to notice the inward-tilting metal fence crowning the tall walls that flanked the main entrance.

Staff members, lawyers, and visitors would enter the prison through the front doors, which required an electronic key, and which led to a small reception, offering tea, coffee, and some sweets. On the reception desk there was a small sign saying, 'You only have three choices in life: Give up, give in, or give it all you got.' To reach the spaces where those incarcerated were held, one would have to pass through four additional locked doors. Incarcerated people would enter the building from an altogether different place; they would arrive and leave in police cars or with the prison service's escorts and be shuffled through the electronically monitored gates at the back of the building. Inside the prison, secure doors locked with numeric codes and swipe cards and thick, plexiglass windows kept the people detained confined from the outside world. However – and again, in line with the decriminalising ambition of the detention regime – the prison's interior design was supposed to induce a sense of relative freedom, permitting incarcerated people to move around between their dormitories, where up to four people would sleep in the same room, and the common room, where the meals were served. The common room, which was the room where staff also spent most of their working hours, was decorated with pots with plants, some framed IKEA posters, and pieces of handicraft and artwork made by incarcerated people. A TV was constantly on, alternating between Swedish news, cooking shows – and reality TV shows (see also Canning, 2019a). Incarcerated people also had unrestricted access to a computer room, a gym, and a library room containing a few books. Smokers could go outside into a confined space called the 'smoking cage'.[4]

In her writing on the architecture of migration-related detention, Chak (2016) argues that the very idea that we can mediate and manage the endemic violence of these institutions serves, in fact, to reify it. The aesthetically appealing and comfortable architectures of confinement become 'a tool of moderating violence [...] so that we don't question the logic behind their very existence' (Chak, 2016: 17; see also Keshavarz, 2018). Marianne, the director of the deportation prison and herself a former prison officer, wished that the logic would go unnoticed, even to those incarcerated. Marianne explained that they therefore made efforts to create a 'homely' atmosphere that would 'limit the number of occasions when detainees are reminded that they are confined [*frihetsberövade*]'. For detention officials, too, it was important that any association to prisons was eliminated. On my first visit to the prison, I met Joseph, who had studied public administration but spent the past decade working in psychiatric care. He initially worked 'on the floor' in the prison but had now assumed a position as decision maker and was monitoring detention decisions and undertaking quality evaluations. He took these legal responsibilities sincerely and liked to express this by making sure to dress smartly. He was the only detention official I met who wore a shirt and a suit jacket for work. Joseph sat me down in his office, located on the second floor of the building, took the Swedish Aliens Act from the bookshelf, and read in its commentary, 'It is evident that detainees should *not* be equated with prisoners [...] when it comes to our possibilities to restrict their everyday life.' He continued,

> The public has such skewed ideas of who is detained here. Most people in here have not committed any crimes and they are here for a variety of reasons. They are not here because they are dangerous. I usually say we have a normal distribution of people in here. Some are sweet, others are idiots, a third category just go around their own business. But I have read that they call the detention centres 'Sweden's Guantanamo camps', and they think that we are some sort of guards here, but we are not. We are not here to guard people – not even to prevent them from escaping. The tall fences, the plexiglass, and the climbing protection arrangements are doing that job for us. Our role is more like housing administrators.

Marianne and Joseph's emphasis on the non-punitive, and even 'homely', character of the deportation prison, and the service-oriented role of staff, contrasts with the criminalising approach to incarcerated migrants characterising Ellebæk. With its prioritisation of caretaking and maintenance functions, the Swedish deportation prison represented what Khosravi (2009: 44) has termed a 'hostile hospitality', where care and compassion function as disciplining and responsibilising mechanisms. Hence, productive tensions were formed between care and coercion, hostility, and hospitality. These seeming tensions – which as Chak notes, ultimately work in a mutually reinforcing manner – were reflected in the design of the deportation prison, and in the role of the staff.

Deporting with care

The composition and role of the staff in the Swedish deportation prison differed significantly from Ellebæk. The Swedish deportation prisons employed people from a broad variety of occupational, social, and national backgrounds. Some were students of law, criminology, or human rights; they would usually work as caseworkers (*handläggare*) and were in charge of monitoring detention orders and maintaining communication with lawyers and other agencies involved in the deportation process. Three of the caseworkers were actively working on deportation cases, which entailed holding so-called return dialogues and pressuring detained people to cooperate with authorities. The deportation prison also employed 'supervisors' (*handledare*) who worked on the floor in the detention wings, and who oversaw the day-to-day logistics, such as serving meals, making the daily inspection rounds, and monitoring the people detained and answering their questions. Staff holding these roles had diverse occupational backgrounds. Some had previously worked within the Prison and Probation Service or the military; others had worked within the healthcare sector or the National Board of Institutional Care, and yet others were truck drivers or former warehouse workers.

Marianne, the director, took pride in the deportation prison being an 'ethnically diverse' workplace (even though all managerial and decision-maker positions were occupied by white staff members). Marianne particularly valued how staff members with 'non-Swedish background' (*icke-svensk bakgrund*, a term encompassing first- and second-generation migrants, in this context in particular denoting racialised people with what is commonly referred to as 'non-European background') held language skills and 'cultural competences', which they could use to smoothen interactions with detained people. Several detention officials also had personal experiences of arriving in Sweden to seek protection, of the asylum system, and of encampment. Jaromir, who had arrived in Sweden after he fled war in former Yugoslavia in the 1990s, was one of them. He said, 'I'm empathetic to their situation as I was also a refugee once, and I know what it's like to be forced to wait.' Jaromir saw his own experience of forced displacement as something that facilitated a common understanding between himself and the people detained. In his research on detention and deportation in Sweden, Khosravi (2017a: 175) discusses how the notion of cultural proximity of racialised staff members with detained individuals is instrumentalised for deportation enforcement. He concedes, 'the 'potentiality of migrants' cultural competences is recognised and valued only in the service of expulsion of other migrants'. The celebration of 'diversity' among staff is thus not antithetical to racism, but an affirmation of the importance of race as an ordering mechanism in the deportation prison (see also Bosworth, 2018).

In contrast to Ellebæk, detention officials in the Swedish deportation prison had a proactive role in deportation enforcement. For this purpose, staff were expected to mobilise all their legal, interpersonal, and psychological skills, language, and cultural competences – and, as a last resort, physical force. Their involvement in the deportation process could indeed entail anything from dusting off a bag of plastic dinosaurs and baking cakes with detained children (see Canning, 2019a), to engaging in actual casework, to assisting in deportations. Regardless of their formal mandates, all staff members were expected to partake in facilitating deportation enforcement. Joseph told me, 'The prospects of return should be present throughout our conversations with them. If we come to discuss for instance passports, we can tell them that well, if you get your passport, you will be out of here sooner.'[5] According to Joseph, the principal role of staff was to 'help detainees to figure out their attitudes towards leaving Sweden and make them understand their situation'. One way of doing so was by manipulating their hopes, dreams, and future aspirations. Joseph put it bluntly, 'detention is a graveyard for dreams. Here, we help them bury their dreams of a possible future in Sweden and plant a seed of a dream of another future elsewhere.' Killing incarcerated people's dreams was an act of care, he insisted, since the vast majority of those detained had no prospects of obtaining legal residency in Sweden. It was therefore better that they aligned their dreams with the state's deportation fantasies as soon as possible, rather than maintaining 'false hopes' of getting a chance to remain (see Lindberg and Edward, 2021). Staff therefore considered detained people's attempts at resisting deportation by filing appeals, refusing to cooperate, or physically resisting deportations a 'waste of time' (Eule et al., 2019), whereas swift and effective deportations were a more 'humane' way to an inevitable end. Charles, a rowdy caseworker who had worked in the prison since its inauguration, explained that his strategy was to make the inevitability of deportation clear to the incarcerated person from the very beginning, to discourage any attempt at resistance.

> Our role is to make sure that those who are not allowed to remain understand and accept this decision. We do it through conversations and a sort of psychological game, to make them understand that there's no point in resisting. They don't always get it, but the ball is in their court. They think they can play it so that if they wait us out, they don't have to leave, but that's not how it works: the police will always figure them out after a while, even if they think they have guarded their alias well, and it might take time if the police have to send requests to Libya, then Morocco, then Tunisia … but they often get so tired of us after a while that they take out their passport.

Charles not only holds high trust in the enforcement capacity of the Swedish police; he also makes it clear that incarcerated individuals carry the responsibility for their own confinement, and for the violence that might eventually be used on them, should they refuse to cooperate.

As Walters (2016: 438) has argued, the 'political dream' of deportation is 'that the migrant places themselves on the plane, without the need for guards, restraints or any spectacle of enforcement'. However, officials' own deportation fantasies of swift, rational, and humane deportations regularly failed to materialise, not only because of detained people's resistance, but also due to bureaucratic or political hurdles, and to the uneven application of laws such as the Dublin Regulation. Like their Danish colleagues, detention staff encountered people who got stuck in repeated Dublin procedures, or who were oscillating back and forth across the Danish-Swedish border. Marianne commented on these cases with a mix of fascination and frustration, 'It's magical – magical! – You drop them off at the airport one day and two days later the police have apprehended them, and they are back here again' (Eule et al., 2019: 158). Such circular mobilities were far from the smooth, linear deportation process that detention staff envisioned. The staff did not only feel unease with failed deportation attempts; Greta, a senior caseworker with several decades' experience working in deportation prisons, also found 'successful' deportations taxing, especially when they involved coercive force.

> We had a chartered Frontex flight to Afghanistan some weeks ago. There were so many policemen. And protestors with megaphones and all. Fourteen detainees were going to travel, but in the end, only twelve left because the other two filed appeals against the deportation that authorities didn't have time to process ... and those two were of course very happy. But the others were sad, afraid, anxious, which I understand, and they had many questions. Some of my colleagues didn't want to take part in it but I was there to talk to them. But it has a price, it's hard ... and the next morning I woke up and read that there had been a bomb detonating in Kabul, and I have been wondering how they are doing, are they there now ... mm. Sometimes, it's really hard.

For Greta, deportation was not necessarily a successful outcome of incarceration; unless the person in question agreed to travel, she said she preferred that they were released. When she sat down with the people awaiting forced deportation to Afghanistan (deportations that are prioritised politically but contested, and which have been met with fierce resistance from non-deported people and their support groups), she witnessed their fear and anxiety, and felt that fear sticking to her, too. Such confrontations were rare, and something her colleagues would selectively avoid. I was also told that authorities sought to alter the deportation prison from which chartered flights departed, as a way of diffusing resistance attempts but also of easing the emotional burden on staff. Indeed, the deportation prison was structured in such a way that it was easy for staff to neutralise the violent realities of detention and deportation, casting themselves as caregivers, and displacing responsibility for the harms of detention from the system onto the detained people themselves.

Seeing like a welfare state

Detention officials' morning shift commenced at 07:00. After a brief meeting, where incidents from the previous shifts were reported and new arrivals and departures announced, the officials would usually sit down with a cup of coffee on the couches in the common rooms. The couches became the starting point of my fieldwork. Since staff were not allowed to be alone with detained people, they would always move around in pairs in the common room and in the dormitory corridors or sit down two and two (or as was often the case when the morning shifts began, five or seven) on the couches, placed in front of the TV. From their position, they had a good overview of the room.

Sitting on the couch did in no way equal passivity, they explained. From the couches, officials would 'feel' the atmosphere, identify changes in the behaviours and attitudes of the people detained, and, they explained, make them 'feel seen'. Greta told me, 'You have to be able to read the atmosphere. You've got to have your tentacles out, get to know them a bit, so you can get a sense of what's going on … and maintain eye contact. I think that's important, making them feel seen.' Greta would greet every person who passed by the couches with a jolly 'good morning', and always address them by their names. This, she explained, made those detained feel recognised and enabled staff to establish 'humane' relationships with them. In addition, 'seeing' was also a means to exercise control. Apart from making observations from the couches, staff undertook inspection rounds in the prison five times a day, where they entered detained people's rooms, conducted headcounts, and checked the facilities for any damage. Marianne explained, 'some think it's a lot of control, but it's because we are responsible for these people, their health and well-being – what if someone lies dead in their room and we don't realise until the day after?' If a staff member observed anything they deemed suspicious, it was noted down and shared at the next staff meeting. These reports could contain information such as 'Michel and Amadou seem suspiciously interested in the kitchen and the windows' (interpreted as an indication that they were planning an escape attempt), 'Hannah isolates herself and does not speak to anyone' (leading to her being 'flagged' for mental ill-health and risk of self-harm), and 'David is anxious about his deportation' (warranting a meeting with a caseworker).

Deporting with care 77

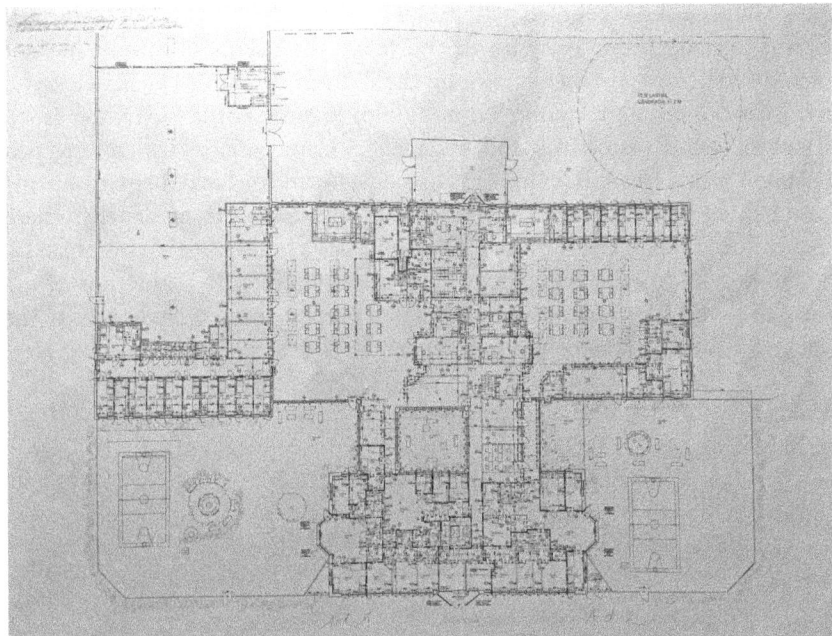

Figure 3.1 Evacuation plan of a Swedish detention centre

In her description of a Swedish deportation prison, Canning (2019a) elaborates on how the multifaceted practice of *seeing* detained people enabled staff to combine care with pacification and control. The welfarist gaze serves to make detained people intimately known to authorities, registering not only their attitudes and behaviours, but also their dreams and aspirations. While officials' compassion and concern for the well-being of detained people were surely genuine, their recording gaze was also perceived as controlling and intrusive by those incarcerated. Reza, one of the detained men who had spent several months in the prison and who would occasionally sit down with us on the couches, noted, 'They are always sitting around here, doing nothing but stare at us.' David, the man who was anxiously awaiting deportation, shared that the routine inspection rounds stressed him out, because each time, he feared they were coming to pick him up for an unannounced deportation. Unannounced deportation procedures were activated if the person in question had previously resisted or declared that they would not cooperate in the deportation process (see Borrelli, 2021); the case of the family described in the beginning of this chapter is one example.

In addition to their caring gaze, staff sought to mediate the harmful impact that the deportation prison had on incarcerated people by encouraging them to partake in daily activities. Angelica, a physiotherapist who was responsible for the scheduled activities, explained that the idea of the activities was to make them 'wind down and relax, get a sense of routine in their everyday life, and help them maintain the diurnal rhythm'. The activities on offer included circuit training, Saturday bingo, basic pottery activities (such as making pearl pegboards and bracelets), 'krim' yoga – which Angelica explained was a form of 'calming' yoga developed for locked environments – and baking cakes (which, I was told, was particularly popular when there were children detained; see also Canning (2019a) on officials' use of sticky chocolate cake to cope with sticky time in confinement). At the time of my visits, the weekly schedule with activities pinned on a whiteboard in the common rooms contained the following:

Monday	14.30 Resident meeting
Tuesday	07.15 Yoga
	14.30 Swedish church visit
Wednesday	09.30 Make a key ring
	15.45 Circuit training
Thursday	09.30 Drawing
	13.00 Quiz
Friday	Clean your room
	10.00 Yoga
Saturday	Ping pong tournament
Sunday	Bingo

Angelica admitted that the activities might seem banal and infantilising, and that they were usually poorly attended. Still, she insisted, activities could 'help detainees take their minds off bad things', such as the pains of imprisonment, or their anxiety over deportation. She continued,

> I thought they would make pearl bracelets where it said 'fuck Sweden' or something like that … and they did write 'fuck the police' and 'immigration can't take me', but other than that, it was ok. And at least they can always say no to this. When you are locked up, there is not much you can decide for yourself, including what you eat, when you eat, what to do, and so on – but at least they can decide whether or not they want to partake in our activities.

Angelica rightly identifies the harmful nature of the deprivation of autonomy and control over one's own life and daily routines that is part of confinement (Turnbull, 2018). Allowing detained individuals to refuse participation in infantilising activities might seem like a feeble compensation for this deprivation of 'free choice', but the activities also served to channel negative emotions such as anxiety, fear, and anger into manageable forms, such as a pearled bracelet stating 'fuck the police'. This way, the activities served to displace incarcerated people's attention from the structures and conditions causing their anger, anxiety, and deprivation of liberties in the first place towards 'manageable' feelings expressed in pacified forms.

The management of harms caused or amplified by imprisonment also took place through extensive documentation practices. Through standardised routines, forms, and protocols, staff were to ensure that risk behaviours (such as escape attempts, resistance to deportation, or acts of self-harm) were recorded and, ideally, prevented. The forms also legitimated expanded coercive controls: they authorised staff to confiscate the personal items of incarcerated individuals, which they deemed could be dangerous, and to enter their dormitories several times a day and wake them up for 'headcounts'. They also authorised comprehensive visitations, where personalised spaces and items were inspected, ostensibly in the name of ensuring the 'safety and security' of the people detained, while those detained were held confined in a separate room. I witnessed a couple of those visitations during my fieldwork, which were conducted since staff were suspecting that some of those detained were plotting an escape attempt. All detained men (the section where women and families resided was not searched) were then ordered into the gym where they were offered lemonade while the staff, equipped with plastic gloves and bags, searched their rooms and personal belongings. Before being let back into their rooms, all detained people were asked to sign the visitation order.

The welfarist gaze, which was supposed to prevent disruptions, resistance, and harm, did not only scrutinise detained people's belongings for potential causes of such disruptions. A contested issue at the time of my fieldwork was the recently introduced suicide screening forms, which were mandatory for detention officials to fill in for each detained person upon arrival. The protocol, I was told, had been developed after a detained man died from hanging, and was supposed to prevent similar incidents by making staff screen detained people for suicidal intent at the point of their arrival in the prison. The protocol included questions such as, 'Have you ever attempted suicide? Have you ever been treated for depression?' and, 'Have you ever felt like life is not worth living?' A suspicious answer to any of the questions could lead to solitary confinement or referral to a psychiatric clinic. Staff found the questions to be blunt, but straightforward. While understanding of their intent, they were ambivalent about having to use them in practice.

I sit down with Livia who is about to begin the registration screening of an incarcerated man. He is reserved, and she is tired, as she hasn't had time to have her morning coffee yet. He speaks some Swedish, so Livia first tries to hold the conversation without an interpreter to get it over with. We have been in the room together for about two minutes, going through the formalities of the protocol, when she double-clicks on the suicide screening form on her computer. It instructs her to ask if the man suffers from any illnesses: 'Physical? Psychological?' – to which the man answers 'yes', 'yes'. 'Did you ever try to commit suicide?' is the next question. The man doesn't understand and asks her to repeat the question. Livia gets nervous, starts gesticulating, and tries to signal what she means: cutting wrists, swallowing pills? The man still looks puzzled, but answers, 'yes'. Livia turns to me, 'no, this doesn't work. We need an interpreter.' An interpreter joins us via telephone, and Livia tries to continue with the questionnaire. The man looks down at the table. He says he is stressed out and needs to have a smoke. He hasn't smoked for twenty-seven hours, he says, so he needs it badly – and he needs his medicines. Livia persists and wants to finish with the protocol, as the man is not formally allowed to enter the prison facilities before the suicide screening is completed. She continues, 'have you been treated for depression? ... have you ever felt like life is not worth living?' 'I'm mentally ill', the man insists, 'I need my medicines. Why do you say you will help me but instead you put me in prison and want to deport me?' He is now visibly upset and makes clear that he will not answer any more questions. Livia skips most of the remaining questions and chooses to focus on confiscating his phone, which also needs to be done before they finish. Eventually, the man is allowed to enter the prison and goes out for a smoke. Livia turns to me, 'it's totally worthless, this suicide screening. So intrusive. I think you just have to trust your own judgement.'

The vignette not only demonstrates the awkwardness with which the suicide screening was used in practice. As the detained man points out and Livia admits, it is also a shallow performance of care, unlikely to capture the state of mind or mental health of the detained person, and likely to create confusion, if not animosity. While ostensibly put in place for the safety of those incarcerated, such documentation practices also obscure the original cause of the violence. Indeed, the protocol can be understood as a paperwork performance (Borrelli and Lindberg, 2020), which serves to write off institutional responsibility for harms either directly caused, or likely to be aggravated, by incarceration and the threat of deportation. In her research on migration-related detention in the United Kingdom, Mary Bosworth (2016) comes to a similar conclusion regarding the role of bureaucratic forms, which primarily serve to ensure that staff have their 'arses covered' in case a detained person suffers any mental or physical harm in confinement. She concludes that bureaucratic forms magically transform detention from a violent realm into a humanitarian one (see also Fischer, 2015), effectively averting the question of what the original cause of harm is.

White lies, ruptures, and resistance

Through the mechanisms described in the previous section, detention officials carved out a 'humane' role for themselves in the Swedish deportation prison. This role enabled them to calculate, codify, and depoliticise the violence endemic to confinement. Uses of coercive force were principally outsourced to other state actors – the police and the prison service, who were authorised and trained to use such force – while the systemic violence of confinement was mediated through the forms and bureaucratic routines that served to mediate the harms it inflicted on incarcerated people. There were also bureaucratic scripts for how detention officials should manage their emotional reactions to their work. These scripts, I argue, can be understood as white lies. They were 'white' lies in that their purpose was to avoid hurting the feelings of staff, but they were also white in the sense that they were premised upon the assumption that the deportation prison was a fair, just, and necessary element of the border regime and the global mobility apartheid it serves to sustain. This assumption, in other words, was premised upon whiteness as the norm and affirmed and normalised the racial order (Bonilla-Silva, 2019) that the border regime is premised upon. To sustain the lie that detention was useful and legitimate required that staff developed stories about their work that foregrounded some of its elements while downplaying others.

Sara and Peter were two white junior detention officials who usually worked night shifts, since it was compatible with their academic studies, and since the nights offered more time to socialise with detained people. One evening, as we sat down on the couches in the common room, Sara, who was training to become a lawyer, told me that detention was the only part of the Swedish Migration Agency she would feel comfortable working for. Making life-altering decisions in the asylum office would have been way too emotionally challenging and morally problematic for her, she explained, but in detention, she was merely enforcing others' decisions. Peter, who had studied philosophy at university, added,

> Yeah, but it's not like what happened in Nuremberg. I would never take a job where I would have to say that I was just following orders. But here it's not like that, all the cases have been processed at three levels: the Migration Agency, the Migration Court, and well, the Supreme Migration Court although the cases rarely make it all the way to there. But my point is, you must believe that the system works. At first, I thought I could never work for the Swedish Migration Agency, but then I realised I actually fit in well here … but sure, it is still a form of structural violence, locking them up like this, and we must not forget the power position we are in.

Peter refers to the post-Second World War Nuremberg Trials, where high-ranking Nazi officials were tried for war crimes, including the Holocaust.

Peter invokes Hannah Arendt's (1963) famous coverage of the trial of Adolf Eichmann, which informed her writing on the banality of evil, where she develops a critique of the bureaucratised system that permits officials to thoughtlessly follow murderous orders. Yet Peter claims that, in contrast to Eichmann, the system he and Sara are working for is fair, democratic, and just. While not prepared to take decisions, they are confident that others are doing their job, permitting them to deflect responsibility for the 'orders' they were enforcing among the 'many hands' of bureaucracy (Thompson, 1980). Just like Livia and Greta discussed in the introductory vignette, Sara and Peter also felt misrepresented when the media and activist groups criticised them for controversial detention or deportation cases. Sara said,

> We often become the bad guys. That's what people read about in the newspaper: that they have detained another family. But what they don't know is that we played bingo that weekend and that the little boy won six out of nine rounds and was super happy, and that we baked a cake together with him. Sure, it's always a pity when we detain families. But it's important that there is a balance in what comes out.

Sara and Peter's belief in the Swedish deportation regime is based on their trust in the infallibility of Swedish bureaucracies, on the one hand, and on the idea that their 'humane' work stands apart from the deportation system, on the other. In their research on staff perspectives on detention, Puthopparambil and colleagues (2015) similarly find that staff variably positioned themselves as proud enforcers of a fair and just immigration control system, which they trusted, yet were not personally responsible for, or, as detached from the system, insisting that their role was only to care for people in a vulnerable situation, not enforcing deportations (see also Wettergren, 2010). This was something I discussed with Lars, the director of another deportation prison, where I spent a day conducting fieldwork. Lars had a background in the military and a degree in psychology. He had elaborated his own sociological theory of staff emotions, which he outlined for me over a coffee.

The walls of Lars' office are covered with books. On the shelves, I spot titles about Swedish migration law, legal philosophy, political theory, prison research, and psychology. Lars says that many detention officials are struggling to make sense of their role in detention and the larger political and social structures they operate within. For him, it is important that his junior colleagues grasp these layers of complexity. Otherwise, they might end up in a situation where staff blindly 'follow orders' without further reflection – the ultimate implications of which, Lars explains, are captured in Zygmunt Bauman's Modernity and the Holocaust, *or Hannah Arendt's* Eichmann in Jerusalem, *two books that Lars picks down from the shelf. He begins to draw an image on a whiteboard to illustrate his point. I copied the image into my notebook (see Figure 3.2).*

> It is important that we see our role in the system [he draws the man in the middle], and we must be able to see what we are doing and what the consequences are. The way I see it, officials change in two different directions. Or there are several, but I see two. Either you end up being cynical, cold, and stop engaging in people's life stories. Or, you become emotionally affected, you develop sticky relationships to colleagues, you seek safety in your team but you distance yourself from the organisation as such, you consider it evil. And – you start making exceptions. A lot of exceptions. This is what I think [Lars draws the two axes on the whiteboard]: on the horizontal axis, you have individual considerations at one end, where everything becomes an exception, you end up without boundaries, perverted – on the other side of the spectrum, everything becomes structured, black and white: you become cold, cynical, dehumanised, and pathologically rulebound. And these people will trigger each other. On the vertical axis, you have the holistic understanding of our role in the process, in the entire system, and you have to be able to explain detainees' situation in relation to the system, too. At the other end, we have the small details in everyday life that matter – the yoghurt or the possession of telephones – which should reflect the holistic picture, and staff should help bring clarity here as well. But not focus too much on the household, those who make a big deal out of whether or not we serve vanilla yoghurt must be able to step back and see how this fits into the larger system ... or, those who want us to carry a metal key chain instead of using a string and swipe card, they have to think about how this fits into the system as a whole, how does that help us fulfil our role? Anyway. These are the ideal types – and we want staff to be somewhere in the middle ... And at the end of the day, what we do here is locking people up. And it is important that we understand what effects this has; that it affects ourselves and others [Lars now draws a skull symbolising the people detained]. I'm thinking here of what you said earlier that we are carrying out legal decisions here, and you have to be able to stand for it. Not denouncing responsibility for your job – you cannot say 'I didn't know' – even though our democracy is not like Hitler's, but some argue that it is. We need this knowledge to be able to see our role and reflect on what we do.

Lars contends that whether we are in Hitler's genocidal dictatorship or in the Swedish democratic welfare state, officials should not follow orders blindly, or 'thoughtlessly'. Therefore, Lars wished for detention officials to perform their tasks fully aware of their implications; they may – and should – be critical of the system, and it is through this critique that they will sustain its legitimacy. Indeed, the critique offered by Lars, Peter, and Sara remains within the self-referential logic of the benevolent and fair state system, and therefore, also builds on a reductionist and individualist understanding of this system. When comparing – and contrasting – their

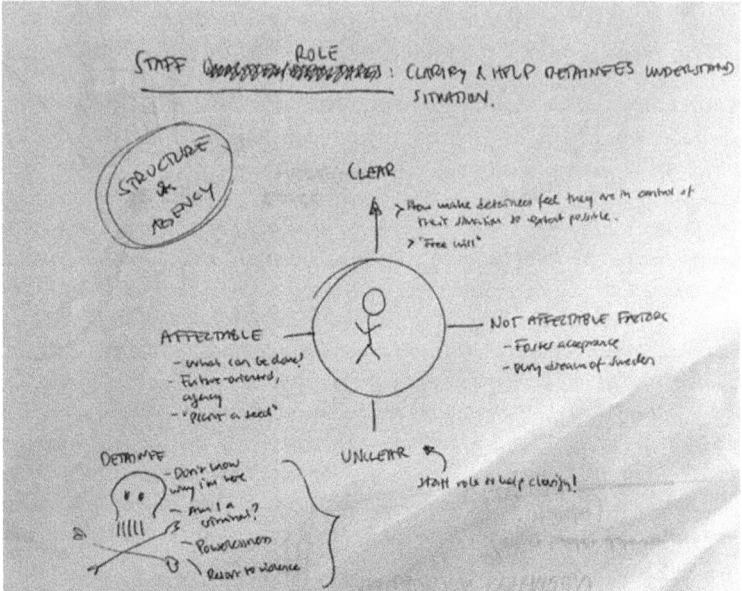

Figure 3.2 Notes based on drawing by Lars

work to the horrendous acts of extermination perpetrated by state officials in Nazi Germany, they trivialise and render impossible a critique that highlights how contemporary formations of encampment and expulsion, and the bureaucratic management of life therein, take inspiration from and build on previous ones. They also denounce the possibility that such violence is inherent to and has indeed underpinned the historical development of 'liberal democracies', including the Swedish welfare state. This is not to say that Swedish deportation prisons are *like* Nazi extermination camps. Yet, when the officials evoke the comparison with the Holocaust, and the reflections of Hannah Arendt, only to mark their own *difference* and resistance to this analogy, they refute not only the moral implications of such analogy (and the critique of their position it would inevitably provoke) but also the existence of a relationality between 'the modes of racial governance and orders of racist exclusion, humiliation and death' (Goldberg, 2009: 1280) upon which border regimes ultimately are built.

The enclosed system of emotional and moral comfort, which staff created for themselves, enabled them to maintain the white lie that their work is good, humane, and possible to set apart from other historical and contemporary manifestations of state violence. Yet, the humanitarian inclinations of the staff were founded upon and necessitated a dehumanisation of those incarcerated, whether as villains warranting monitoring and control, or victimised figures 'needing' their care. Hence, their justification mechanisms must not only be considered as 'coping mechanisms' but as mechanisms of upholding racial hierarchies in detention. As such, this system of legitimation was fragile, regularly disrupted, and vulnerable to criticism. Staff members' belief in a humane deportation prison was disrupted during forced deportations, which several staff members found difficult to handle and preferred not to partake in. It was also challenged by the processes of gradual securitisation of the deportation prison, which was underway during the time of my research, and which challenged officials' insistence on working for an essentially non-violent detention regime. Marianne explained to me that while detention used to be considered 'dirty work' within the Swedish Migration Agency, the increased political focus on deportations had made it more publicly acceptable to talk about the prison 'for what it was: a place where people are locked up'. In contrast to their colleagues in Ellebæk, the Swedish detention officials had limited training in using physical violence; instead, they built on what they called a 'dynamic security' approach, which entailed 'building trustful relationships' with detained individuals and using dialogue techniques to ensure their 'calm' and cooperation. As Livia once noted, 'You are less inclined to beat up somebody you know and have talked to!' However, this approach to security was changing with the ongoing restructuring and 'professionalisation' of the operation of deportation prisons, which essentially consisted in reinforcing control and security measures in the prisons. According to the new rules, which were implemented all over the country, staff were supposed to carry more sophisticated alarm systems, and be trained in self-defence and so-called pacification techniques, which staff were supposed to use if, for instance, a detained person tried to escape. Some staff members, notably those who had a background in the prison service, the police, or the military, welcomed this trend, while others remained sceptical. Greta told me, 'I don't like this new security logic and the harsher attitude that comes with it. I prefer talking to them, calming them down when they are upset, but these aspects are forgotten with all this focus on security.'

Officials' discomfort with becoming directly involved in coercion can be illustrated by an event that took place on a night shift during my fieldwork. That week, a group of young men had staged a series of escape attempts, and one of them eventually succeeded in escaping through the courtyard. To prevent further escapes, staff stepped up control efforts, constrained the freedom of those incarcerated, and conducted several of the above-mentioned comprehensive visitations, where they searched through their belongings for sharp items or other prohibited objects that they suspected could have facilitated the escape. During one of these searches, staff found tools that they believed could be linked to the escape. Two young men were singled out to be punished for their alleged involvement in the incident. These are my notes from the evening after the comprehensive visitation.

I arrive too early for the night shift. Some detention officials are discussing the two men who have been placed in solitary confinement.[6] One of them is suspected of involvement in the escape attempt; the other man has had a verbal conflict with staff over the opening hours of the smoking cage. The exchange ended with the man throwing his coffee cup on the ground, so that an official was speckled with coffee stains. Ronny, one of the supervisors, explains that this man also 'has a history of being obstinate'. The officials are now discussing an incident that just occurred in the solitary confinement cell, when the man who threw the coffee cup called upon staff because he needed to go to the bathroom. The two officials who attended to his call had then ordered him to keep the door open so that they could keep an eye on him because, as they said, they wanted to make sure he did not commit any act of self-harm (even though he had not demonstrated any intention of doing so). The man had refused, since he found the situation degrading, so staff had let him back into his cell where he was compelled to urinate on the floor. Ronny sighs and tells me that they are uncertain of how they should deal with this. Should they wipe the floor for him or let him do it himself, with the risk that he uses the broom to threaten staff? Zita deplores that the man now complains about feeling dirty, and snorts, 'He has caused this situation himself – and now he calls us racists! Ronny offers to go and clean the room if someone keeps him company and watches over the man. Suddenly reminded of my presence, he turns to me, boxes me on the arm and says, half-jokingly, 'wait, perhaps we shouldn't talk about this when you're around'! I don't say anything, but in an attempt to smooth over the conversation and change topics, Ronny starts to explain that he has nothing against those who are detained, and although they are often accused of racism, he really isn't – he is the opposite. He does not define what this opposite means.

The incident drew my attention to the discomfort with which staff handled a highly intrusive, coercive task, which lay outside their formal training and experience. The humiliation of the detained man is the perverse result of their attempts to demonstrate care and caution, and to manage a perceived security threat simultaneously. An hour later, when the night shift staff arrived, I spoke to Karl, a more experienced detention official who had talked to the man in solitary confinement. Karl did not hide his irritation with his colleagues. 'Why the hell would they ask him to keep the door open? He is not at risk of committing suicide! Of course, he gets pissed off.' The incident illustrates how caretaking intentions and the securitisation of the detention environment clashed with detention officials' own understanding of their roles, generated novel *in*securities, and triggered new animosities between themselves and those incarcerated. Additional insecurities were, in this case, also triggered by my presence, and in the utterance of the word 'racist', which to staff was as contagious as to their Danish colleagues. Indeed, staff strongly resented when detained people questioned their caretaking intentions or called them racists – an allegation that they all firmly denied and denounced. In their understanding, racism equalled prejudiced attitudes and racist language, which they disassociated themselves from – even though both racialised staff members and detained people testified that such forms of racism prevailed in the deportation prison. Meanwhile, what was obscured or overlooked was how racism functioned as a structuring logic of the deportation prison, and how it was expressed also through staff members' acts of care and compassion.

Detained people also regularly resisted and challenged the legitimacy of the detention and deportation system. An illustrative example is a conversation between several detention officials and Samir, a man in his early twenties, originating from a North African country that was unknown to the migration authorities. He had spent an unknown period of time in Sweden prior to his incarceration and had been confined in the deportation prison for some weeks at the time of my fieldwork. Prior to this, he had been shuffled around between different deportation prisons for several months. The police had attempted to deport him to different North African countries, but since he refused to cooperate with authorities and had no identity documents, he had been denied entry and subsequently returned to Sweden. One afternoon, I sat down on the couch in the common room with Samir and a couple of staff members. Samir turned to the officials and asked them, jokingly, and in fluent Swedish,

> What do you dream of at night? I'm having nightmares these days. I don't dream about my family anymore but I dream that my mum is the migration agency [*mamma Migrationsverket*] and my dad the police [*pappa polis*] and you are having a custody dispute and I'm your kid. They don't let me into my country, so they drive me back, I get on another plane, but it's money before papers over there. And then I come back and knock at the door of the police and say hey here I am again. Police say I cost 3,000 Swedish kronor per day, and I don't want them to pay that for me, so I promise I won't eat more, I'll live off coffee and ciggies. Now I have been in all detention centres in Sweden except for one, they move me around, I don't know why. At some point I've got to go and see the last one … and when you don't have space for me anymore you throw me out on the street.

The detention officials looked at Samir, then at each other. Yasmin, one of the supervisors, rolled her eyes and leaned over to me, whispering, 'it's ok. He's been talking about this all day.' Samir stood up to go out for a cigarette, and she continued, 'But we get that he is stressed. He was supposed to have travelled today but now he's going to court instead. It's not ok, we had another one like him who was here for nine months, was deported but refused entry at the border and came back here again … nobody wants them.' Yasmin referred to other cases of people whose deportation order was complicated to enforce, because they had refused to disclose their identity or to cooperate with authorities in the deportation process, or because of practical obstacles to enforcement. Some of them ended up oscillating between living as destitutes, taking up jobs in the informal labour market, getting caught by the police, and being sent to regular prison or to deportation prisons. When Samir returned after his cigarette break, he started singing 'Clandestino'[7] by Manu Chao, first in Spanish, then attempting to translate it into Swedish.

Samir was caught in deportation limbo. His way of mocking authorities' attempts at getting rid of him and while claiming to care for him was ingenious: by likening migration authorities to disputing parents, and answering the police's statement of how much the circus of his repeated deportations cost them by promising to refuse their food, he challenged the authorities' claim to benevolence, highlighting instead their limited ability – and willingness – to control and care for those who, like him, were 'Clandestino'; illegalised, and unclassifiable. His case history also demonstrated the chaotic functioning of deportations (Hiemstra, 2014), which stood in sharp contrast to the imaginary of a rational, fair, and orderly deportation process that detention officials relied on to legitimise their work. Samir also knew that if the repeated efforts to deport him kept failing, he would eventually be thrown out on the street. He knew, in other words, the limitations of the welfarist caretaking gaze, and was familiar with the fact that incarceration was only one of several tools that would be mobilised to expel him.

Concluding remarks

In the Swedish deportation prisons, care, compassion, and the seeing gaze of the welfare state are utilised as techniques of expulsion. During my fieldwork, the often well-meaning officials were seeing, attending to, and trying to alleviate detained people's immediate suffering, while 'unseeing' the violence endemic to confinement and deportation enforcement, and its role in causing their suffering. The staff registered attitudes and behaviours and identified 'risk profiles' among detained people but left unanswered the question of the risks they were exposed to as a result of their incarceration.

Staff reluctantly partook in the gradual securitisation of the detention environment, accepting it on the premise that comprehensive visitations and solitary confinement were used for the sake of suicide prevention, and that twisting somebody's arm was a de-escalating pacification technique, rather than an act of violence. Such codification of violence 'institutes the oxymoron of an exercise of force stripped of any notion of violence' (Makaremi, 2018). It does not ensure the safety of detained people against the violence of the state, but it facilitates its normalisation. Next to codification, the normalisation of violence was enabled through racialisation, which in the Swedish deportation prison took place through inferiorising tropes of detained people as objects of care, and detention officials as benevolent. This way, the Swedish deportation prison, if less overtly harmful than its Danish counterpart, exemplifies how violent state action is rendered more digestible and normalised through 'humanising' reforms. In his book on Manus prison, Behrouz Boochani (2018; see also Bhatia and Bruce-Jones, 2021: 84) identifies oppression to have been perfected where 'everything is logical': where an imprisoned man is banned from playing the guitar, because its strings might be used for suicide; and where smoking, as one of the few remnants of 'freedom', is prohibited for the safety of those imprisoned. Boochani explains how these bureaucratic rules are exercises in power that gradually but systematically deprive people of their autonomy and personhood. These forms of border violence, which operate *through* performances of care, humanitarianism, and rationalisation, do not fundamentally change the conditions of incarcerated people as much as they serve to 'humanise' the detention officials (see also Bosworth, 2016).

The incarceration and deportation of foreign nationals are carried out at the 'threshold of public, political and ethical acceptability' (Walters, 2019: 176). This threshold of acceptability is located on a continuum where violence can take multiple forms. However, whether it is manifested through overt, punitive violence like in Denmark, or in the form of codified 'force' redressed as care and rationalisation, like in Sweden, the violence in deportation prisons has similar effects: it reduces those incarcerated to threatening or threatened things, and breaks them down physically, mentally, and socially. These effects, and the critique and resistance against this violence articulated by detained individuals, were known to officials in Ellebæk and in the Swedish deportation prison. It manifested in the Danish physiotherapist's calculation of the per cent of humanity left in a person after some time in confinement, in the suicide-preventive schemes put in place in both prisons, and in the Swedish detention official's anxiety about what subversive words would be articulated on a pearl bracelet. For detention officials, it was not a matter of being ignorant of the violence of confinement. But their reactions to it – or lack thereof – were marked by a belief that these harms were inevitable, that detention was a necessary part of the border system, and that this system was the only one possible.

I sent two fieldnotes to Julia Suárez-Krabbe, including the preface to this book, which takes place in a Danish deportation camp – a context which she, as a scholar and activist in Denmark has also worked extensively on – and the above notes from my encounter with Lars. I asked her to help me think through how far denial is really a precondition or a necessity for sustaining state violence, as has been argued in the literature on bureaucratic violence (Arendt, 1963; Bauman, 2013), and in research on migration-related detention, respectively (Bosworth, 2014; Mountz, 2020). In our conversation that followed, Julia reflected,

> I am interested in how whiteness can be decolonised. Fanon said that decolonisation cannot happen without the help of European masses. Since then, immigration has increased. So, what are the grounds upon which white people construct their subjectivity, which replicates and partakes in this system, and imagine it as if this was the only way of doing things? Where everything else is perceived to be – or made – impossible?

> The characters, Niels and the Swedish guy [Lars], they 'see' and they don't see what is happening. The Swedish guy uses a particular rationality to be critical and yet not critical. He is caught up in a logic that individualises structural problems. He has the book titles, and he makes reflections on responsibility and individual roles in the system, etc. And yet, he remains completely in the rationality that Maria Lugones (1994) connects to the politics of purity, which is individualisation. This is how we see whiteness collapsing into itself. When people have this fragmented relationship with reality, Niels and the Swedish guy ... they see parts of a greater picture, but at the same time, not really. They cannot step out of the script they have been given, and which they have naturalised since they were born, including the knowledge traditions they have chosen to rely on, which remains the only realm of possibility for them. They are only able to think about rationality and actionality – but this reasoning implodes, collapses into itself. The reflections never challenge the basic truths they live by: individualism, individual responsibility, the 'usual' way of thinking (critically) in society, of being a critical worker who operates within the system. In the Nordic countries, this is a common way for people to relate to law and authority. Here, you trust these structures so much – perhaps you have good reasons to, because of how they have enhanced your own life. On the other hand, it's like the Matrix! Remaining in the Matrix gives you privileges. It's easier to be there and to deny and decide that this is the reality where you want to live. It is not necessarily a *denial* that other realities exist, but it is a *decision* that you want to remain there. [...] There is a made-up logic within that logic: you see that you partake in dehumanisation, you do violence to people in detention centres without recognising it as violence by keeping a self-image of yourself as humane and critical and friendly to these people, although this perception is also based on an idea of their inferiority.

Julia and I continued talking about the self-enclosed nature of this logic, which, as Julia added, relied on a rationality 'that needs to be enclosed within itself, for it cannot bear reality'. On the one hand, this rationality precludes any critique which does not speak within that same framework, and which is therefore conceived as 'irrational'. This includes perspectives that question the perceptions that non-deported people are imbued with difference and danger, and that what is at stake is the order built upon the violent policing of these differences. On the other, there are worlds beyond this enclosed logic. Julia concluded,

> Niels says he still doesn't understand the reasons behind the deportation camps. But I think he does, it's a way not to take responsibility. The fissures – the cracks in the system – are not on the individual level but they are found in how we relate to each other. As white and non-white, there are more nurturing ways of being in the world together.

Notes

1 The police officer in charge of the raid of the church camp was also involved in a mediatised police intervention in a monastery in 1993. That time, the raid became a major backlash for the police, whereas this later intervention seemed to have more widespread public and political backing.
2 Decisions on detention can be taken by the Swedish Migration Agency or the police according to chapter 10 of the Aliens Act. Grounds for detention include the purpose of 'establishing the identity' of the person in question (§ (1)), if it is deemed necessary for establishing whether the person has a legal right to remain in Sweden (§ 1(1)) or is probable that the person will be deported (§ 1(2)), or for the purpose of preparing or enforcing an existing decision on deportation (§ 1(3)). Children may be detained with their parents, or in exceptional cases alone, if there is no legal guardian in Sweden (§ 2(2–3)). In 2018, at least fifty-seven children were detained; in thirty-three of the cases, the best interests of the child had reportedly not been taken into consideration (Red Cross, 2018). Detention orders for investigating the right of a person to remain in Sweden may last for two weeks. Detention while awaiting deportation can last for two months, but can be extended to a maximum of twelve months if the person fails to 'cooperate' in the deportation process. Migrants who have received a deportation order from a criminal court can also be held in detention while awaiting deportation: for these people there is no time limit to detention (Aliens Act, chapter 10, § 4(2)). The average stay in detention was 31.5 days in 2017 (Global Detention Project, 2018).
3 In 2020, the number of incarcerated persons in detention fell to 2,528, allegedly due to the ongoing COVID-19 pandemic, which resulted in the Swedish Migration Agency reducing the holding capacity in their facilities for the purpose of limiting the potential spread of the coronavirus (see Migrationsverket, 2020: 55).

4 Detained persons could receive a daily allowance of SEK 24 (around EUR 2), which enabled them to buy cigarettes or snacks from a vending machine.
5 This quote has also been used in Eule et al., 2019: 164–165.
6 *Avskiljning* or 'separation' in solitary confinement is authorised in accordance with chapter 11, § 7 of the Aliens Act up to seventy-two hours as a means to prevent or sanction escape attempts or behaviour that jeopardises order and security. A decision on 'separation' needs to be continuously reassessed and a new decision taken at least every three days. If separation in the detention facility is not deemed sufficient, e.g. because the detained person is deemed to pose a risk to order and security in the deportation prison, staff can decide to transfer them to 'secure confinement' in police custody or pre-trial detention in accordance with chapter 11, § 7 of the Aliens Act. The deportation prison where I conducted fieldwork had two solitary confinement cells, located in an enclosed corridor. The rooms were small with no furniture except for a bed nailed onto the floor, and staff could observe the person held there at all times through a small window.
7 'Entre Ceuta y Gibraltar / Soy una raya en el mar / Fantasma en la ciudad / Mi vida va prohibida / Dice la autoridad Solo voy con mi pena / Sola va mi condena / Correr es mi destino / Por no llevar papel / Perdido en el corazón / De la grande Babylon / Me dicen el clandestino / Yo soy el quiebra ley / Mano Negra clandestina / Peruano clandestino / Africano clandestino / Marihuana ilegal' (from the album *Clandestino* by Manu Chao, 1998).

4

Politics that kill, slowly: the Danish deportation camps

Steve: I wanted to ask … for me, personally, not that it's something personal but I want to know, how is this place being run? How long does someone have to be here? How long do I have to wait here?

Niels: I cannot give you a personal answer because I simply don't know. We have no insights into the individual case, which means that I don't really know your background or why you are here. What I do know is that you are supposed to be here. Or, that you have to be here. In the long run, any inhabitant can stay here eternally.

Steve: Eternally?

Niels: Eternally. This is three years ago, the government made a decision about what they called sort of … placement or housing by which phase you're in. There are reception centres […] all the centres for when you are in process […] and departure or exit centres, Sjælsmark and Kærshovedgård. And the ambition is that any foreign person who has no legal residence in Denmark will be housed in either of [these centres]. That is the political intention at the moment. And that means that as long as an individual – and that could be you – has no legal access to stay in Denmark, you will live here. And that's why I say eternally, or as long as the place exists, or, whenever. Literally, you can say that these individuals who have no perspective to gain residence permit in Denmark, they will stay here in this centre until the day they die. That's the political ambition; how it will sort of be in real terms, I don't know.

(Edward, Elsted, and Hansen, 2019: 02:00–04:36)[1]

In 2013, the Danish Social Democratic-led government, with support from the Social Liberal party, the left-wing Unity List, and the right-wing Liberal Alliance, announced their agreement to establish two 'departure centres' (*udrejsecenter*; henceforth deportation camps), Sjælsmark and

Kærshovedgård. A new political invention, the deportation camps were added to the 'motivation enhancement measures', introduced in the Danish Aliens Act in 1997 (§§ 34, 36, 40, 41, and 42a), which were designed to pressure people whose asylum applications had been rejected to cooperate with authorities in the deportation procedure. Formally adopted as a way of ensuring 'purposeful accommodation' of people seeking asylum, the deportation camps were supposed to separate those whose applications had been rejected and to send 'a very clear message telling them [rejected asylum seekers] that this is the last stop in Denmark and that now you must go home' (Danish Ministry of Justice, 2013). Two years after the political agreement, Niels – whom the reader encountered in the prologue – and his staff installed themselves in the barracks, and Sjælsmark opened to receive its first residents. Steve was among them.

I recall first hearing this recording at a campaign meeting arranged by Steve and other resident activists in Sjælsmark deportation camp in 2016. The self-organised movement Castaway Souls of Denmark were arranging a series of protests against the deportation camps, which as they described, were 'killing them slowly' (Castaway Souls, 2016). As part of his activism and to understand the rationale behind the camps, Steve conducted several interviews with Niels, the director of Sjælsmark. In the above extract from one of their conversations, Steve asks how long he will be held in the camp. In a calm, matter-of-fact manner, Niels explains that the political intention is that as long as residents do not agree to leave Denmark, they will have to stay in the camp – even if that means they will remain there for the rest of their lives. As the interview continues, Steve asks Niels to share his opinion on this arrangement. Niels replies that as a professional public official, he must keep his personal opinions to himself; his role is to 'carry out the job'. However, he remarks, 'as a professional, I can say that this act of putting pressure on people does not seem to have any effect. That means that from a professional point of view, it might seem ... pointless' (Edward, Elsted, and Hansen, 2019: 14:41–15:07).

A seemingly pointless policy that subjects non-deported people to the prospect of indefinite waiting under conditions that practically if not legally amount to *de facto* confinement. Such is the setup of the deportation camps, which over the years have turned into central sites of contestation in Denmark's deportation-oriented asylum regime. The conversations between Steve and Niels touched upon many of the same issues I later came to discuss with Niels. A crucial difference is, of course, that the conversations between Niels and me, or between Niels and the prison management – whom he would 'annoy' with his straightforward questions – were about theoretical scenarios and organisational concerns. In contrast, when he spoke to Steve about the possibility of people spending the rest of their lives in Sjælsmark, he spoke to someone for whom the prospect of remaining in the camp until the day he died was a possible scenario. For Niels, the politics of slow death was puzzling; for the people residing in the camp, it was a lived reality. The violence of this condition was only amplified by the seeming 'pointlessness' of the policy, although the deportation camps had their rationales, too.

Incarceration is a costly means for governments to contain and control non-deported people. From a coldly bureaucratic and financial perspective, deportation prisons are resource-intensive and legally well-monitored, given the range of provisions for minimum conditions and procedural safeguards that states have to comply with (such as the EU Return Directive, Asylum Reception Directive, and Articles 3 and 5 of the ECHR). Politically, they can be costly, too, since the use of the penal system and of coercive force for the purpose of deportation enforcement risks drawing public criticism and generating resistance (as demonstrated by detention officials' anxiety over reactions to forced deportations in Sweden). The human toll of incarceration is also significant, and there is no evidence that incarceration renders deportations more effective. Therefore, governments take to alternative measures to pressure non-deported people to leave, including confinement-like configurations, such as the Danish deportation camps, or the withdrawal of access to essential welfare provisions, which is practised in Sweden (Ataç, 2019). These approaches are manifestations of 'slow violence', which shift the governing rationale from care and control to the creation of injurious conditions that are supposed to deter non-deported people from remaining in the country. This governing logic, which operates through indirect violence and formal abandonment (Davies et al., 2017: 1270), compelled Niels and his prison officer staff to change the control-oriented approach that characterised their profession. Meanwhile, it compelled Steve and other people confined in the deportation camps to navigate a complex system of bureaucratic regulations and camp rules, which were designed to make their lives 'intolerable' by minimising their autonomy over their lives, and by exposing them to harm without touching them.

Infrastructures of intolerability

In 2016, Inger Støjberg, then Minister for Immigration, Integration, and Housing for the Conservative Party, was probed about the restrictive laws adopted with the purpose of tightening control over non-deported people, which critics argued were balancing at the very edge of human rights conventions. Støjberg answered that the deportation camps were meant to 'make life as intolerable as possible' for non-deported people, to make them feel unwanted in Denmark (Støjberg quoted in Skærbæk, 2016). Her statement set the tone for what would become a heated a public debate over the threshold of legality, morality, and indecency of the deportation camps (see e.g. Canning, 2019b; Clante Bendixen, 2021; Freedom of Movements Research Collective, 2018; Red Cross, 2019).

Sjælsmark was the first deportation camp to open in 2015, followed by Kærshovedgård, which came into operation in 2016. In 2018, the Red Cross asylum camp Avnstrup was converted into a third deportation camp, and later turned into a camp for non-deported families. In 2020, the three camps altogether counted 686 residents, but had the capacity to house 1,200 people, which roughly corresponds to the number of non-deported people who Danish immigration authorities count as being in a so-called departure position. According to the Danish Immigration Agency (2020), 200 of the people in this position had remained stuck in the condition of being non-deported for more than five years. Most residents were people whose asylum applications had been rejected, or who had had their protection statuses withdrawn since Danish authorities, under the new, restrictive asylum laws, considered it safe for them to return to the countries they had fled from. Since 2020, the Danish Return Agency is the authority that decides who must reside in the deportation camps, how often they must report to authorities, and which additional 'motivating' measures (such as voluntary return advice, incarceration, or pocket money) will be used in each individual case. The camps, importantly, exist in continuity with the pre-existing archipelago of asylum camps, and people are shuffled back and forth between them as their asylum applications are rejected, reassessed, and reopened. Sjælsmark was my primary fieldwork site, although I also came to visit the other camps regularly over the years.

Sjælsmark deportation camp is located just a few kilometres away from Ellebæk prison and from Sandholm asylum camp. The same gunshots from military training exercises that prison officers referred to in Ellebæk also echoed among the military barracks in Sjælsmark. The group of residents initially sent to Sjælsmark encompassed single adults and couples whose asylum applications had been rejected and who were deemed 'cooperative' in their deportation cases. Moreover, there were people awaiting deportation to an EU/EES member state according to the Dublin Regulation, and people whose asylum cases were classified as 'manifestly unfounded' and were bound for swift deportation. When I conducted fieldwork in Sjælsmark, the camp was not even half full and the streets ghostly empty; since then, Sjælsmark has expanded, the empty streets filled with the echoes of people who came and went. For some years, the camp hosted families with children, and the abandoned cafeteria building was temporarily converted into a kindergarten, which was subsequently closed when the families were

Figure 4.1 Departure centre Sjælsmark

moved to Avnstrup. The fences, which at the time of my research were merely symbolic, were reinforced, and new monitoring mechanisms put in place.

Those who were deemed 'non-cooperative' in the deportation process risked being sent to Kærshovedgård, a converted open prison located in Mid-Jutland. Kærshovedgård lies well hidden in a forest, and with the closest town located nine kilometres away and no public transport available, residents' only means to leave the camp is by walking or using donated bicycles. When I first visited in 2016 shortly after it opened, there were only a few residents, and reconstructions were still underway. Stoves, fridges, and kitchen items were removed from the resident buildings, as were pool tables and other leisure equipment, since non-deported people – in contrast to people imprisoned under the criminal code – had no right to cook their own food or to activities. The material conditions and regulations thus became significantly more restrictive compared to when it served as an open prison for imprisoned citizens (Danish Helsinki Committee, 2017). As Kærshovedgård was turned into a deportation camp, fences were also erected, and biometric controls installed at the camp gates. In 2021, the 278 people held in Kærshovedgård under these conditions of *de facto* confinement included single men and women whose asylum cases had been rejected. In addition, there were 112 criminalised foreign nationals, who had lost their residence permit or been sentenced to deportation in addition to their prison sentence, and thirty-six people on tolerated stay, an open-ended status for people who have received a deportation order (§10 and §25 of the Danish Aliens Act) but who cannot be deported due to the risk of *refoulement*. A significant number of the people residing in Kærshovedgård have been non-deportable for several years, some up to decades.

In 2018, Avnstrup asylum camp, located in Lejre municipality in a former tuberculosis hospital, was transformed into a deportation camp housing up to 400 people. As a result of protests organised by families living in Sjælsmark supported by advocacy groups, families were promised improved conditions in Avnstrup by the Social Democratic government that came to power in 2019. Its reputation as a better or 'softer' camp was earned by it being run by the Danish Red Cross, in contrast to Sjælsmark and Kærshovedgård, which are run by the Prison and Probation Service. Avnstrup is not surrounded by fences and has cooking facilities where residents have certain opportunities to prepare their own meals. However, the families quickly identified that these improvements were mainly cosmetic: with its remote geographic location, and novel restrictions on residents' freedom of movement – which I shall return to shortly – they described Avnstrup as 'another prison, but without fences'.

The three deportation camps differ in terms of their respective groups of residents, the legal and *de facto* mobility restrictions imposed upon residents, and in their so-called house rules. What they all have in common is that they are designed to ensure that residents are kept apart from Danish society. Much like the asylum camps, social exclusion and isolation is ensured by residents being separated from their family members, friends, and communities in Denmark (see Syppli-Kohl, 2015). By regularly moving residents around between the camps, authorities also prevent solidarity and a sense of community from developing among them (Canning, 2019b). Social isolation also operates through stigmatisation and symbolic criminalisation: the prison facilities, the fences, the uniformed prison officers, and intensive police presence made up a penal spectacle that induced fear and resentment among residents in the surrounding society. Ever since the inauguration of the deportation camps, their location has been the subject of heated political debate, with neighbours reacting strongly against hosting the camps in their municipalities. As Steve noted in one of our conversations,

> The neighbours play an important part in creating this criminalisation. The fences around the camps, the officers in uniform, they instil fear into the neighbours – this is what the state wants, for the citizens to feel this fear, but also that the citizens work with the state. And people say, if you say they aren't dangerous, then why are they in military barracks, why are there fences? So, these things are interlinked! The state makes these policies to instil fear into citizens, and to make them accept that the lives of rejected asylum seekers are made unliveable. They teach their citizens not to value the lives of these people, and when people then react by calling them criminals or security threats, this permits for the state to react with more dehumanisation.

Under the guise of addressing the safety risk allegedly posed by non-deported people, the deportation camps create the conditions that put non-deported people at risk and in fact construct them as risky subjects. The dynamic that Steve describes above was perhaps best illustrated by the 2018 plan of the Conservative-led government coalition, launched in response to the 'concerns' raised by neighbours to Kærshovedgård over the alleged criminal threat posed by residents, to relocate criminalised foreign nationals from Kærshovedgård to Lindholm, a deserted island which used to house research laboratories for infectious veterinary diseases. The plan was subsequently dropped by the Social Democratic government in 2019, allegedly because it turned out to be too expensive. However, 'the island' as social imaginary where the supposed threat posed by the criminalised foreign national can be contained, isolated, and extinguished is already practised in the present organisation of the deportation camps. Their remote geographic locations effectively hide residents behind fences and forests, immobilising and concealing them while fuelling popular imaginations that they pose an unknown, unidentifiable threat to society. As Alison Mountz (2020) has argued in her writing on the centrality of the 'island' and other hidden geographies as tools of dehumanisation and border enforcement, such politics of concealment removes unwanted people from public consciousness, entertains imaginations of them as an unknown, racialised threat, and invisibilises the oppression they are subjected to while in confinement. Mountz proposes that the island has become the idealised political fantasy of exclusion, where time, space, geography, and law are manipulated to dehumanise and devalue the people confined. The Danish deportation camps can partly be understood through this island imaginary, although located on land.

Legally, deportation camps are not considered comparable to detention – as prison officers in Sjælsmark were keen to emphasise, residents were 'free to leave anytime' (even though most people had nowhere to go where they were legally permitted). In practice, however, the duty to register and to report to authorities regularly, and the risk of being criminalised for failing to do so, leave residents *de facto* confined in the camps. Residents also lack access to the legal safeguards awarded to people who are *de jure* detained (in accordance with § 35 or § 36 of the Danish Alien Act), notably the right to appeal an order to be moved to the camps, and the stipulated time limit of eighteen months. The duty of residence (*opholdspligt*) stipulates that residents are obliged to spend their nights in the deportation camps. In addition, they should register regularly with authorities (*meldepligt*) and notify authorities if they leave the camp during the daytime (*underretningspligt*). In Sjælsmark and Kærshovedgård, the residence duty is controlled via electronic keys, which need to be updated on a regular basis, or the key will be deactivated, and the person registered as absconded. The duty to register must be fulfilled in person, and the frequency ranges between three times a week for people whose asylum applications have been rejected, to every day for criminalised foreign nationals and individuals on tolerated stay in Kærshovedgård. In Avnstrup, there is no electronic monitoring of residents' coming and going, but in return, residents are obliged to report to authorities twice a day (between 07:00–10:00, and 17:00–22:00, respectively). The punishment for failing to register has gradually increased through a series of restrictive legislative amendments. Following a first round of restrictions in 2019, 100 residents were arrested within the course of three months for having failed to register in the camp (Linddahl, 2019). In 2021, the punishment for failing to register two days in a row increased to sixty days in prison, demonstrating how the registration system directly contributes to the criminalisation of residents. Residents are also at constant risk of being detained in Ellebæk as a 'motivating' measure (§ 36(5) of the Aliens Act), which rarely 'succeeds' in making them cooperate in the deportation case, but traumatises those affected, and disciplines others. The deportation camps have been criticised by numerous human rights organisations and legal experts for their 'prison-like conditions', and in three cases, the Supreme Court has found that the regulations of the camps disproportionately infringed upon residents' freedom of movement (Amnesty International, n.d.; Danish Institute for Human Rights, 2016; Danish Helsinki Committee, 2017). The time spent in semi-confinement was deemed of central importance, and following two key rulings in the Supreme Court, the Ministry for Immigration stated that foreign nationals *on tolerated stay* could not be held in deportation camps for more than four years. However, the rule does not apply to all residents in the camps, but only to those on tolerated stay, who are subjected to the strictest regulations. This means that people who are relocated to deportation camps following a rejected asylum case or withdrawal of protection may still remain confined in the camps indefinitely. It also demonstrates how those tried under the Danish penal code were granted stronger legal protection than people whose fates were determined by administrative immigration law.

If the camps' geographic location and the registration duties ensure residents' spatial isolation, the temporal indeterminacy of residents' stay was – as discussed in the dialogue between Steve and Niels – an equally important technology of exclusion. In the camps, time is weaponised as a technique of deterrence and control; and their everyday time is also meticulously regulated through administrative rules, which circumscribe their autonomy and, as Niels once bluntly put it, 'take the meaning out of life for residents'. These rules include the catering arrangement, which obliges residents to have their meals in the cafeteria inside the camp, and prohibits them from cooking their own food. They also include the prohibition to work or study, and the withdrawal of daily allowance for those considered 'uncooperative' in the deportation process. There are also unwritten rules, such as the prohibition to personalise one's room, to arrange for spiritual practices, or to engage in recurrent, 'meaningful' activities which might contradict the motivating purpose of the camps (for a full list of camp rules, see Freedom of Movements Research Collective, 2018: 26–27). As a result, the daily lives of people held in the camps were highly circumscribed. The prison officers guarding the camps were supposed to monitor residents and ensure their compliance with the rules of 'intolerability'.

The regime of intolerability

> They are supposed to stay here, but most of them often leave. If they abscond, we notify the Immigration Service and the Police, their rooms are cleaned out, we collect their luggage. But nothing happens. Some of them reappear and are simply reinscribed into the system. And so, it goes on … people have a life around here, they do not depend on the centre. Some have family and friends on the outside. And what can we do about it – nothing! They can do whatever they like, just not on the centre's premises.

Back in 2016, all staff working in Sjælsmark were uniformed, trained prison officers who had previously been working in low or high security prisons, or in Ellebæk. Being used to enforcing rigid control in prisons, they were, as Niels mentioned in our initial conversation, struggling to figure out exactly what their role was going to be and what kind of authority they were supposed to enforce in a deportation camp. The first thing that puzzled them was their lack of means to control the whereabouts of residents. The quotation above is from Eskil, a prison officer in his forties with a previous career in the Danish prison system, who describes his feeling of confusion when realising that there was 'nothing' they could do about the coming and going of residents. Yet, the prison officers soon realised that the fact that residents did *not* show up in the camps and instead disappeared was not necessarily undesired. Niels explained to me that 'there are two categories of people here: those who pass through quickly – that's why the camp is located close to Kastrup airport. And there are those who've got their minds set on staying.' To these two categories, Eskil wished to add the great majority who, before or soon after arriving in the deportation camp, simply disappeared.

> Statistically, you could say that it works when people disappear and are deregistered in our systems. On the other hand, it might create a bigger problem

when people disappear from the system but remain in the country and end up on the street. It's worse for them and for our society, we get more crime, more illegal work ... but sure, statistically it works, when they disappear from here.

Prison officers kept no statistics over how many people disappeared on their way to or after having arrived in Sjælsmark (nor did the Immigration Service at the time). Some considered this a success of the 'motivating' measures; others took it as a sign that non-deported people did not care about the camps and their intolerable rules, and simply continued leading their lives in Denmark, disregarding their deportation orders. Regardless of where people ended up, by making them disappear from the system, the deportation camps produced a semblance of enforced onward mobility, which might not be exactly what the government's deportation fantasies had envisioned, but close enough.

Apart from having no authority to control residents' coming and going, prison officers also had limited means to sanction and control their behaviour. Like in Ellebæk, officers were stripped of their rehabilitative tasks, and knew nothing about residents' deportation cases; but in contrast to Ellebæk, the officers in Sjælsmark were stripped of their mandate to use physical violence. Some officers found this frustrating. Mads, who also came straight from the prison world, said, 'I found it difficult to get used to not running after people. It's a bit irritating, not being able to sanction them when they break the rules.' Others enjoyed being relieved of the constant anticipation of violence that haunted them inside locked prisons. Gert, a senior officer whose favourite spot in the camp was an armchair in the reception building, which permitted him to stretch out his feet comfortably on the desk, and look out over the empty streets, told me, 'Here is like being on holiday compared to prison! Conflicts with residents don't escalate, and I'm not interested in what residents do here. They can do whatever they want, and their problem is not our problem.' Like Gert, several officers shared how, when arriving in Sjælsmark, they had felt their blood pressure drop, their shoulders relax, and their gaze soften: unlike in prison, they did not 'constantly have to be on their guard'. They enjoyed the freedom of being able to interact with residents and 'be more of a human' than a control agent, as Mette, another officer, noted. Eskil agreed and suggested that the officers' role in Sjælsmark was something akin to 'social workers, but in uniforms. Or actually', he added with a wink, 'we are mostly looking tough in our uniforms'.

The official duties of staff included managing daily logistical tasks, such as monitoring the gates, registering visitors, distributing mail to residents, and updating their electronic keys, and cleaning out the rooms of those who had left. Every other week, they were supposed to distribute 'pocket money' to residents who were considered 'cooperative' in the deportation process. But since this, at the time, applied to almost no one, the event instead became a ritual of rejection, where residents lined up in front of a building to confirm their presence, and prison officers confirmed that they were there, and that there was nothing for them to get.[2] Given their lack of control functions, staff considered their role as being 'social' and predominantly positive, but the people living in the camps testified how interactions with staff were often intrusive, blunt, and abusive. With free access to residents' rooms, officers were authorised to enter people's private spaces unhindered at any time; they could conduct surprise raids in their search for banned objects, and they would assist the police in unannounced deportations. Women living in the camps recounted how staff would walk in while they were having a shower; men testified that the officers interacted with them with manners that were arrogant, racist, and degrading. One day, Anne, an officer in her forties who thought she had built up a decent rapport with residents, complained to her colleagues that she had got into a conflict with a man she was usually on good terms with. Anne had entered his room to have a chat and saw writings on his wall that made her concerned: 'He said it was poetry, but how could I know? It could have been some terrorist message, for what I know. I don't read Arabic.' Anne had started taking pictures of the writings and told the man that this was for security reasons. He got upset and asked her to leave. 'He must understand why I did this, I don't understand why he got so upset', she told us with a shrug. Anne seemed unaware of the racist undertones of her own suspicion, and of the stress it had caused the man to be portrayed as a suspected terrorist. A couple of hours later, she shared that they had another talk and that 'the man was now happy again'. Happiness, along with gratitude and compliance, were the character traits that officers preferred among residents.

Officers' limited duties in the camp were usually not enough to fill their work hours. When they were not patrolling the camp or monitoring residents, they would therefore spend most of their time in the office building or 'service centre' (which, as Bashir, one of the residents, pointed out, was a curious name for a reception that was not allowed to offer any services), browsing the web, or taking turns at the reception desk. Sometimes, one of them would drive off to a nearby town and buy Danish puff pastries for the others. The service centre also had a back door, which led out to a patio surrounded by what was probably the camp's most functional fence: an opaque, wooden hedge, which was under construction at the time, but where staff would soon be able to enjoy a coffee, a cigarette break, and an occasional hot dog barbecue in relative privacy. Sitting down for a cigarette on the patio, the prison officers readily admitted that their role in the camp was mainly symbolic, and so were the security arrangements, and the manifestations of militarised state power represented by the fences, electronic gates, and surveillance cameras. Henriette, a senior officer, tartly noted, 'we are part of a political masquerade here. We are prison officers, but you know over here, most of the time, nothing happens.' Gazing out over the empty streets, she smattered her fingers against the table where we were sitting, repeating: 'Nothing happens.' Much like in Ellebæk, most prison officers took little interest in migration control matters. Some of them were irritated with the 'lack of gratitude' that residents showed for the welfare provisions they received 'in spite of being illegally here', as Gert noted. 'They get food, shelter, what can they complain about? It's them who are dirty, they don't clean the place. No wonder they think it's shit here, but it's on them.' Yet, there were also officers who were critical of the setup in Sjælsmark and felt uncomfortable with the intolerability regime. When I sat down with Jonas in the cafeteria, he told me,

> This group has become so politicised. They are supposed to go back to their home countries, but I recognise many of them from when I worked in Ellebæk – they are just being sent back and forth between these different camps. And these are people we are talking about! They should at least get a dignified return. They have no private life, no money, no activities, and someone else decides what they should eat. They are just waiting to be sent off somewhere else. We should be able to offer them something to make them happier and feel better ... I don't think it makes people motivated to sit around and do nothing, it just makes them more frustrated with the system. Or that's how I would feel.

Jonas, and other prison officers with him, contemplated that at the very least, they could try not to make matters worse for residents. That was the reason why they all appreciated Abolfazl, who was known among them as the Gardener, since he tried on his own initiative to retain a sense of normalcy, and to make the camp a little less hostile, for himself and for others. He did not complain or make any fuss. If more residents were like him, they contended, the atmosphere would perhaps not be so bad, after all. The officers regretted that they could not award his exemplary behaviour, just like they regretted not being able to discipline the others. Altogether, however, they considered their role in the enforcement of the intolerability regime as marginal; it was the facilities and the camp rules that were supposed to make residents' lives intolerable, not the way staff treated them. But they were not there to make residents' lives any easier, either.

There were, however, certain social functions permitted for staff to take up in the camp. For this purpose, the Red Cross were contracted to offer emergency healthcare, a limited set of daily activities, and so-called voluntary return advice (which was later taken over by the Danish Return Agency). The Red Cross's work in Sjælsmark – and later on also in Avnstrup – illustrates the ambivalent role of humanitarian actors within the deportation regime. The Red Cross are by no means new actors in the Danish asylum system: since 1984, they have been contracted by the state to run asylum camps. As argued by Syppli-Kohl (2015; see also Lindberg, 2020b), this places them in a position where they are part of the repressive asylum regime of the Danish government, at the same time as they are claiming to operate in the 'best interest' of asylum seekers. Like other 'humanitarian' border workers (see Andersson, 2016: 1068; Rozakou, 2012), they were supposed to alleviate the suffering caused by the border regime they partook in enforcing. Yet not all Red Cross workers did necessarily consider this position to be tension-ridden or problematic. A staff member whom I interviewed in the Red Cross coordination office in Copenhagen suggested, 'it's maybe a Northern European thing, to believe that we can operate on state contracts and solve our issues with them without jeopardising our independence'. In Sjælsmark, the Red Cross workers considered it of great importance to demarcate their difference from the prison officers. Having installed themselves in a separate wing of the camp, and carrying bright Red Cross vests at all times, the NGO workers insisted that they were 'on the residents' side' against the intolerability arrangement, even though the rules of intolerability limited them in terms of the support they could offer.

The Red Cross were only allowed to offer activities that could motivate residents to comply with their deportation order. Any activity that would contradict the purpose of the motivation enhancement measures was prohibited; therefore, the Red Cross only offered English courses, even though Danish classes were in higher demand. They also gave computer classes and curriculum vitae workshops, where residents were supposed to think about what skills they could bring with them from Denmark 'back home'. The two Red Cross workers in charge of these activities admitted that these workshops were poorly attended, but their English classes usually attracted between two and five residents. I sat in on some of these classes, which usually took place in the morning hours. Participants were instructed to fill in English sentences with the correct pronouns, to read aloud texts on Persian carpets, or to look at pictures from the US presidential White House and list its interior decorations. They were told to read in silence about how to make a pizza and memorise the ingredients. The classes usually ended with the teacher doing the hangman game on the whiteboard. Hannah, one of the two Red Cross workers, had previously worked in asylum camp Sandholm, which in contrast to Sjælsmark, was 'full of life' and where, as she put it, 'people still had hope'. When I asked her what she thought was different in Sjælsmark, she said she found it 'ghostly'. She went on, 'and the prison officers … they are a bit square. We always must ask for permission for everything and explain why the activity is conducive to activation in the resident's home country. We are not allowed to do anything meaningful with them.' I asked what would count as 'activities' – anything that would make life less intolerable in the camp? 'Yes, pretty much', Hannah replied. Next to their limited activities, the Red Cross were starting up a so-called voluntary return advice unit, which Hannah hoped would help 'inspire residents, make them happier, show them that there is a way out of their situation'. Even though all activities the Red Cross offered were aligned with the motivation enhancement measures, Hannah insisted that their presence in the camp served an important role as a 'counterweight' to the Prison and Probation Service: 'The Red Cross should be a social watchdog to make sure people are ok.' The more restrictive the policies, the greater the need for the Red Cross to be there to 'humanise' their implementation, she contended; even if that entailed maintaining residents' lives at a very humanitarian minimum – and 'helped' them getting deported.

Since I conducted fieldwork in Sjælsmark in 2016, the Danish deportation regime has indeed continued to move in a more restrictive direction. Meanwhile, the role of the Red Cross in its enforcement has expanded since they overtook responsibility for Avnstrup deportation camp. While they maintained that they operated at a 'critical distance' from state authorities, their role is better described as being positioned on a 'continuum' alongside state actors (Kalir and Wissink, 2016: 34). In Sjælsmark, they could claim to perform a 'purely' humanitarian function, and distance themselves from repressive control measures; in Avnstrup, this symbolic differentiation was more difficult for them to maintain. As Akelio, who had experience of being housed in several Red Cross-run camps in Denmark, once told me, 'they might help saving lives elsewhere, but here, they help killing us slowly'.

A politics that kills, slowly

I revisited Sjælsmark in August 2017. The camp then housed around 150 residents (who actually lived there), including families with children, many of whom had spent several years in the Danish asylum system. Some of the children had been born and raised in the camps. The staff had changed, too: prison officers had been called in to staff prisons elsewhere, and the majority were now civil employees with various backgrounds, many of whom had previously worked in asylum camps run by the Red Cross or a municipality. The Red Cross ran the kindergarten in the centre, and a bus came to pick up children for school every weekday. Still, the basic logic of the camp remained the same.

We drive around in the golf car, which the camp staff have acquired in order to move around in the camp since it expanded. Much changes, but much stays the same, they explain to me. Niels tells me that they are currently housing a family with a mother who is suffering from cancer. The family knows they are not eligible for asylum, but they thought the mother might receive better treatment in Denmark than in their country of origin. Their asylum application has been rejected, but their deportation cannot be scheduled yet as the mother is about to die from her illness. This means she is going to die in Sjælsmark. Normally, Niels tells me, they would send her to the hospital but since they are rejected asylum seekers, the hospital will not allow the family to stay there overnight to watch over her due to their lack of legal residency. Staff in Sjælsmark have therefore tried to arrange a hospice in the family's room, so that they can be together until she dies. For Niels, this is a novel situation: had this been a regular prison, the imprisoned person would normally have been pardoned or allowed to leave prison to die with the family. But that is not possible in Sjælsmark. The woman is expected to die there, and afterwards, the family will be deported and get to bring her body. 'I don't know what that will look like', Niels says, and we drive on.

The 'effectiveness' of the intolerability regime in terms of its impact on deportation rates has been – and remains – politically contested. There is no evidence that they have succeeded in making more people comply with their deportation order, but this failure has itself been politically productive. Citing the substantial costs of running the camps – allegedly DKK 300,000 per resident per year – the government has been able to justify the adoption of further restrictions to put pressure on non-deported people to leave, and vowed to externalise asylum processes to a country outside Europe. Meanwhile, from a bureaucratic point of view, the deportation camps have only aggravated the limbo situation that they were allegedly meant to address. When I interviewed a group of immigration caseworkers in 2016 about their perceptions of the effects of the deportation camps, Nebe, one of the officials, told me,

> I doubt that they really leave the country. Instead, they abscond, or leave for Sweden where they become Dublin cases – and then they are back here again, and some of them return to Sjælsmark. I mean, even they have got to eat … The reality is that some of them risk remaining there forever. The situation is troubling regardless – some of them end up in a no man's land where they can never get a residence permit and never be sent back. If they really fear for their lives, it won't be a punishment to be put on a catering arrangement in a departure centre. I understand that they would rather remain there than go back home.

Nebe's observation corresponds with that of prison officers, with residents' own accounts, and with reports by media and civil society organisations showing that the deportation camps have rendered a growing number of people stuck in limbo, or pressured them to go underground, either in Denmark or elsewhere in Europe (Danish Helsinki Committee, 2017; Freedom of Movements Research Collective, 2018). Aya, an activist and resident in Avnstrup deportation camp, summarised why:

> Many people think a rejected asylum seeker means people who don't have the right to stay but won't leave because they are enjoying themselves here. But the truth is that we are stuck in the system. We can't go back because of human rights conventions that Denmark signed, because back is war, back is occupation, back is a place where life is not safe. But we are not granted the right to stay, so we are stuck here, for years and years. We don't leave, we are just waiting to live.

Deportation camps have been utilised in other countries and proved equally harmful. The so-called return centres tried in Norway in the early 2010s did not enhance deportations but broke down residents mentally and pushed them underground (Valenta and Thorshaug, 2011). Similarly, the German deportation camps, which were designed to 'wear down' people's resistance to deportation and make them 'realise that they have no future [in Germany]' (Ellermann, 2010: 419), did exactly that, but did not enhance deportation rates. The policies underestimate the resolve of non-deported people to endure intolerable conditions to evade deportation; something which Nebe and other bureaucratic officials were well aware of. To the extent that the Danish deportation camps had an effect on deportation rates, it was because they pushed people underground or pressured them to move on to other European countries, which enabled the Danish government to pass on responsibility for their cases to these states. Sometimes, they would reappear as Dublin cases; in other cases not, which is a matter I shall return to in Chapter 5. But if the camps were part of a political masquerade, as the prison officer Henriette put it, it was also a performance that came at high human costs. Indeed, if we understand them as a policy of orchestrated abjection, they have to some extent 'succeeded' in creating conditions that cause non-deported people's premature death.

The intolerability regime was supposed to remove the meaning of life for residents of Denmark's deportation camps, so that the 'freedoms' awarded to them (compared to those imprisoned in camps like Ellebæk) lost their meaning in practice. In theory, they were free to leave at any time, but in reality, they had – as Aya noted – nowhere they could legally go. In theory, residents were not confined in the camps, but in practice, they had very limited access to the financial and logistical means to leave the camps and to participate in society. If they left the camps without authorisation, they also risked criminalisation according to the house rules outlined above. In theory, camp staff had limited authority over residents and few ways of sanctioning them, but in practice, the camp rules also enabled staff to monitor and regulate even the most intimate aspects of their lives, such as what, where, and when they could eat; who they could receive as a visitor and when; what personal items they possessed; and their daily habits. As the prison officer Eskil once noted, residents were 'stripped naked in front of the system'. Or, as Mohamed, a seven-year-old activist in Sjælsmark, put it, residents had 'no room of their own'. Issa, a resident in Sjælsmark, described his experience of the false semblance of freedom offered to residents in the camps in the following way:

> Even though you are allowed to leave the camp, there are certain regulations which make it very difficult for you to live. You can't have any activities that keep you going. It's like a wall between you and the rest of society, one that you can't see ... As a normal person, you choose to do things when you want to. You can eat when you want, exercise whenever you want, decide how you want to live your life. In the camp, we are deprived of all choices. And you can't make any plans for your life [...] and this situation could go on forever. Maybe some of those who are there must stay there for the rest of their lives ... and bearing this in mind is a burden you carry. It creates craziness. When life doesn't have a purpose, when it's made purposeless ... it makes you go crazy. Knowing you have potentials, dreams. And this is just to make you sign a paper. (Issa, quoted in Freedom of Movements Research Collective, 2018: 30)

Issa draws attention to the temporal violence of the deportation camps, manifested in the deprivation of autonomy and power over one's everyday life and habits, and in how the system deprived residents of their future hope, potentials, and dreams (see Lindberg and Edward, 2021). The orchestrated purposelessness created, as Issa notes, craziness – a craziness which manifested in the widespread mental and physical ill-health within the deportation camps. In Sjælsmark, there were residents who resorted to substance abuse (for which they also risked criminalisation). There were others who turned silent and apathetic; and yet others acted out, trashed the facilities, set fire to their rooms, or attempted to kill themselves. Several reports have detailed how the deportation camps have caused depression and anxiety-related conditions among residents, and aggravated pre-existing traumas (see e.g. Canning, 2019b; Clante Bendixen, 2021). As residents and activists in Sjælsmark and Avnstrup have emphasised, mental ill-health, anxiety, depression, and aggression are expected reactions to a politics designed to make life intolerable. Therefore, they insisted that their emotional responses to the intolerability regime were political and criticised the ways in which their reactions were either pathologised, criminalised, or blamed on themselves.

For some residents, the long-term exposure to stress, anxiety, and depression generated long-lasting physical conditions (and vice versa), which remained untreated in the camps. While residents formally had access to emergency healthcare services, run by the Red Cross, this access was limited in practice, since healthcare personnel were instructed only to provide healthcare that was deemed 'necessary, urgent, and pain relieving'. A standing joke among residents in Sjælsmark was that no matter what their health condition, if they sought help from the medical clinic, the Red Cross nurse would dismiss them with a prescription to 'take a painkiller and drink some water'. As a result of this medical neglect, minor and curable medical conditions remain untreated, only to become aggravated over time and eventually turn into acute conditions. Behrouz Boochani (2018; see also Bhatia and Bruce-Jones, 2021) has called such minimum access to medical support in detention and deportation camp settings a form of cruel care, which deflects responsibility for the injuries caused by the system onto the suffering bodies and offers little remedy for them.

Another consequence of the deportation camps was that they directly contributed to the criminalisation of non-deported people. In addition to the military and prison facilities and uniformed prison officers running the camps, which fuelled public suspicion and fear against residents, the intolerable camp rules criminalised residents. Most of the rule transgressions committed by people residing in the camps could be directly attributed to the motivation enhancement measures, including violations of the registration duty. In 2019, authorities registered more than 40,000 violations of registration duty in the deportation camp Kærshovedgård, resulting in 234 convictions (Berlingske, 2020). Other misdemeanours could be attributed to the prohibition to earn an income, such as travelling without a ticket on the bus, some were criminalised for smoking weed or consuming alcohol on the camp premises, which some residents used as a way of coping with the intolerability regime. Residents would also easily be criminalised for getting into conflicts with staff (see Freedom of Movements Research Collective, 2018). Aside from adding to the restrictions and stigmatisation they experienced, criminalisation diminished residents' legal prospects to remain in Denmark, since it might entail a deportation order that could jeopardise their possibilities of obtaining legal residency, even if their asylum case was reopened.

In exposing residents to social, mental, and physical harms, the deportation camps can be understood as operating according to a logic of 'slow violence', where residents were kept 'alive, but in a state of injury' (Mbembe, 2003: 21) – or as Aya once put it, 'alive, but not allowed to live'. This slow violence operated on several axes that injured residents

> psychologically, through the mental stress imposed upon them through the rule of intolerability and by depriving them of both their present and future hopes and aspirations; physically, through the psychosomatic and physiological

conditions they acquired from residing in the centres; and legally, by pushing them into illegality or criminalizing their very existence and means of survival. (Suárez-Krabbe and Lindberg, 2019: 93)

The staff in Sjælsmark were aware of the detrimental effects that the intolerability arrangement had on residents but had different opinions on whether they were legitimate. Eskil thought it was 'fair', since non-deported people could simply 'choose to cooperate and go back where they belonged' if they did not like it in the camp. Jonas, on the other hand, thought the arrangement was 'shit', arguing that 'it is not decent to treat people this way, in a democratic society'. Henriette said, 'you can't think about what's happening or what's awaiting them all the time. It's not that all of them are sent to ongoing war, many of them are Dublin cases, but still, it must be crap. You have no money, you have nothing. Not even bus tickets. It must be quite awful for them. But there are rules we have to follow.' Thinking of the rules, but not feeling responsible for their implications, enabled prison officers to selectively ignore or overlook the camps' adverse and injurious effects. Because the violence was structural and indirect, it enabled a diffusion of responsibility for the suffering it caused.

Contesting deportability: the politics of presence

'You see, in my country, death would be quick. But in Denmark, they are killing us slowly. And the state doesn't even recognise its own role in doing it.' Bashir was among the younger men who were staying in Sjælsmark and who participated in the self-organised protests initiated by residents in spring 2016. His statement reflects the dual frustration with being subjected to the 'slow violence' of the Danish deportation camps, and with the state denouncing its role in perpetrating this violence. This logic of responsibilisation, in addition to the dehumanisation and criminalisation of non-deported people taking place in the camps, was what Castaway Souls of Sjælsmark/Denmark were mobilising against. With the support of other activist movements in Denmark, the group initiated a series of demonstrations, art interventions, and a protest camp arranged at Copenhagen's Red Square, where they demanded the right to have rights, freedom to stay and to move, closure of asylum camps and prisons, and an end to the intolerability regime (see Arce and Suárez-Krabbe, 2019). By drawing attention to how the conditions that 'left them to die, slowly' were orchestrated politically and sanctioned by law, they challenged the *ir*responsibility of the Danish government for the slow violence of the intolerability regime. Through these actions, the camp residents – like in struggles by non-deported communities elsewhere – emerged as 'haunting figures' of Denmark's violent deportation regime, insisting on their right to be seen, heard, and have their presence recognised (Nyers, 2019: 130). The protesters challenged the 'political hierarchies of visibility and audibility' (Minor Keywords Collective, 2021: 29) that determine who is allowed to participate in the political conversation in Denmark, and the political debates surrounding their condition, which had almost exclusively been waged *about but without* them.

In Sjælsmark, prison officers paid little attention to the demonstrations. When I asked them if they had heard of the protests, most of them shrugged, and repeated their mantra, 'if they don't like it, they are free to leave at any time'; but Mohamed, one of the organisers of the protests, noted, 'they say we are free to say what we want, but they refuse to listen, so what's that freedom worth? When residents smash windows, or harm themselves – are we still free to do what we want?' Even if authorities did not heed their demands, they did not go unheard; after the protests, several participants of the movement were forced to relocate to Kærshovedgård (Arce and Suárez-Krabbe, 2019). Dispersal is a well-documented administrative strategy used by immigration authorities to discipline people living in camps and to disrupt solidarity networks (see Gill, 2009; Hiemstra, 2020). However, protests continued emerging in Kærshovedgård in 2017, and again in Sjælsmark in 2018, when the families who had by then moved into Sjælsmark mobilised to draw attention to the detrimental effects of the camps on their children's mental health and well-being. A range of civil society organisations mobilised in their support (see Folkbevægelsen for asylbørns fremtid, n.d.), and reports were published documenting how the children in Sjælsmark suffered from chronic anxiety, stopped eating, and refused to attend school. Among them was a report by the Red Cross (2019), which concluded that 60 per cent to 80 per cent of the 130 children residing there qualified for a psychiatric diagnosis, which the medics assessed risked turning into a permanent condition (it should be noted that the Red Cross remained in charge of healthcare services in the deportation camps during this period). The protests resulted in the Social Democratic-led government, which took power in 2019, promising to offer the families improved living conditions in deportation camp Avnstrup, which was run by the Red Cross, and where they would get the possibility to cook their own food. Once they were moved to Avnstrup, however, residents criticised the fact that the metal fences in Sjælsmark had merely been exchanged for intensified reporting duties, which prevented them from leaving the camp and amplified their social isolation; and although they were permitted to cook their own food, they could only select groceries from a limited list of items delivered by Hørkram, a large food service company, which did not cater to or satisfy their different dietary needs.[3] Healthcare services remained limited, and children continued to be denied access to adequate education (see 'Avnstrup on Strike' in VisAvis, 2020). As Aya, who was part of the renewed protest movement in Avnstrup, noted, the changes that came with the residents' relocation to Avnstrup did not generate any substantial improvement of their situation but served to 'deflect attention from the core issues: deprivation of autonomy, of future hopes, and of the right to liveability'.

Alongside these visible struggles, non-deported people continuously challenged the intolerability regime through acts of contestation that took place on the level of everyday life. By forming social relationships with people outside the camps, they circumvented their involuntary dependency on the state. The so-called house rules that were designed to regulate residents' everyday lives rendered mundane activities into acts of resistance: including refusing to eat in the cafeteria, bringing cooking utensils into the camp and cooking for oneself, or decorating one's room, which might indicate an intention to remain rather than leaving. Residents also challenged their enforced isolation by maintaining friendships, relationships, and community bonds beyond the confines of the camp, and by finding work in the informal sector. Although the camps rendered people 'stuck' temporally, physically, and existentially (see Hage, 2009), the fact that they remained in the camps also directly challenged the official function of the camps, which was to make them leave. They contested their deportability as well as the legitimacy of their deportation orders by staying put, waiting out the state, and by trying to reopen their asylum cases. Some of them succeeded in turning the same asylum laws that produced their exclusion into an avenue to regularisation: between 2016 and 2018, forty-seven residents in Kærshovedgård successfully appealed their deportation order and obtained asylum (Ibfelt and Skov-Jensen, 2019). Others continued their everyday practices of transgression, of living and hoping against the deportation regime, residents enacted a 'politics of presence' (Minor Keywords Collective, 2021: 30) against state authorities' attempts at making them disappear.

Concluding remarks

In her book *Ghostly Matters*, Avery Gordon (2008) draws attention to the ways in which power might manifest in acts of violence that cause bodily injury or death; or it might cause harm 'without ever seeming to touch', or in that which 'causes dreams to live and dreams to die' (Gordon, 2008: 3). In contrast to deportation prisons, the deportation camps operate through slow, indirect violence. They are set up to kill dreams: slowly and methodically, not through the immediate threat of a gun, as Bashir pointed out earlier in this chapter, but through indirect forms of control that expose non-deported people to injuries and indeed, premature death. The intolerability regime can be translated as a denial of the 'right to liveability' (Rodríguez, 2018: 24), which operates through the orchestrated withdrawal of the means of making a life liveable, removing access to mobility and settlement; to healthcare and education; and to relationships, family, and community. The Danish deportation camps, and the deportation-oriented migration and asylum policy they are part of, actively seek to remove the dreams of a future in Denmark for the non-deported. While they ostensibly fail to increase deportation rates, they are, in this regard, 'successful failures' (Whyte et al., 2020: 143), as they sever the hopes and aspirations of people to make a life for themselves.

Slow violence has long-lasting implications. As Alison Mountz (2020: xvi) has argued, abusive systems of power continue to 'haunt' the lives of those who have been exposed to them long after they ceased to have their immediate effects. At some point during the summer of 2016, Steve and I started recording our conversations about the Danish deportation camps and their slow violence. By then, Steve had been living in Sjælsmark deportation camp for more than one year. This is how Steve, back then, reflected on the toll of the slow violence perpetrated against people living in the deportation camps.

> When I say a convicted criminal has more right as a human recognised in this society, another aspect is that he or she knows that one day, he or she will be out of jail. So, their lives still have a purpose. But for someone living as a rejected asylum seeker, this purpose of life is intentionally taken away from them. While you live in the camp, time pauses … you know Daniel in the deportation camp? He has been in Denmark for nine years, in Europe for maybe fifteen to twenty years. Those are wasted years. This pause has no end.

Deportation camps steal people's time by keeping them in an indefinite state of 'not arriving' (see Khosravi, 2018: 41): caught within the Danish archipelago of camps, or in circulation between different institutions of asylum, detention, and deportation in Denmark and across Europe. The camps not only render non-deported people stuck but also 'stick' onto people's minds and bodies. Steve and I spoke about the camps again in 2021, when four years had gone by since he left Denmark. I shared with him the draft version of this chapter and asked him to share his thoughts on it. We ended up talking about what had and what had not changed since he left, and about what was still haunting him. He explained,

> I thought when I left Denmark that I left this behind. I left anxiety and depression behind. Or at least, I thought had found a way of making myself become more … human in the sense that I can try to live normally, whatever that means. But you know when I wrote you early this morning, I was still trying to go to sleep. I have this since Denmark. My eating habits are disordered, my

sleeping interrupted. I have anxiety when nothing is happening. And I can't be happy when good things sometimes happen. Because I know that now a new struggle begins ... I'm so confused, I don't know how to live a life. There's no structure, how to live a life again. And I'm struggling to do that. You think this is something that's left ... in the chapter it is mentioned that the system is exporting people with their problems to somewhere else where the state doesn't see it. You are finally erased, good for you. If we can't kill you and you are not dead, we must find another way, you disappear from the public, away from where we can see you.

Steve speaks about the long-lasting injurious effects of the slow violence he lived through in the Danish deportation camp. His testimony demonstrates how the 'political masquerade' of the deportation camps wears people down mentally and physically to the extent that it affects their ability to live a liveable life, even long after they have left the camps. Steve also contended that if he still felt changed by the camp, not much had changed in the camps themselves. 'They do not change the laws, only the conditions. None of what we see happening now is new, nor does it change anything. There have been people living in the camps for fifteen to twenty years, and governments came and went during this time, but they were still in the camps.' Steve highlights here the impossibility and inadequacy of relying on reform as a way of addressing the injurious effects of the deportation camps. Instead, since 2016, Danish governments have intensified their efforts to pressure non-deported people to leave, increased their investments in deportation enforcements, and expanded the scope of people who risk being sent to deportation camps by removing the protection status for refugees from Syria and Somalia, many of whom have nothing to 'return' to, and whom authorities have little or no prospects to forcibly deport. This way, the camps keep being filled with people enduring the deportation limbo; some of them will do so confined in the deportation camps, others might take the risk of moving on. Their lives will be put on hold, and at the same time, their presence will continue to haunt the Danish deportation regime.

Notes

1 Steve's recorded interviews with the director of Sjælsmark later became a short film, which has been screened at multiple festivals across Europe. The trailer to the video can be accessed at https://vimeo.com/325701061 (accessed 10 August 2022).
2 The system of pocket money has since been elaborated. In Kærshovedgård, residents may earn up to DKK 427 every fortnight if they 'cooperate' in the deportation process; comply with their residence, registration, and reporting duties;

and fulfil their so-called education and activation contract, which obliges them to partake in certain activities such as cleaning their rooms and completing unsalaried 'internships' in the camp.
3 The 'list solution' was developed in response to families' ongoing protests against the restrictions to their autonomy. However, instead of granting residents' access to cash allowance, which would enable them to purchase their own food, they were given the option to select from a total of 300 items from the food service company Hørkram (of which eleven were different parts of chicken). The food items do not correspond to residents' cultural preferences; for instance, there is no way for them to know whether the meat is halal, and the range of spices available is highly limited.

5

The idea is to exhaust them: minimum welfare provisions in Sweden

> Exhausting them – that's the idea behind the amendment. In the short term, I'm sure there will be lots of problems, increased burden on the police, on civil society, and destitution, which is also a cost on society ... But sure, there were costs associated with keeping them under control in the Swedish Migration Agency's accommodation units too. That was also bureaucratically complicated ... and they don't care. So now we kick them out on the street and let them freeze until they've thought things through – and maybe they will change their minds. The point is to exhaust them.

At the end of the previous chapter, we heard Samir, a young man from a North African country who soon had been held for the maximum time in a Swedish deportation prison, reflect on what would happen to him if authorities did not manage to deport him. Previously, people like Samir, whose applications for protection had been rejected but who resisted deportation, used to be allowed access to shelter and a reduced daily allowance from the Swedish Migration Agency until their deportation could be enforced. However, according to a legal amendment adopted in 2016 as part of the Swedish government's restrictive turn on asylum and migration, instead, as Samir rightly noted, they would be 'put on the street'. The 2016 amendment to the Act (1994: 137) *on the reception of asylum seekers and others* (LMA) withdraws access to housing and social benefits for people who refuse to leave 'voluntarily'. This amendment was what I was discussing with Hasse, the caseworker at the Swedish Migration Agency quoted above, who worked at one of the agency's return units. The return units were, bureaucratically speaking, part of the asylum reception system. Yet Hasse's job was not primarily to provide accommodation but to administer the departure of people whose asylum applications had been rejected – a job that he noted had gained increased political recognition since 2016. Hasse explained to me that the political rationale behind the LMA amendment was that cancelling non-deported people's access to a bare minimum of social welfare and 'making them freeze' would eventually wear them down and make them comply with their deportation order. Reflecting on the implications of the law, Hasse weighed its societal and human costs against the 'bureaucratically complicated' option of allowing people whose asylum application had been rejected to remain inscribed in the system. The latter option had been frustrating for officials since, in their experience, people did not care about their deportation order and remained anyway. I take his concluding remark, which he expressed in a rather cynical tone, about the political intention to 'exhaust' non-deported people as an invitation to explore the instrumentalisation of access to welfare as a means of deportation enforcement.

Alongside detention, the Swedish authorities use formal abandonment (Davies et al., 2017) and derecording (Kalir and van Schendel, 2017) as means of putting pressure on non-deported people. These techniques signal a shift in governing rationales; in detention and during the bureaucratic preparation of the deportation process, non-deported individuals are 'meticulously inscribed within the bureaucratic machinery of expulsion' (De Genova, 2017: 255), with its caretaking as well as coercive functions. In contrast, the Swedish exhaustion strategy operates through the withdrawal of access to welfare services and care, and through bureaucratic derecording (Davies et al., 2017; Kalir and van Schendel, 2017). This governing rationale can be described as a form of 'violent inaction' (Davies et al., 2017: 1263), where the non-deported are met with indifference by state authorities; they might be present on the territory but treated 'as if they no longer exist' (Kalir, 2017: 66). If the deportation camps in Denmark signalled a shift from meticulous control towards a politics of semi-confinement, deprivation, and selective looking away, the Swedish approach to non-deportable people constitutes a step further along the state violence continuum towards the violence of 'active inaction'. The policy is justified by a welfare chauvinist imaginary wanting to reserve welfare for 'natives' (Keskinen et al., 2016), and by neoclassical assumptions that non-deported people are incentivised to remain in Sweden due to 'economic pull factors'; accordingly, withdrawing their access to welfare services is not only fair but believed to incentivise them to leave (Mayblin, 2019). The policy approach is also embedded in a narrative of 'humanitarian deportations' (Borrelli, 2021: 3484): Swedish state authorities have an explicit preference for 'voluntary' deportations, which do not require them to resort to physical force. Thus, by withdrawing access to minimum welfare provisions, authorities are able to put pressure on non-deported people and subject them to injurious conditions, without having to touch them.

Enforcing 'voluntary' return

On a rainy October morning in 2017, I was waiting in the entrance hall of the office building in one of the Swedish Migration Agency's return units.

The unit was a former open prison, but with no remnants of fences or surveillance systems, located close to one of Sweden's larger airports. It offered temporary housing to people whose asylum applications had been rejected while authorities were administering their deportations. Unlike the Danish deportation camps, it was not mandatory for non-deported people to live there. Instead, the accommodation was presented as an offer to those who cooperated with authorities in the deportation case, and for those who refused to leave but whom authorities still thought might 'change their minds' and cooperate. Staff working in the accommodation units therefore summoned residents regularly to attend so-called return dialogues, where they discussed different deportation scenarios.

*I meet up with the manager of the unit, Kristoffer. We get a coffee and sit down in the staff office area together with two return caseworkers, Mariam and Susanne. A whiteboard covers one of the walls, and it is full of tables and flow charts, which are meant to capture the formal steps in the so-called voluntary departure process. Scattered across the tables are colourful Post-its representing different cases the unit is currently dealing with. The 'aim' is to move a case smoothly through the tables towards the end goal: deportation. On the other walls are various posters with motivational slogans for staff (I read, 'Respect!' 'Communication!'), and drawings of staff members – Kristoffer explains that the return unit recently had staff meeting days (*planeringsdagar*), where officials were asked to describe and evaluate their personality traits. They have kept the posters on the walls, to remind themselves that it is a tough job that requires them to work with themselves continuously. We turn towards the whiteboard with the flow chart, and Kristoffer hands me a leaflet so that I can situate their work in the deportation process better (Figure 5.1).*

*He explains to me that the left column illustrates the different stages in the voluntary return process: rejection of an asylum application, repeated return dialogues, perhaps an appeal, followed by more return dialogues, ending with 'departure from Sweden' (*Resa från Sverige*). The right column illustrates a 'ladder of coercive measures' that authorities may take if a person does not cooperate with authorities in the deportation case; withdrawing LMA, reporting duty (*uppsikt*), where a person is obliged to register with the migration agency or the police on a weekly basis (Swedish Aliens Act, chapter 10, § 6–8), detention, and finally, handing over the case to the police for enforcement. As a first step, caseworkers at the return units screen the case to make sure no obvious mistakes have been made in the asylum process. Kristoffer says that their staff have usually worked within the Swedish Migration Agency for some years, and they are used to*

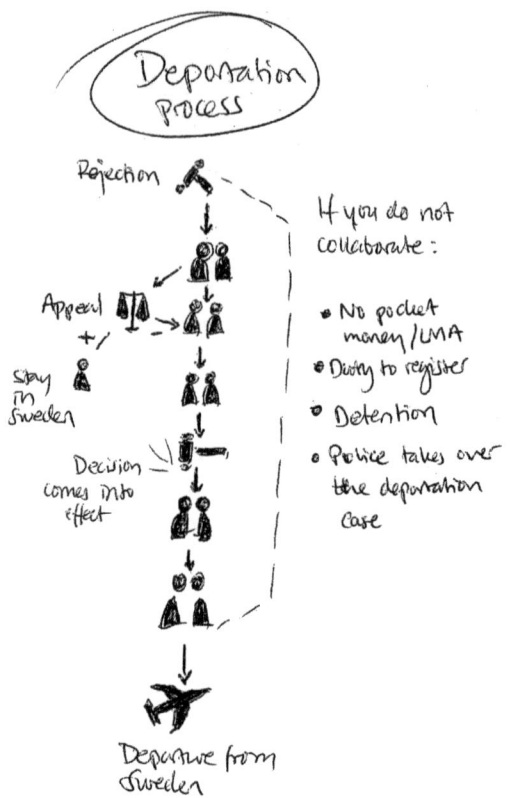

Figure 5.1 Illustration of the 'return process' by the Swedish Migration Agency

dealing with challenging cases and situations. This is even more important now, he continues, since 'the competence of asylum caseworkers is … low. They employed lots of new, young people in 2015, and they got no proper training. So, we see ourselves as the last resort and guarantor that asylum seekers will have their rights respected.' If an asylum case is rejected, the person can either decide to comply with the deportation order, or appeal to the migration court; meanwhile, the return caseworkers start preparing for the return process. 'We do not force anyone', Kristoffer emphasises, 'we work with voluntary return. Or you can say that it's voluntary but under the force of law.' Pointing to the first 'return dialogue' column, he explains, 'for those whose applications have been fast-tracked, like people from the Balkans, we try to discourage them from appealing, as the turnover rates are so low anyway, and we don't want to give them false hopes. It is better for them to leave as soon as possible.' Mariam, who has been silent so far, now fills in,

> Basically, what we do is we tell them that a no is a no. Rejection means you must return. We have a form for this that they must sign. If they don't cooperate, we hand the sheet over to the police and they enforce the decision. This way, we show clarity. They should never be able to say: 'you didn't tell me!' because we can show with this form that we have told them. It is important to emphasise that responsibility is now on them. We can help them plan a good return procedure, support reintegration, prescribe medicines – it's up to the applicants and their behaviour determines the outcome. We must show dignity and respect. And a certain amount of assistance. That's all we can offer.

Susanna adds, 'Yes, we need to make sure they know what the deal is. It might sound mean, but we must be clear: you are not allowed to stay here. We sometimes challenge them and ask, what will you do here? What will you live off? Where will you find a job?' Kristoffer continues,

> In some cases, there are some positive incentives we can offer if they comply with the deportation order. People of certain nationalities can apply for reintegration support from ERIN[1]... but it's a bit tricky, it seems a bit arbitrary who actually gets it, and that undermines our credibility when we offer it, of course. But we try always to be available here, to talk to them and to take their concerns seriously.

I ask what 'incentives' they can use for those who are not eligible for assisted voluntary return support, and Kristoffer says,

> For those who qualify for assisted voluntary return, we can always say that the support will be withdrawn if they do not comply and that we will hand over their case to the police. But in some cases, it's tricky. You see here, we are supposed to hand over the case to the police if we believe there is a need to use force. But there are also those who we know that the police cannot deport by force. Which is the case for some Afghans, and people from Somalia, Iran, Uzbekistan ... and they know this too. It's a bit weird, we sit there and say we are now going to take all these measures, put you in detention or hand you over to the police but we both know that will not happen ... and we end up in a catch-22 situation.

From Kristoffer, Mariam, and Susanna's overview, we learn about the different measures available to authorities to pressure people to comply with a deportation order without them having to resort to physical force. We also learn that staff conceive these measures as *voluntary* – or, voluntary under the 'force of law'. For this purpose, the officials stressed the importance of making non-deported people *know* and *understand* their limited prospects of remaining in Sweden. By framing the issue of deportation as a question of knowing and understanding the right information – that is, the information provided by Swedish migration authorities – responsibility for the deportation case was deflected onto the non-deported people.

Caseworkers emphasised the importance of voluntarism, and 'returning at one's own accord' (*självmant återvändande*) was their preferred terminology to describe this part of the deportation process, before the police intervened to use coercive force.

In 2018, 46 per cent of the 18,761 concluded deportation cases were registered as 'voluntary', whereas 44 per cent were handed over to the police for enforcement, either because the person had absconded, or because coercive force was deemed necessary in order to enforce the deportation order (Migrationsinfo, 2019). However, the numbers do not reveal if 'voluntary' returns have been enforced with the use of detention, withdrawal of welfare, and so on. All officials I spoke to were aware of this contradiction; some of them merely saw 'voluntariness' as part of the bureaucratic lingo. Others were concerned with what the euphemism obscured: namely, the fact that migration officials and non-deported people 'lived in different realities', as Palle, a junior caseworker at another return unit expressed it; that many still feared going back to the country they had fled from, and that this fear had not been adequately accounted for in deficient asylum procedures (see Asylum Commission, n.d.). Palle reflected,

> It's hypocritical to say, 'it will all be fine if you go home'. Unfortunately, the return conversations are laden with negativity. We have nothing to offer. We just say: if you stay in Sweden we will withdraw your LMA and you will end up on the street. So 'motivating conversation' is just wrong. We only offer negative motivations – like 'you'd better watch out'.

In Palle's view, 'motivation' was an ill-disguised threat. Kristoffer told me, 'to say that we work with motivating measures … I think that sounds a bit like "Arbeit macht frei"'. Or, as Hasse noted, presenting non-deported people with the 'choice' of deportation with or without coercive force was 'a bit like telling them to choose between two evils'. Mariam contended, 'We can talk nicely to them, or we can try to buy them. That's it – if there's no readmission agreement, maybe that's the final little thing that convinces them to leave. That they can rent a room for a year or so, buy a taxi, or an animal. That's what we are doing, we're buying them out.' Hence, if threats did not work, officials could use extortion.

The migration officials I talked to emphasised that at the end of the day, all they could aspire to do was to 'help' non-deported people make 'the decisions that were best for themselves', as Hasse put it. The point here is not to question the genuineness of their empathy or intentions. But as we were discussing the officials' motivation strategies, we kept returning to how the discursive distinctions between 'voluntary' and 'forced' deportations, between 'assistance', threat, and extortion, collapsed in practice. As deportation scholars have highlighted, the language of *voluntariness* and *assistance* does important legitimation work for the deportation regime, by obscuring the always underlying threat of force and by disfiguring the *de facto* 'absence of viable options' (Andríjasevic and Walters, 2010: 996) into a semblance of 'deliberate choice' (see also Gibney, 2013; Koch, 2014; Lecadet, 2018; Webber, 2011). 'Voluntary' deportation procedures are also perceived as a way of enhancing the efficiency of deportations at lower costs, while giving deportation an air of humanitarianism (Bendixsen, 2020). While the rhetoric of assistance was prominent among the Swedish officials, they did not deny the coercive underpinnings of their work. In this way, their attitudes provided a realist contrast to the rosy stories that figure in the official 'soft deportation' campaigns by governmental institutions and NGOs that have been dissected elsewhere (Kalir, 2017: 56).

As Kristoffer mentioned, there were also cases where neither threat, nor extortion, nor assistance offers worked. Migration officials at the return units were particularly challenged by the cases where the deportation could not be enforced without the active 'cooperation' of the non-deported (e.g., due to a lack of readmission agreements, because deportable people refuse to disclose their identity, or because forced return would violate the principle of *refoulement*; see SOU 2017:84). These were the cases Kristoffer referred to as 'catch-22' situations, and according to the migration officials, they made up a substantial share of the deportation cases they dealt with. Handing over these cases to the police was virtually useless, as Kristoffer explained, since coercive force, incarceration, and chartered planes would not make any difference. And indeed, in their 2018 yearbook, the Swedish Police reported that out of the 10,529 deportation cases handed over by the Swedish Migration Agency to the police for enforcement, 4,980 cases were classified as difficult or very difficult to enforce (Polisen, 2019: 100–101). These people, who remained in Sweden either because they considered other options worse or because they could not be deported, were caught in limbo (SOU 2017:84). Their cases kept being brought up in conversations with migration officials, who referred to them as 'sourdough cases', and with police officers. Karin, a senior border police officer, was less concerned about these cases, as she was confident in her ability to 'wear them down until they comply'. Margareta, on the other hand, who worked in the Swedish Migration Agency's central organisation (in a 'quality unit' that has since been shut down) with – according to her – the Sisyphean task of updating standards and manuals for streamlining the deportation process, answered in a cynical tone when I asked her about these cases,

> They insist that people become stuck in limbo, but actually, these cases are very few. Those who refuse to cooperate, they choose to put themselves in limbo, so to speak. For this group, where deportation cannot be enforced

without their cooperation and we cannot use force; it is *we*, the authorities, who are in limbo!

In these situations, she went on to explain, the fact that non-deported people knew that authorities could not forcibly deport them rendered 'voluntary' measures and incentives useless. Margareta's claim that it is the authorities who are left 'powerless' and 'in limbo' reflects a bureaucratic logic where non-deportability causes knots or fissures in an otherwise smooth flow diagram. However, with the amendment to the LMA, migration authorities had been provided with a novel strategy to resolve this bureaucratic catch-22: if people could not be deported, they could be derecorded.

Destitution as deterrence

The LMA regulates access to social welfare for people seeking protection in Sweden. Since 1994, people who arrive to seek asylum can choose between being housed in accommodation centres operated by the Swedish Migration Agency (*anläggningsboende*) and run by municipal or private actors, in which case they receive food and accommodation and a daily allowance of SEK 24 per day for single adults. Or, they may choose to stay in private accommodation (*eget boende*), usually with family and friends, in which case they may receive a daily allowance of SEK 71 per day to cover food, medicines, and other essential expenses – yet as of 2020, this allowance might be withdrawn if they choose to live in a 'socioeconomically challenged area'.[2] In 2019, around 56 per cent of people seeking asylum were estimated to live in private accommodation (Prop. 2019/20: 10). Prior to 2016, people whose asylum applications had been rejected continued to receive a reduced daily allowance and could stay in the Swedish Migration Agency's accommodation until they left Sweden. However, the amendment to the LMA that entered into force in July 2016 withdraws access to the Swedish Migration Agency's accommodation units and to daily allowance and subsidised medical care for anyone who does not leave the country within the stipulated deadline for voluntary departure, which ranges between two and four weeks (chapter 8 § 21 of the Aliens Act).

This drastic change in policy was justified with logistical and administrative arguments: when an 'exceptionally' high number of people arrived in Sweden to seek asylum in 2015, the Swedish Migration Agency's accommodation units were filled up. Evicting those whose asylum applications had been rejected, it was argued, would make more space for new arrivals (Prop. 2015/16: 146). The LMA amendment was also supposed to serve a deterrence function, by preventing people from 'becoming stuck' in reception facilities and delaying deportation procedures, instead incentivising them to leave (SOU 2018:22). Exceptions could be made in cases where the withdrawal of benefits was deemed to be 'manifestly unreasonable' (*uppenbart oskäligt*): for instance, families with children, and people with disabilities or health conditions of a severe *yet temporary* nature, could retain LMA until they left the country (Migrationsverket SR 13/2016). Exceptions were also made to those whose deportations were suspended for reasons outside their control (SOU 2017:84). However, the preparatory work of the LMA amendment stated that exception clauses should be used restrictively, and for people deported back to Sweden according to the Dublin Regulation, no exceptions would be made. The law thus rendered access to minimum welfare conditional upon certain requirements: either demonstrating vulnerability, as illustrated by the exceptions made for children and people who were severely ill, or 'performing' in accordance with authorities' wishes by cooperating in the deportation process.

When the law was passed, authorities counted around 12,000 open deportation cases, and 4,300 people were expected to be affected by the amendment. Most of them stayed in private accommodation, and would have their daily allowance withdrawn, whereas those who stayed in accommodation provided by the Swedish Migration Agency received an eviction notice (FARR, 2016). In principle, most caseworkers at the Swedish Migration Agency who worked with deportation processes considered exclusion from welfare services to be a logical consequence of a rejected asylum application. Mariam, for instance, argued that there should be no 'contradictory incentives' that might 'encourage' non-deported people to remain in Sweden. Others thought that it lent 'clarity and consistency' to the deportation process. Margareta told me that the amendment had made the Swedish Migration Agency introduce a new category in their online system SKAPA, which permitted authorities to finalise these cases more swiftly, since no more bureaucratic action (such as granting daily allowance or other welfare benefits) could be taken. The category, I was told, was particularly useful for the catch-22 cases that Kristoffer mentioned earlier, where the person could not be deported by force and refused to comply with the deportation order. Referring to these cases, Susanna explained, 'we simply put them in a locker. Once we withdraw LMA they simply stay there.' And, she continued, 'the police don't want them in their registers, it's a political thing, and for us it also looks better: we can complete the case file and send it to the archive'. The LMA amendment thus allowed state authorities to strategically use derecording as a last resort, by placing the people whom they could not deport out of bureaucratic sight and out of politicians' concerns. However, the amendment also presented officials with new dilemmas. It compelled them to make assessments of who was vulnerable or cooperative enough to retain their basic means of subsistence, and Hasse, who was an experienced return caseworker, told me of a particularly difficult case that he had recently encountered:

> There was a woman who was ill in cancer, and there was no way of knowing whether she would get better. She was evicted from her accommodation unit and her allowance was withdrawn because her disease was not of 'acute but temporary character'. But how can you assess that – you only know what's temporary afterwards, right? I wouldn't want to be in the person's shoes who would have to make that decision.

According to the migration authorities' legal guidelines, health-related issues only guarantee continued access to accommodation if the condition temporarily impedes deportation enforcement (see SR 13/2016). In the case Hasse describes, the temporary nature of the woman's illness could not be guaranteed, since it was likely that she would die from cancer. It is noteworthy that the decisions on the nature of her illness and the decision to make her destitute were taken by migration authorities, and not by healthcare professionals. It is unclear whether the decision makers in this case had considered the fact that her destitution might aggravate her health condition. Alongside the thousands of other people affected by the LMA amendment, the woman in Hasse's story went from being treated as a subject of care and control to being formally abandoned by state authorities.

In their 2018 report on Sweden, the European Commissioner for Human Rights (2018: 7) wrote, '[The LMA] amendment had severe humanitarian consequences for a number of individuals, who ended up living in the streets. It also resulted in increasing numbers of people seeking support and help, notably asking for food, and in a reportedly serious deterioration of health situations.' NGOs working to support young, non-deported people have similarly reported that the LMA amendment has aggravated the social marginalisation of this group, and increased the burden on civil society, which has filled the gap in welfare provisions (Jansson-Keshavarz, Lundberg, and Obenius, 2021). In 2020, during the COVID-19 pandemic, NGOs providing legal advice and essential services to non-deported people reported having to turn away people with symptoms, knowing they had nowhere else to go (Inci et al., 2020). Yet, the amendment is in line with policies adopted across European countries as part of their deterrence approach to non-deported people. By reducing their access to essential welfare to an absolute, humanitarian minimum, the idea behind the approach is to disincentivise non-deported people from staying, and to strategically make them disappear from the registries of bureaucratic authorities. Research from Norway (Johansen, 2013), the Netherlands (Kalir, 2017; Van der Leun and Bouter, 2015), Switzerland (De Coulon, 2015), Ireland (Lentin and Moreo, 2015), and the United Kingdom (Bloch and Schuster, 2005; Mayblin, 2019) has shown that destitution as a mechanism of deterrence has failed to enhance deportation rates. Instead, and as the EU Commissioner also highlighted, it has pushed non-deported people into destitution, and as a result the responsibility for their bare survival has been outsourced to civil society (Rosenberger and Küffner, 2016).

This formal abandonment of non-deported people, who most likely remain in the country under extremely precarious conditions, needs to be understood not as an unintended side effect of the deterrence policy but as a governing technique in its own right. In academic debates, these approaches have variably been described as a 'politics of exhaustion' (Ansems de Vries and Guild, 2018: 1), 'violent inaction' (Davies et al., 2017: 1263), and an expression of necropolitics (Mbembe, 2003; see also Mayblin et al., 2019), which permit authorities to 'solve' the problem of non-deportability by treating people as if they do not exist. It is an example of indirect state violence, which facilitates harm, without ever needing to touch – and without overtly breaching human rights obligations.[3] While exhaustion, derecording, and inaction describe how the policies work, their implications are better captured through the concept necropolitics, which underscores the racialised imaginaries facilitating this form of indirect or slow violence. Ultimately, the politics of 'letting die' relies on a racial matrix of human hierarchisation where non-deported people are considered disposable, and as such, can rightly be left in a condition where they are merely (or barely) prevented from physically dying (Mbembe, 2003). Moreover, discourses of voluntarism and responsibilisation are important for understanding how these minimum rights approaches are justified, since they construct non-deported people as the cause of 'their own vulnerability and exploitability' (Luibhéid, 2013: 2). Like deportation prisons, the politics of abandonment performs and reproduces the boundaries of membership and human worth.

The dilemmas of derecording

If the LMA amendment was supposed to perform 'clarity and consistency' in the exclusion of non-deported people from the welfare state, it also amplified tensions internal to the welfare state apparatus in at least two ways. First, it contradicted the principle of bureaucratic inscription fundamental to the work of deportation enforcement officials.[4] At the Swedish Migration Agency's return units, caseworkers argued that making non-deported people destitute would simply make them lose contact with authorities. Susanna said, 'now with the amended LMA, they don't have any incentives to remain in the system. What should we do, ask them for their address and then be like ah, you live under the bridge over there? That's just absurd!' Similarly, Palle told me that he had experienced non-deported people laughing at him when he had first communicated the decision of the Swedish Migration Agency to make them destitute and then, in the next moment, asked for their address (which they had to provide to authorities as to show that they remained 'available' to authorities for enforcement). 'And', Palle continued, 'it's even worse if we accept someone back according to Dublin. Then we say welcome back, we had to take you back here but now we will put you on the street. And one wonders, what the message is here?' Some return officials shared that they would make exceptions in cases where rejected people had demonstrated their willingness to cooperate with authorities in their deportation process and allow them to remain in the accommodation unit for some extra nights without registering them. Otherwise, they contended, people would lose their trust and any incentive to remain in contact with authorities. As a discretionary measure, the LMA amendment therefore also allowed authorities to expand their repertoire of enforcement strategies.

In the Swedish deportation prison where I conducted fieldwork, detailed in Chapter 3, staff told me that they had realised that the police were releasing people from detention as a way of pressuring people refusing to cooperate with authorities in the deportation process. Yasmin, one of the detention officials, explained that 'once there was a guy they had to carry out of here, he didn't want to leave because he had nowhere else to go … it's like, you call the police to take them here and then you have to call them again to get them out of here!' I observed a similar scenario on a Saturday afternoon in late September 2017.

We are on the couch in the common room. Livia walks in, bewildered. 'There is a man waiting at the reception and he says he wants to return to his country of origin. His asylum application has been rejected and his case has been handed over to the police because he absconded, but now he quarrelled with his girlfriend and has no place to stay.' Livia explains that the man claims that the police referred him to detention, but she is not sure if that can be trusted. 'And we obviously can't detain him', she says,

> Since he is showing up here, there are no longer any grounds for detention – he is no longer hiding from authorities! But I get it, he has nowhere to go and no money. We can just refer him to the municipality or to the social services. It's a bit ironic, we had this other guy who just escaped. I just spoke with the police, and they joked and said you have to be nicer to them so they don't run away from you … there are many we can't please!

The incident ended with the man simply being told to leave, as there was nothing they could do for him. Livia suspected that the police would want to place him under registration duty, but since the incident occurred during the weekend, they probably would not make that decision anytime soon. The officials found the incident ironic: they had people trying to escape from the deportation prison, while others were desperately trying to be incarcerated. The story can be read as a way of banalising incarceration – as Khosravi (2009) has highlighted, detention staff used stories such as these to convince themselves and others that detention was not so bad after all. But it also demonstrates how incarceration and destitution are used as complementary measures to govern non-deported people, for whom law enforcement proliferates into a 'continuum of liminal spaces', encompassing direct and indirect state violence, coercive control, surveillance, and formal abandonment (Schmid-Scott, 2018). In a way, the man who asked to enter the deportation prison to access food and shelter challenged the derecording logic, as he demanded recognition by authorities and access to basic welfare provisions. But his action also testifies to the precarity of his condition, where a deportation prison is the only place for him to access minimum social assistance.

The second tension or dilemma that the LMA amendment amplified was within the 'social arm' of the welfare state, which was now ascribed an even more prominent role in migration enforcement. Minimum rights policies are examples of how social welfare is instrumentalised for the purpose of 'internal bordering' (Tervonen et al., 2018: 139), and social services are mobilised as gatekeepers of essential welfare service provisions. As such, the active role of social services in border enforcement is not a novel phenomenon. Defining categories of deservingness and delineating membership are integral parts of social work, and social services continuously partake in defining the boundaries of the welfare state by determining who can access social support and under what conditions (Spencer, 2016; Tervonen et al., 2018). In the context of border enforcement, research from across Europe has demonstrated how social services have increasingly been mobilised as *de facto* border enforcement agents, who not only determine access to welfare but who are also obliged to check the immigration status of welfare users, and gather and share their personal contact information with police and migration enforcement authorities (Lundberg et al., 2017).[5] In these contexts, social workers and welfare providers are confronted with conflicting responsibilities: to guarantee access to basic social rights for anyone present on the territory, on the one hand, and to uphold the boundaries of membership in the welfare state, on the other (Björngren and Staaf, 2014). The LMA amendment needs to be seen in the light of the proliferation of internal bordering practices, and as a rather extreme form of, as Nordling and Persdotter (2021: 155) have phrased it, 'bordering through destitution'.

At the time when the LMA amendment entered into force, people whose asylum cases were rejected and other people living as undocumented in Sweden could turn to the municipal social services and apply for emergency assistance, which was meant to cover food and basic needs (but not accommodation), in accordance with the *Social Services Act* (2001:453). Decisions on who was eligible for this support and the amount offered were at the discretion of the social services, and varied greatly between municipalities (Nordling, 2017), but in principle, Livia, Palle, and the other migration officials were right in referring non-deported people to social services as a last resort when they lost their LMA. However, in a 2017 ruling, the Supreme Administrative Court (HFD 2017 ref. 33) concluded that social services were *not* obliged to provide support to people whose asylum applications had been rejected and who were at risk of deportation – including families with children. The court stated that these people should receive assistance from the Swedish Migration Agency, which the LMA amendment effectively precluded. Consequently, non-deported people lost access to any legally guaranteed social support. Social services still retained a certain possibility to grant them emergency assistance to 'avert dangers to life and health' (in accordance with chapter 2, § 1–2, SoL), yet at their own discretion (according to chapter 4, § 2, SoL). In their analysis of the ruling, Kjellbom and Lundberg (2018) conclude that the court ruling affirms the prioritisation of migration control over non-deported people's access to essential welfare.

I discussed the court ruling in the light of the amended LMA with Dalia, a social worker in a Swedish municipality that is known for having a more generous interpretation of the rights of non-deported people compared to other municipalities. She told me that the ruling placed social workers in a difficult situation.

> As social workers, it's just not in our imagination just to reject them and stand by and watch while people don't have enough food for the day or roof over their heads … and the idea behind the emergency assistance is that it's supposed to be of temporary nature. When they wrote the law, they didn't count on there being a group who are in a permanent emergency … and this places a greater responsibility on social services. You can't just say 'no, you've been in acute need of assistance for so long that it's enough' – it's the other way around, if you are in a long-term emergency, we have a greater responsibility to help.

For Dalia, the LMA amendment confronted her with a professional dilemma. As a social worker, she was trained to *see* and meet the needs of people, whereas the new regulations implied that instead she should look away from those in need. Her reading of social workers' approach to need – the direr your condition, the stronger your right to social assistance, no matter for how long you are in acute need – directly contradicted the logic of migration enforcement. Dalia continued, 'We have had discussions …

what is our role? Is it to motivate them to return? No, our sole task is to alleviate suffering. But that role is in direct opposition to the work of migration authorities and the police.' Far from all social workers took a similar position; like migration officials and border police officers, there were also social workers who maintained the differentiation in humaneness and deservingness between destitute citizens and migrant 'others' (see Kazemi, 2021). Yet among the social workers I interviewed, there was a widespread understanding that the hostile political climate towards people seeking protection – which was not confined to the LMA amendment but encompassed a broader range of 'displacements' in Swedish migration and welfare policy (Jansson-Keshavarz, Lundberg, and Obenius 2021: 319) – had changed the conditions of social work. They witnessed how people who were already in a precarious condition were made even more vulnerable, while their possibilities to assist them were becoming more limited. They also noted how responsibility for the provision of social welfare to non-deported people was gradually pushed onto civil society actors (see also European Commissioner for Human Rights, 2018); something they thought was 'foreign' to a welfare state. Maria was another trained social worker I interviewed, who had previously worked at one of the Swedish Migration Agency's accommodation units for people arriving as unaccompanied minors. She told me that seeing how people were denied access to social welfare by state authorities had made her resign. When we spoke over the phone, she explained her decision to leave in the following way:

> I used to feel proud of my job. But what I was proud of was that we used to treat unaccompanied asylum seekers the same way we treat Swedish unaccompanied children, and this changed in recent years. We saw how they were now reduced to a gender and a casefile. So, my inner compass told me I had enough. I had empty beds in the accommodation unit while kids were sleeping rough on the street [...] I resigned in protest.

After her resignation, Maria established an NGO that provided accommodation and basic welfare services for young people whose asylum applications had been rejected – the same people she had seen state authorities abandon.

Maria's resignation was a reaction to the discriminatory differentiation between citizens and 'foreign' children, which for her challenged the social imaginary of an inclusive welfare state. Concerns over what happened when the welfare state was mobilised for exclusion were also raised by migration officials. Palle, the return caseworker, told me as we finished our interview, 'I feel like I started questioning the system. But I think, if you are going to work here, you have to buy into the system ... at least to a certain extent.' At the time we met, Palle considered resigning and applying for a doctoral position to research deportations from the perspective of non-deported people. Whether he did or not, I do not know. But the unease expressed by him, Maria, and other state officials illustrates some of the fissures and cracks in the ideology of a fair, inclusive, and egalitarian welfare state that the derecording strategy generated. The belief in the system was also shared initially among many who sought asylum in Sweden, but who were later challenged in their belief by the discrimination and disregard they experienced in their encounters with the welfare state. Their reactions to and ways of navigating the sudden changes from bureaucratic inscription to formal abandonment are important for understanding the implications of the necropolitical operation of the welfare state for non-deported people and their life chances.

Challenging deportability by moving on

In 2015, around 35,000 children arrived to seek asylum in Sweden and were registered as so-called unaccompanied minors. Many of them were Afghans. Their trajectories through the Swedish asylum system and towards deportability have become the focus of a heated public debate, and large-scale mobilisation by civil society, since they have demonstrated the discrepancy between the imaginary of a benevolent, humanitarian asylum regime, and the discriminatory, arbitrary, and harmful outcomes it generated. The treatment of this group has been discussed extensively in research detailing how the children have been exposed to racist political and societal rhetoric, framing them as tricksters, criminals, and welfare abusers (Djampour, 2018), to institutionalised suspicion, and to degrading treatment during asylum processes (Wernesjö, 2019). They have also been subjected to highly intrusive medical age assessments (Kazemi, 2021), which evoked associations to the Swedish history of racial biology, and their prospects of remaining in Sweden were constantly changed through a virtual flood of legal amendments, which amplified their uncertainty for the future (Elsrud, 2020). Recognition rates for Afghan citizens are low in Sweden, compared to other European countries, and many of the young people – who by the time they received their asylum decision had been re-classified as adults – ended up deportable, despite the volatile situation in Afghanistan (UNAMA, 2019).

Many of them refused to leave, and appealed to suspend their deportation orders. Some of them initiated demonstrations. Most famous became the sit-in protest organised in August 2017 by a group of young Afghans outside the parliament building in Stockholm, where they demanded an end to deportations to Afghanistan and the right to remain (see Khavari, 2018). During the two month-long protests, which acquired the name 'Young in

Sweden' (*Ung i Sverige*), thousands of people showed up to document, support, or join the strike, including a steady stream of journalists and politicians. *Ung i Sverige* mobilised support from civil society organisations, including grassroots movements such as *Vistårinteut* ('We cannot take it anymore') and *Stoppa utvisningarna till Afghanistan* ('Stop deportations to Afghanistan'). Like the demonstrations by people confined in the Danish deportation camps, the protests can be understood as a politics of presence; a refusal to be derecorded, a demand for participation in society, and an insistence on recognition of the violence that they had endured while in Sweden (see Khosravi, 2017b). The protesters and their support groups did not succeed in suspending deportations to Afghanistan, but they pressured politicians into proposing legislation that enabled some young people to regularise their status in Sweden temporarily. The 'high school law' (*gymnasielagen*), adopted by the parliament in June 2018, enabled unaccompanied minors who had arrived in Sweden prior to 24 November 2015 (when the 'temporary' law entered into force) to apply for a temporary residence permit that would enable them to finish upper secondary school (see Elsrud, 2020). It offered them a temporary respite but did not protect its holders from being deported to a country in conflict once it expired; indeed, the new law rejected the young asylum seekers' claims to be recognised as *refugees* in need of protection, and instead conditioned their safety upon performances of deservingness as part of a diligent, grateful, and hard-working future workforce (Wernesjö, 2019). Therefore, critics called it 'a prolonged deportation process rather than a real opportunity to remain in Sweden' (Khavari, 2018), which did not resolve their condition of being in limbo.

Some young people who refused to comply with their deportation orders to Afghanistan challenged the deportation regime in other, less visible ways. Some went underground, relying on the support of friends, family, communities, and social networks. At the Swedish Migration Agency, officials were well aware of their continued presence, and regretted how their 'futile hopes' to find another way to regularise their status interrupted authorities' efforts to archive their cases. Commenting on the case of non-deported Afghans, Susanna said,

> They are among our most challenging cases. They have been here for a long time, and they have been through a lot. They were minors when they first arrived and have now become adults. Many of them are suffering from mental ill-health, and there are so many actors involved: the school, their accommodation units, friends, civil society actors, all of whom give them contradictory advice. And the laws keep changing all the time, which gives them hope. It's difficult for us to inform them correctly. And if they don't have identity documents the police can't deport them. So, we just put them in a locker, together with Somalis and Iraqis.

Susanna argued that the young people's hopes to remain were based on false information; but many saw the constantly changing laws, and the multiple and sometimes contradictory advice they were offered by various actors, as opportunities that were, at least, true enough for them to act upon (Eule et al., 2019). Aside from those who decided to stay and wait for novel opportunities to arise from the messy legal landscape of Swedish asylum law, Susanna also directed her frustration at the thousands of non-deported people who 're-escaped' (Elsrud, 2020: 501) to other European countries in order to evade deportation from Sweden, which in theory should not be possible due to the Dublin Regulation. Indeed, since 2016, there have been reports of an increase in Dublin take-back requests from Southern European countries (see European Migration Network, 2016; Ibfelt and Skov-Jensen, 2019; Schibbye, 2019), which contradicted officials' assumptions that most people moved along a linear, northbound journey through Europe. Swedish migration officials were unsure of whether this trend could be attributed to the new, restrictive, and deterrence oriented migration policies in Sweden, or to civil society actors, who were giving non-deported people 'false hopes' by encouraging them to move on. Mariam exclaimed, 'Do they even know what Dublin is!? I don't get what they are thinking!'

Nevertheless, people kept leaving. In 2017, Swedish news media started reporting about the growing number of young Afghans who, after their asylum applications had been rejected in Sweden, had shown up in the Swedish church in Paris (Kyrkans tidning, 2017; see also Schibbye, 2019). The Swedish church, which is at once a religious and a cultural centre, became a meeting spot for young people, mostly men, who had escaped deportation in Sweden, and who had acted upon rumours of the French asylum system being more lenient towards Afghan refugees. As more people kept arriving, the Swedish church in Paris began to offer them food, a cup of coffee, a shower, and a place to wash their clothes, since they were otherwise sleeping rough in informal tent camps or under bridges across Paris while waiting for their asylum application to be registered with French authorities. The church hired a coordinator, Klara, who also helped them translate official documents from French, arranged access to legal advice, and initiated Swedish-French language classes. I visited the Swedish church in Paris in March 2018. Around this time, Klara had recorded some two hundred young people passing through the church; some showed up only once, while others returned regularly. New people kept arriving every day.

The church café is a large open room. At one end, two Swedish-speaking women are having coffee and cake while their children are playing. Next to them, young men are sitting around the wooden tables, some of them alone, others in groups, sipping tea or coffee. Others are charging their phones, crashing on the couch upstairs, using the internet, or doing laundry. Klara runs between the laundry room downstairs and the entrance upstairs, greeting and chatting to the young men, some of whom she knows well, others whom she seems to meet for the first time. Klara explains to me,

> It started with rumours … some guys arrived here and did not get Dublin even though they had been rejected in Sweden. They should not be able to do it because their fingerprints are in the database and they should be returned to Sweden. But sometimes their fingerprints are not there. I would say it is chance that determines whether they are detected or not. And if you are well informed, there's a chance you can influence the outcome yourself. I had to learn myself that the system doesn't function. That it's so unfair. One gets asylum here and the other gets sent back to Sweden. There is no justice.

I sit down with Abas and Rohullah. They are brothers and arrived in Sweden three years ago, Abas was a minor, Rohullah eighteen at the time. Abas explains that they both invested a lot in building a life in Sweden, learning the language, going to school, and preparing for a future there. But when their asylum applications were rejected, they did not dare to stay, and left for Paris where they heard there was an opportunity to get asylum despite Dublin. But now, they have a problem. Rohullah has been categorised as 'normal procedure' and awaits his first asylum interview, but Abas has been categorised as a Dublin case, and risks being deported back to Sweden. Rohullah smiles as he is telling me this story, shaking his head. But he is concerned, too, as they don't know what to do next. They are either sleeping on the streets under dire conditions or moving around between temporary shelters. Right now, they regret their decision and would like to go back to Sweden, even though thinking of Sweden makes them angry. Abas explains,

> I got three rejections. The first time, they didn't believe me. The second time they claimed I was older. According to their counting, I would have worked since I was one year old back in Afghanistan. It makes no sense. The third time, they told me that it was dangerous for everyone, but not for me. But if it is dangerous for everyone, I suppose it's also dangerous for me? No, not for you, they said. Then they said the EU had paid to return me to Afghanistan. They said so, the migration officials. I said what do I care who you paid what, I have my own problems. I don't care anymore. If you get asylum, it's only a matter of chance.

The brothers are torn. They don't want to leave and jeopardise Rohullah's new-found chance to get asylum in France. If they manage to wait for eighteen months in Paris, the deadline for Abas' Dublin transfer to Sweden will expire, and he might be able to file a fresh asylum request. But, Abas sighs, 'The waiting is the worst, it takes over everything. Your life pauses when you don't have papers.'

The story of Abas and Rohullah, and the estimated 4,000 other young Afghan citizens who have escaped deportation from Sweden (see Reguera and Mahmoud, 2020, though the number keeps increasing) demonstrates both the risks and opportunities arising from the uneven operation of the European deportation regime. Contrary to Mariam and other migration officials' disbelief in the Afghans' hopes for regularisation, their cases show how the legal condition of being rejected, illegalised, and non-deported is never fixed, and always negotiable (Wyss, 2021). The systemic *illegibility* of migration law renders access to rights and residency contingent upon authorities' unpredictable legal interpretations, upon luck, and upon non-deported people's own ability to identify and act strategically upon the offerings of the moment (Eule et al., 2019). While in theory, the Dublin Regulation and the harmonisation of asylum law across European states should prevent Rohullah and Abas from finding a second chance to get asylum, in practice, the system does indeed remain a lottery (Brekke and Brochmann, 2015; Schuster, 2011). For Afghans, asylum recognition rates vary between 6 per cent and 98 per cent between European states (ECRE, 2019), with France being among the more generous countries: in 2018, 67.5 per cent of Afghans obtained asylum in France, whereas recognition rates in Sweden were at 33 per cent.[6] Therefore, it might not appear as surprising that in 2018, the Swedish Migration Agency reportedly recorded that there were more Afghans who re-escaped to other European countries than deportations to Afghanistan (see Elsrud, 2020).

A second important insight from the brothers' story is the inherently transnational character of deportation regimes (Drotbohm and Hasselberg, 2015), which offer opportunities to escape, but also present risks to become trapped anew. An activist in the Danish deportation camps once noted that the Dublin Regulation effectively renders Europe an 'open prison' for non-deported people, either making them trapped within the confines of a state that does not want them or making them 'stuck in transit' (Brekke and Brochmann, 2015: 145), in a precarious condition of onward mobility (Wyss, 2019). These onward movements, and the protracted uncertainty, disruption of communities and relationships, and dire living conditions they produce, can be understood as part of the politics of exhaustion that Hasse presented in the beginning of this chapter (see Ansems de Vries and Guild, 2018). However, they also show how the deportation limbo is a site of negotiation, and is generative of new practices of control, evasion, and appropriation. If 'luck' and 'chance' remain precarious exceptions in a migration control regime set up for people to fail their migratory projects, they are also what make people endure, move on, and re-appear, contesting the efforts of states to make them disappear.

Concluding remarks

The politics of minimum welfare, of exhaustion, and of derecording enable Swedish state authorities to govern non-deported people using minimum force. Through the logic of voluntariness and responsibilisation, non-deported people are made responsible for their vulnerable condition; it is up to them, the narrative goes, to inform themselves of their condition, and to make the 'right' decisions and comply with the attempts of the state to deport them. Officially, these measures all fall under the category of what constitutes 'voluntary' return measures, which is Swedish authorities' preferred way of enforcing deportations. Such discourses of benevolence and free choice function to conceal the structural violence of making people destitute, and the symbolic and legal violence of compelling non-deported people to act under the false pretence of freedom. The violence therefore goes unrecognised, for 'violence that occurs gradually and out of sight [...] is typically not viewed as violence at all' (Davies and Isakjee, 2019: 214). It simultaneously makes non-deported migrants disappear, from bureaucratic registries, and sometimes, from the country. At the same time, it enables state violence to disappear, making it difficult to trace, other than through its effects.

The hiding away of these indirect forms of state violence is made possible by the devaluation of non-deported people's lives. The harms caused by this violence are unevenly distributed among different groups. Without comparing the direness of their conditions, a young man in good health might have higher chances to survive without formal access to welfare than a woman of older age who is dying of cancer. A family with young children might find it more difficult to make the decision to move on within Europe, considering the risk to end up destitute and without alternative support networks (although some do, as this option is preferable to deportation). Access to formal or informal support is also determined through gendered and racialised notions of deservingness; in Sweden, there were specialised (and state-funded) NGOs working to support primarily young Afghans who had been through the asylum process, whereas there was significantly less support available to people like Samir, the detained North African man who appeared in Chapter 3.

To some extent, the purported failure to protect those in most dire need contradicted state officials' imaginary of a humane and egalitarian welfare state. The 'displacements' (Jansson-Keshavarz et al., 2021) in the support mandate for social workers, in particular, caused many to question the conditions of their job, some to protest, and some, like Maria, to resign. While the welfare state as such is a bordering device, and while limited access to welfare is a common strategy of deterrence among European states, I concur with Davies et al. (2017; see also Khosravi, 2010) that the institutionalised and organised nature of abandonment in wealthy, bureaucratised welfare states makes acutely visible the political prioritisation of some lives over others. Moreover, the radical forms of exclusion it generates need to be seen in the context of a civil society unprepared to fill the 'gaps' in welfare provisions. The examples I have provided from Denmark and Sweden indicate the importance of abandoning simplistic understandings of welfare states and bureaucracies as egalitarian institutions and neutral distributors of 'universal' rights.

Finally, the effects of the deterrence strategies of the Nordic welfare states extend beyond their borders. The significant number of people who have left both Denmark and Sweden after a final rejection on their asylum application testify to how responsibility for providing protection, for processing applications, and for enforcing deportations are pushed onto countries in Southern Europe. Their trajectories illustrate the transnational expansion of the deportation limbo, and how it generates a proliferation of sites of enforcement, and of contestation (Sanchez Boe, forthcoming; Schmid-Scott, 2018). They also demonstrate the inadequacy of limiting an analysis of deportation policies within the confines of a single state apparatus or legal framework. We need, therefore, to consider how deportation regimes expand: inwards, outwards, and onwards.

Notes

1 For some nationalities, the Swedish Migration Agency offers financial support for 'reestablishment' and 'reintegration' (via the European Reintegration Network (ERIN)), as return is expected to be 'difficult due to severe conflicts' (Migrationsverket, n.d.). These countries include Afghanistan, Iraq, and Nigeria, among others. The assistance amounts to SEK 30,000 for adults, SEK 15,000 for children, or a maximum of SEK 75,000 per family and is conditioned upon 'cooperation' with authorities. The cash payment is only transferred after return, and several caseworkers were aware that cash payments were only handed out on an uneven basis, which undermined the credibility of the measure among prospective recipients.
2 In 2020, another amendment was introduced, which withdraws daily allowance for people who during the asylum process settle in certain 'socioeconomically challenged areas' (*utsatta områden*) which have a high share of residents with migrant background. The amendment, which constitutes a form of indirect spatial and social regulation of asylum-seeking persons, was formally supposed to prevent 'negative social consequences' of their choice of housing.
3 Article 3 of the Universal Declaration of Human Rights, the UN Refugee Convention, and the European Asylum Directives establish the obligation of states to admit asylum seekers and grant them provisions so as to avoid

destitution. Article 11(1) of the International Covenant on Economic, Social and Cultural Rights establishes the right of everyone, regardless of nationality or legal residence status, to enjoy an adequate standard of living and access to 'adequate food, clothing and housing, and to the continuous improvement of living conditions'. Article 12 stipulates states' obligation to recognise everyone's right to enjoy 'highest attainable standard of physical and mental health'. Article 34 of the EU's fundamental rights charter obliges states to ensure social assistance and social security for all persons present on their territory. However, the conventions leave wide discretion to states.

4 The LMA amendment – much like the Danish deportation camps – has not had any recorded effects on deportation rates. The Swedish border police has reported that the change has made more people abscond, and therefore impeded on their possibilities to enforce deportations (Polisen, 2019), and the Swedish Migration Agency has come to a similar conclusion (see Sellin, 2018).

5 In 2016, the Swedish police demanded the social services in Malmö to share the contact information in a number of cases of non-deported persons. This resulted in the detection and subsequent deportation of four families. A political discussion ensued regarding the responsibility of social services to protect the identity of welfare recipients on the one hand, and to facilitate the work of migration enforcement agencies on the other. Legal experts filed a complaint of the social services' decision to the Parliamentary Ombudsman, who eventually supported the social services' decision to prioritise law enforcement in cases where the recipient has been issued a deportation order (Justitieombudsmannen DNR 565–2017; for a comprehensive overview and analysis of the appeal see Lundberg et al., 2017).

6 French administrative courts have in several cases cancelled transfers to another Dublin signatory state (including Sweden, Finland, Norway, and Germany) in cases where the applicant in question risked *chain refoulement* to Afghanistan, which French courts deemed would violate Article 3 of the ECHR (cf. decision 1705209 of the Administrative Tribunal in Lyon (28 July 2017) and decisions 17LY02181–17LY02184 of the Administrative Court of Appeal of Lyon; cf. European Database on Asylum Law; ECRE 2019). Yet French courts have also upheld Dublin transfers in similar cases.

Conclusion: state violence and its effects

Sometimes, we get into really deep discussions when we are having the return dialogues, too. About global injustices, about how border and migration regimes are maintaining those injustices. How they serve geopolitical interests and enable economic exploitation ... but it becomes too big to grasp. It's up to you who are studying these issues to address the larger questions. Those of us who are working operationally are just like ants in a huge anthill ... we know that what we are doing is absurd, but we do it anyway. And we get our salary for it. That's how it is. Not everything can be meaningful. I don't think everything can be meaningful.
(Palle, return caseworker, Swedish Migration Agency, 2017)

Many state officials keep being passive and continue to claim we are in a much lesser evil than we could have been. We hear this same thing from different governments in the North, we hear about colonialism, it's always the same argumentation. It's not just about the government. It's about the people, too. Niels once pointed out that if anything needs to change in Sjælsmark, for rejected asylum seekers and migrants in general, it needs to come from the people. And as long as Danish people are indoctrinated and keep benefiting from perpetrating violence against us, nothing will change.
(Conversation with Steve, 2021)

This book has traced the continuum of state violence mobilised in the deportation limbo in Denmark and Sweden. Following a political ethnographic approach, it has centred on the perspectives of frontline workers tasked with implementing the policies designed to pressure non-deported people to leave, and how their efforts often perpetuate the same condition of limbo that they were meant to address, while exposing their target population to social, physical, and mental harm and premature death. The book has thus explored the adverse realities behind government fantasies assuming that deportations are normal, adequate, and politically necessary, and that they can be undertaken in an effective and humane manner (Coutin, 2015). Such fantasies of humane and effective enforcement, I have argued, are particularly prevalent in Nordic welfare states, where there is a widespread belief in

Conclusion 141

the good, benevolent state. The deportation limbo challenges such perceptions and renders visible the violent exclusion that is integral to the (welfare) state project. The deportation limbo and the state violence it mobilises is not an aberration to an otherwise functioning system; it is endemic to a border regime that is designed to prevent racialised travellers from accessing mobility, rights, and resources.

However, as Palle articulates in the quotation above, these 'bigger questions' of what the purpose of deportations is, what interests they serve, and whether they can be humane, fair, or defensible, are rarely asked within the system. Like ants in an anthill, officials feel compelled to carry on with their jobs regardless. The second quotation is from a conversation with Steve, where he comments on state officials' routine attempts to downplay the violent nature of deportation regimes and their own role in sustaining them. He challenges the ahistorical and unfounded claim that at least things are not so bad in Northern Europe as they are elsewhere. He points out how the people living in these countries are invested and complicit in this violence, too. In this concluding chapter, I will depart from the reflections by Palle and Steve and connect them to the main arguments made in this book. I will consider three different *directions* in which deportation regimes – and the state violence they mobilise – expand, and discuss what is the potential and role of research in tracing and challenging them. Rather than offering conclusive remarks, I will throughout the chapter let colleagues and friends, with whom readers are by now familiar, speak with me through the pages in search for alternative future directions.

Limbo and the global expansion of deportation regimes

This book has demonstrated that deportations are what we can call productive policy failures, which sustain a system of global apartheid through regimes of discriminatory, violent regulation of the mobility of racialised people across scattered but interconnected locations (Besteman, 2020). As technologies of citizenship (Walters, 2002), deportations delineate the boundaries of membership and define hierarchies of human worth, structured along the lines of race, class, gender, sexuality, religion, ability, and more (Anderson et al., 2011). Politically, they provide governments with useful folk devils (Cohen, 2002), the securitisation and criminalisation of whom justify the expansion of coercive state powers, as well as new forms of spatial, technological, and social regulation. This way, deportation regimes also generate novel opportunities for investments and profits for private security companies as well as humanitarian and research industries (Andersson, 2016; Besteman, 2020; Golash-Boza, 2015). I have suggested that the *deportation limbo* is a systemic product of the intensified efforts of states to enforce deportations, on the one hand, and of the contestations and struggles waged by non-deported people, on the other. In this book, I have used 'limbo' to refer to the condition of liminal legality characterising the situation of non-deported people, which renders them vulnerable to state-sanctioned violence, including detention, forced deportation, and radical forms of exclusion. I have shown how state authorities use an ever-expanding repertoire of spatial, social, and temporal governing techniques to control non-deported people, including incarceration and encampment, but also evictions, and formal abandonment.

The expansion of deportation regimes shows no sign of decline: on the contrary, deportation measures evolve and travel both within and between states. In Denmark, the government continues its spectacularised hunt for the most remote location that can be found within its limited geography to establish yet another deportation camp for criminalised foreign nationals, while simultaneously trying to find a partner country outside Europe that is willing to host its externalised asylum processing camp. Their fantasy of externalising asylum processing takes inspiration from Australia's colonial offshore detention model, which is practised in Nauru and Manus Island. Similar fantasies are reflected in the expanding archipelago of detention-like reception facilities and hotspots across Europe's southern borderlands, which serve both deterrence and containment purposes (Mountz et al., 2013; Tazzioli and Garelli, 2018). Meanwhile, in Sweden, the government plans for new deportation prisons to be built for non-deported migrants and explores models for increased monitoring and regulation of people seeking asylum (SOU 2018:22). The Swedish Conservative Party has suggested that all non-deported people should be forced to carry electronic ankle bracelets, which would imply a drastic expansion of state surveillance, similar to what has been tried and practised elsewhere in the United States (see Sanchez Boe, forthcoming). If deportation measures travel between states, we are also witnessing intensified police collaborations on the EU level, facilitated through integrated biometric identity systems, which are meant to enhance identification and control of travellers' identity and to facilitate deportations (Statewatch, 2022). As part of their efforts to create a 'deportation union' (Statewatch, 2022: 1), the EU and individual member states are also working to establish more bilateral and multilateral readmission agreements and to strengthen their cooperation with countries of deportation. These processes partly operate through informal exchanges (Cassarino, 2020), discussions in expert networks (Bigo, 2006), and diplomatic negotiations (Collyer, 2016). The informalisation and externalisation of deportation regimes warrant sustained critical scrutiny. For this purpose, political ethnography continues to be useful for tracing these dynamics along the global corridors of expulsion.

These measures all contribute to making non-deported people's lives more precarious and hazardous, and to prolonging their journeys and the time spent in stuckedness in camps, detention centres, and other liminal border zones. Yet, if deportation regimes keep expanding globally, connecting state and security apparatuses, they are also forging new connections between deportable and deported people. These people also actively partake in shaping deportation regimes through their tactics of navigation, evasion, and confrontation with state authorities and other actors who seek to limit and steer their mobility. While their perspectives have not been the focus of this book, the non-deported people waiting in limbo in the Danish deportation camps, or the young people who moved on to Paris, continuously forge new relationships and bonds of sociality and solidarity with their communities in the countries they risk being deported from, and in the countries where they are deported to. They partake in forming the global deportspora (Khosravi, 2017a) consisting of travellers who get caught in cycles of containment and forced onward mobility, and who at the same time continue to undo the nationalist order that states so desperately try to perform and sustain.

From deportation regimes to ordinary expulsions

Tracing deportation processes thus necessitates research to go beyond the nation state as a 'container' of analysis (Wimmer and Glick Schiller, 2002). If deportation regimes expand through global connections, a second direction in which they move is 'inwards', as they encompass more groups of people who hold different legal status. This research has focused on states' efforts to deport foreign nationals lacking legal authorisation to remain, but deportation regimes also impact other populations. Among those immediately affected are foreign nationals whose legal status is made precarious because of ever-more restrictive migration politics, including temporary labour migrants, and people holding refugee status and their families. While they may hold (temporary) legal status, they are also impacted by the intensified policing, rights differentiation, and heightened risk of losing their right to remain, which are the result of states' intensified focus on deportations, even though they are formally not threatened by deportation – or *not yet*. Chapter 1 discussed how the normalisation of temporary and more precarious protection status and a renewed deportation turn in both Sweden and Denmark resulted in more people becoming exposed to the threat of deportation. In Denmark, refugees from Syria, Afghanistan, Palestine, Somalia, and other countries ridden by protracted conflict are having their protection statuses reassessed, and for some – notably women, young people, and those of older age – their protection status is withdrawn. Those among them who receive deportation orders but who fear returning to the countries that they or their parents fled from risk ending up in limbo. Meanwhile, in Denmark and Sweden, permanent leave to remain has increasingly been made contingent upon labour market performance, with the result that people seeking protection are accepted only as cheap if not free exploitable labour (see Rytter and Ghandchi, 2019). Similarly, many of the young Afghans in Sweden whose situation was described in Chapter 5 had little prospects of obtaining asylum, and those who did would only receive temporary protection. Rendering themselves available as exploitable labour remained for some their only option to ensure their economic and physical survival (Khosravi, 2019). These cases demonstrate what some scholars have warned is a hollowing out of the principle of asylum (Schultz, 2020) through the conflation of vulnerability and performance-based 'deservingness' criteria, where protection is rendered contingent on labour market performance, turning refugees into 'humanitarian exploits' (Ramsay, 2019: 11). Their exploitation is enabled through the unevenly distributed susceptibility to deportation; in this way, the 'internal' expansion of deportation regimes reinforces racial, gendered, and classed hierarchies in the labour market and in access to a liveable life among people holding precarious legal status. It does also, to some extent, affect racialised citizens as well.

The political focus on deportation of racialised non-citizens has impacted long-term residents and citizens who, despite having stable legal status, are continuously racialised as belonging to elsewhere, regardless of whether they are born in the country, have ancestors from the country, and so on. The expansion of internal bordering practices, such as intensified policing in certain areas and of certain people, and the introduction of new technologies for conducting identity checks, increases the risk for racialised and minoritised citizens and non-citizens to be made into targets (De Noronha, 2019; Parmar, 2019; Statewatch, 2022). As a technology of citizenship, deportation enforcement becomes a way of identifying and targeting those who, according to prevailing racial matrices, are imagined to be 'others' out of place (Tudor, 2017). Denaturalisation laws are perhaps the starkest example of how, for certain racialised citizens, citizenship remains a conditional status. In Denmark, such a procedure is already in place for cases where a person has been convicted of a terrorist offence, yet a new legal initiative is underway that will allow for the revocation of citizenship and deportation of people convicted of having partaken in organised crime (see Danish Ministry of Immigration and Integration, 2021). The condition of deportability (De Genova 2002) thus extends across the migrant-citizen divide and reconfigures the conditions for citizenship. The above examples also underscore the importance of the reorientation in (a predominantly Eurocentric) border and migration studies that has highlighted the inadequacy of taking for granted statist categorisations of 'migrants' and 'citizens', respectively (Anderson, 2011). Indeed, deportation regimes do not only or primarily delineate the legal boundaries of citizenship, but enforce the racial order reflected and produced through border and citizenship regimes. Here, research on border and migration control regimes needs to enter – and indeed, catch up with – ongoing conversations within scholarship on race, policing, incarceration, and criminal (in)justice addressing not only how mobility freedoms are curtailed but importantly, how they can be abolished (Davis and Dent, 2001; Davis et al., 2021; Gilmore, 2020; Loyd, Mitchelson, and Burridge, 2012; Sharma, 2021).

There is a movement among border scholars who strive to overcome this methodologically nationalist bias and 'de-exceptionalise' transnational displacement, instead considering how expulsions have been and are still used to forge categories of citizens and 'others' – be they indigenous, historically marginalised groups, racialised citizens, criminalised people, or mobile poor (Anderson, 2019; Drotbohm and Lems, 2018; Ramsay, 2019). Such a research agenda entails tracing genealogies and contemporary continuities in the discourses, policy measures, and forms of regulation that produce illegalisation, imprisonment, segregation, and 'ghettoisation'. It enables at once a more comphrehensive and nuanced understanding of the different manifestations of state racism which, while part of the same global system of oppression, target 'dissimilar populations differently' (Leets Hansen and Suárez-Krabbe, 2019: 3; see also Eika et al., 2019), without reifying the methodological statism that (re)produces the state's classifications. Importantly, it also enables us to connect struggles against forced and restricted mobility waged by different oppressed groups who are disproportionately exposed to eviction, incarceration, criminalisation, and deportation (Davis and Dent, 2001; Loyd et al., 2012) and for a radical freedom to move, live, and remain.

Deportation and the challenge of 'liberal' violence

> First we must study how colonization works to decivilize the colonizer, to brutalize him in the true sense of the word, to degrade him, to awaken him to buried instincts, to covetousness, violence, race hatred, and moral relativism [...] at the end of all the racial pride that has been encouraged, all the boastfulness that has been displayed, a poison has been instilled into the veins of Europe and, slowly but surely, the continent proceeds toward savagery.
>
> *(Césaire, 1972 [1955]: 13)*

This book has been concerned with how 'the state' manifests through various forms of violence, which are justified as normal and necessary elements of sustaining the borders of a 'liberal' order rooted in modernity/

coloniality. The varieties of violence detailed have almost exclusively been state-sanctioned, legally codified, and within the confines of human rights obligations; with few exceptions, the violence of deportations remains within the 'threshold' of public acceptability (Walters, 2019: 176). Most state officials I interviewed and observed interacting with non-deported people agreed on the location of this threshold and showed commitment to 'the state' as an inherently 'good' and benevolent structure, which they saw as necessary to sustain social order (see also Keskinen et al., 2019). With few exceptions, officials performed their jobs within their legally codified professional mandates: few went beyond their mandate to make matters worse for non-deported people, and few did so to support them. Like the 'ants in a huge anthill', as Palle put it, they went about their everyday work, witnessing the injurious and at times absurd effects of the policies they were enforcing. Some considered their work to be of humanitarian nature, while others would articulate criticism against the policies they were enforcing; yet others admitted that their profession had left them numb, dehumanised, desensitised to the suffering of others. Hence, as Julia pointed out in our conversation, frontline officials were simultaneously aware and not aware, complicit in and critical of the state violence they were enacting; and none of them questioned its fundamental premise: that the harms inflicted upon non-deported people were justified, even necessary, in the interest of controlling immigration.

One way of making sense of this is to emphasise the officials' 'commitment to blindness' (Gordon, 2008: 207) to the effects of their job, on non-deported people and on themselves. Blindness and denial have been pointed out as central to the continued operation and public acceptability of the 'extraordinary' violence of expulsion, incarceration, indefinite confinement, and destitution (Davies and Isakjee, 2019; Mountz, 2020). Only by denying the violent nature of such practices, the argument goes, or by redressing them as humanitarian interventions, can they continue to operate. Therefore, concealment has been pointed out as an important strategy used in particular in liberal, democratic states to cultivate public ignorance of state violence and its injurious effects (Mountz, 2020; Walters, 2019). However, the broad acceptance of these harms amongst frontline officials and among the broader public cannot be explained by blindness alone. Instead, to understand its operation, we must consider the fundamental role of such violence in the formation of the political identities of 'liberal' welfare states, and their bureaucracies and populations. As Steve mentions in his reflection above, 'as long as Danish people are indoctrinated and keep benefiting from perpetrating violence against us, nothing will change'.

The sharp observation by Aimé Césaire of the brutalising effects that colonisation had, not only on the colonised but also on the coloniser, captures this constitutive role of dehumanisation and violence in the political identities forged through colonialism. So does the comprehensive body of postcolonial scholarship that has demonstrated the violence that underpins liberal European political theory, politics, and society, and which offers important insights to border scholarship about the dehumanisation that borders presuppose and reproduce (Anzaldúa, 1987; see also Grosfoguel et al., 2015; Suárez-Krabbe, 2022). Indeed, for this reason, states, communities, and individuals may not only tacitly tolerate but actively desire 'the violent arrangements supporting their communities' (Kotef, 2020: 30). This active commitment to violence is different from a mere denial or consideration of violence as 'a necessary evil' to sustain the present order. It suggests that violence has become internalised and incorporated into the identity not only of those subjected to it but also of those perpetrating it. To insist that deportation regimes generate and sustain political identities that are premised on a racial order, a hierarchical differentiation in human value that normalises the systematic injuries inflicted on deportable 'surplus' populations, is not to say that state violence is always conscious and desirable by everyone who profits from it, nor that it is inevitable. But it enables us to consider how investments in political and social hierarchies generate not only tacit tolerance but an actual affective and political attachment to the structures that harm; a point made by scholars working on settler colonial societies (Kotef, 2020: 31). It may help explain why, as Julia suggested, most frontline officials had come to accept the current system as inevitable and necessary, despite its obvious, injurious effects; since these injuries seemed to affirm their own subject position, their humanity in face of those who were deprived of theirs. It might partly explain the insistence on and ongoing investments in 'humanising' reforms of border enforcement since a fundamental rethinking of borders would require rethinking – and re-humanising – those oppressed by borders as well as those who structurally benefit from them. As Steve said in one of our conversations, 'they invested so much in building these structures, that they cannot afford to sacrifice them'. Finally, it might suggest that exposing violence is not enough to undo it. However, that is not to say that political identities premised upon violence cannot change; as Julia suggested, it just means we need to look for the fissures.

The deportation research industry and the need for different knowledge

What, then, do we learn from documenting state at the border? What are the potential political uses and misuses of this knowledge? And role can research have in enhancing transformative change of violent border regimes?

As Tuck and Yang (2014) write in their essay on refusals, not everything should be known or researched, nor is research necessarily the intervention that is 'needed' to address social and political problems (see also Simpson, 2008). The research industry devoted to documenting border violence and the suffering it generates runs the risk of reifying those same structures of violence (see Cabot, 2016; Robbins, 2013), and of revealing and exploiting stories that are better left untold (Khosravi, 2020). Hence, we need to consider the conditions under which research should be conducted on, in this case, repressive border or deportation regimes (Coutin, 2015) and for whom this research is imagined to be beneficial. This entails asking who is invited to speak on border violence, in what language can critique be articulated, and who do we expect to listen.

In a conversation we had about the conditions and challenges of 'critical' border and deportation studies, Shahram Khosravi said, 'a recurrent question you get when you talk about borders is, "what is the alternative?" The second question is, "what solution do you suggest as social scientists"? These questions are misleading, because they presume that the problem is located outside the system [...] when in fact, it is the nation state system that is the problem.' The fact that the border regime and the system of nation states that it is supposed to sustain has problems is something that most governments and frontline workers would agree on, and something that border researchers, alongside NGOs, are earning our income from documenting, analysing, and sometimes offering 'solutions' to. However, as Shahram notes, there is a fundamental difference between the approaches that consider these problems to be external to and caused by 'flaws' within the current system, and the perspectives that see the system as inherently and structurally flawed. The first approach prevails in political and public discourse, but does not have room for what Palle, the return caseworker at the Swedish Migration Agency, referred to as 'the bigger questions'. Hence, and as Shahram noted in our conversation, these discourses place limits on the language in which critique can be articulated if it wants to be heard. Shahram shared an anecdote from when he had been invited to give a talk on waiting to staff at the Swedish Migration Agency. After he finished his talk, a participant came up to him and noted, ironically, 'thank you for telling us about all these things we knew nothing about'. Shahram reflected,

> Maybe they only partly heard what I said, and therefore, they only heard the repetition of what they knew already. It is the classic question posed by Spivak, can the subaltern speak? But the other part of the problem is who can *listen*. Not everyone has the capacity to listen when they hear someone speak. We can place more responsibility on the receiver, and instead of asking if the poor can speak, ask whether the rich can listen. We generate so much knowledge, but who can understand it? That is a different question. As for the

other question we get, 'what is the alternative'? This is also a way in which the nation state defends itself by questioning that there exist other alternatives. It asks, how could you abolish borders, when there are no alternatives? It is not because I have the answer, but the question is also misleading, and threatening, suggesting that the alternative is an absence of law, an absence of order. But it's all about which subject position you are coming from. When somebody asks what the alternative is, it comes from the subject position of someone who has something to lose. Those who are crossing the Mediterranean by boat, those who are confined in camps on Lesvos ... for them, there is no alternative. They represent what the nation-state system is afraid of. The lack of order, the chaos; but for them, this system has already brought chaos.

The system defends itself by denying the existence of alternatives. The 'solutions' offered to the chaotic and lethal operation of border and deportation regimes are spoken in the language of reform, regulation, and reinforcement of existing measures. Changes are indeed urgently needed to save lives and minimise the harms inflicted on people who are exposed to border violence, but, as border abolitionists have argued, reformist efforts to 'humanise' and regulate violent borders have not only shown to be ineffective but risk lending normative coverage to the continued operation of an essentially flawed border regime (Anderson, Sharma, and Wright, 2009; Cowan, 2021; Gilmore, 2020; Walia, 2021).

What knowledge and what language is needed to envision alternatives to the border regime? There are ongoing efforts, inside but even more so beyond the confines of academia, to undertake such projects. Speaking to an academic audience, Tuck and Yang (2014: 231) have called for a shift away from the 'pain and damage-centred research' towards 'desire-based research', which centres the knowledge derived from struggles within and against the harmful structures of power, and explores the alternative ways of being and knowing that emerge from them. Boochani and Tofighian (in Paik, 2021) suggest that another language is needed to articulate alternative imaginaries for understanding and challenging the global border regime. They write,

> There's a difference between changing the material conditions [of a social or political problem] and [changing its] intellectual framework. On the one hand, there's trying to change the policies, the power structures, the economic side – all the investment that's involved when it comes to the detention industry. And then, on the other hand, there's trying to change the epistemic, the cultural, the intellectual, the symbolic, the social or colonial imaginary. And if the two aren't addressed hand in hand, then there are huge gaps in the activism. If activism only focuses on one of those dimensions, then we don't see the outcomes that we would like.

Boochani and Tofighian insist that knowledge on how border violence operates is needed to understand and unpack the political fantasies identities that are premised on and sustain this violence, and the hierarchies of human value, which prevent us from, as Julia put it, being in the world together. However, we simultaneously need to speak about, write about, and practise alternative social imaginaries to this chaotic, damaging, global system of states, borders, and deportations.

Epilogue: Abolfazl's death and other afterlives

I opened this book with the assertion that the Danish deportation regime was responsible for the death of Abolfazl Salehian, known in Sjælsmark as 'the Gardener'. The state-sanctioned violence he was subjected to was to a large extent invisible: it was slow, and indirect, structural, and, as prison officers suggested, 'ghostly'. Yet, it was explicitly intended to remove his possibilities to live a tolerable life. I have been uncertain about using Abolfazl's name and story to illustrate the injurious and, indeed, haunting effects of the violence he was subjected to. I only knew him from his time in the camp, and his death prevents me from asking for his consent to have his story shared. I spoke to Steve about the ethics of this mode of representing him. Steve said,

> The guards liked to talk about Abolfazl as a model of a 'good' resident. Someone who doesn't speak up, who follows the rules, and if anything, internalises the intolerable system. What the guards expect from the residents is that they pretend to be happy, that they water the plants, don't disturb the peace, so they can pretend they are not there. Don't cause us problem, they say – so when you die it's not our problem, either. But Abolfazl was also the one who then couldn't stand the system anymore. He died forgotten. Nobody said anything. This is also in line with the system, you know; if everyone could just die like Abolfazl. When we use him as an example we are not trying to portray him or give him a certain status. He is a human who was subjected to the system. His life is a different story. But his death also deserves recognition, to be kept alive. For so many people ... the faces of people who are never seen, the people, families, who die invisible, without anybody ever mentioning it.

I decided to use Abolfazl's name as a way of commemorating him. Those invested in defending the border regime may argue that there is no way of establishing the connection between Abolfazl's death and the slow violence of the deportation camps, since his physical death occurred outside the camp, after he had regained a possibility to live. However, and as Steve also emphasised when he shared his own struggles to rid himself from the haunting memories of Sjælsmark, such claims to disconnection – in time, in space, and in terms of responsibility – are part of how state violence renders itself invisible (see also Mountz, 2020). Boochani has argued, 'when someone killed themselves, the government or the system would say "he killed himself". So, he committed suicide. But in fact, I think it's not that. In fact, it's the system that has killed this person, you know. The system. We should talk about this ... as it happens they are no longer in detention' (quoted in Bhatia and Bruce-Jones, 2021: 83). Deportation regimes travel into the future, through the absences they create, and the haunting feelings they leave behind. We should talk about the often-discounted afterlives of state violence, and how it impacts those who enforced it, those who survived, and those who died from it. And we should, to return to the question that Julia posed in our conversation, talk about alternative identities, imaginaries, and ways of being in the world that do not require the premature death of people like Abolfazl to be sustained.

Appendix: on methods

Rather than being the outcome of a consistent research plan, the research project underpinning this book evolved with the rapidly shifting developments in migration policy that we have seen in Denmark and Sweden in the past decade. As discussed in the introductory chapter, the research was conditioned by access to securitised and locked institutions and took place at a time of intensified politicisation of matters of borders, migration, and deportation. The conditions of access therefore lent insights into the politics and power relations of the migration control field, and of the institutions I studied. While politically and ethically fraught, formal access negotiations can tell us a great deal about 'the field' and our position in relation to it (Kalir et al., 2019). Therefore, our research trajectories are in themselves important empirical material, and in the best case, sharing my own failures and dilemmas can help others with theirs, or at least, make them feel less alone. In this Appendix, I therefore offer a more detailed account of the research process, my access negotiations to the key sites of research, and the ethical dilemmas that came with the choice of these sites. I also enumerate the additional actors who were interviewed for the research project.

In order to gain access to detention and deportation camps, police, and migration offices, I sent out numerous formal requests to the central directorates or to individual units of different state authorities, including the Danish Prison and Probation Service, the Danish Police, the Immigration Service, the Red Cross, and the Danish Return Agency; and for Sweden, various branches of the Swedish Migration Agency, the Prison and Probation Service, social services, and the police. I also approached individual frontline workers and asked those who agreed to be interviewed to recommend other research participants. Many of my formal requests remained unanswered; others were quickly discarded, with reference to either time constraints, practical obstacles, or safety and security issues (see Lindberg and Borrelli, 2019). Some requests were initially met with enthusiasm, usually from individual frontline workers, only to be declined by their superiors or by central coordination offices. However, the numerous organisations involved in deportation enforcement enabled me to try several different entry points. The eventual success I had in securing access cannot be attributed to my negotiation skills, or to a consistent plan. Instead, it is the result of a mix of timing and luck (see Kalir, Achermann, and Rosset, 2019), white privilege (see Introduction), the harmlessness I was ascribed as a young woman, and my middle-class background, which meant that I shared a language in particular with the mid-level managers in state institutions, who were often the ones calling the final decisions.

The first answer that came back positive was from the Danish Prison and Probation Service operating Ellebæk deportation prison and the deportation camps. The directorate forwarded my request to Sjælsmark deportation camp, and Niels, the director, took interest in my focus on prison officers' role in the camp, and agreed to meet me. Migration control was a neglected part of the Prison Service, which had rarely been evaluated, and Niels told me that an external observer could be useful, as I might be able to learn something about how staff were dealing with their unclear mandate in the deportation field. I was granted access to conduct participant observation and interviews with staff in Sjælsmark deportation camp for a time period up to two months, and subsequently, after an additional round of negotiations with the directorate and the local director of the Prison and Probation Service, I was granted access to Ellebæk. In Sweden, I sent out requests for interviews to all the by-then five Swedish deportation prisons and visited four of them. In one of them, I was granted access to conduct fieldwork. The reason, I believe, was the interest that the director, herself a former prison officer, took in my prior research on the Danish camps. The other interviews were negotiated individually with frontline workers who agreed to participate in the research and/or by their managers.

Most of the research took place between 2016 and 2018, with additional follow-up interviews in 2020–2021. In Denmark, I conducted one month of fieldwork in Ellebæk detention camp, and two months' part-time fieldwork in Sjælsmark deportation camp. I also visited Kærshovedgård and Avnstrup on several different occasions. The fieldwork in Sweden encompassed one full month of ethnographic observation in a Swedish detention camp and visits to three additional detention camps, visits to four departure housing units run by the Swedish Migration Agency, and interviews in a further three return units. In addition to ethnographic observations, I conducted interviews with other state agencies involved in the deportation process. In Sweden, these included interviews with two migration officials working for the central organisation of the Swedish Migration Agency, seven border police officers, three social workers, two legal advisors, and eight representatives of NGOs working to support non-deported people. In Denmark, I interviewed three officials at the Danish Immigration Service, five officers at the Foreign Police, and seven legal advisors and human rights advocates, and conducted two interviews with representatives from NGOs supporting non-deported people. All interview and observation studies were conducted in Swedish and Danish, respectively, and were subsequently translated into English.

The intensity of fieldwork and the methods used have varied between field sites, partly due to access restrictions, and partly due to the nature of each field site. My observations have been triangulated with information retrieved through interviews, document analyses, and secondary sources, including policy and legal documents, and NGO and media reports. The empirical material informing this work thus encompasses fieldnotes from participant observations, interview transcriptions, and supporting artefacts and documents, including images, legal texts, news reports, and policy documents. The process of data analysis, interpretation, and theorising has been iterative, and as previously stressed in this book, always collaborative. It has emerged through a constant moving back and forth between fieldwork; conversations with colleagues, some of whom have read and commented on my work; and conversations with people living the deportation limbo.

A peculiar part of the research entailed disseminating the findings to state authorities. The Danish Prison and Probation Service evidently saw a possibility that my research could be instrumental for them, and I was asked to write summary reports to them upon the completion of my fieldwork. As discussed in the concluding chapter, on such occasions, researchers may be summoned as 'experts' to give advice on reforms, whereby we risk lending normative coverage to border practices. Our research might also be used in unanticipated ways (see Bosworth and Kellezi, 2016; Mutsaers, 2015). My reports to the Danish Prison and Probation Service focused on officers' reflections on their working conditions. I tried to formulate my critique of the institution, and the violence I had observed there, as something structural and endemic, rather than a matter of individual staff attitudes (and I am quite certain I did not succeed). I was invited to share my research findings from Ellebæk and Sjælsmark with the Danish Prison and Probation Service, and the presentations were received with moderate enthusiasm. While officers seemed to appreciate the acknowledgement from an external actor that they worked under harmful conditions, a critique of their practices and of institutional deficiencies presented without solutions was deemed useless. I learnt that to be considered relevant or to achieve 'policy impact', academic critique needs to be formulated in the language of reform and repair. I am quite certain that my reports ended up collecting dust on some shelf in the director's office.

Next to my research on the perspectives of state officials and non-state actors involved in governing the deportation limbo, I have worked with and learnt from non-deported people who are also struggling to criticise and challenge the deportation system, and to provide alternative support structures for those who are exposed to it. The material in this book draws on previous and ongoing engagements with these movements, which in the Danish context have included collaborative research and writing projects (see Freedom of Movements Research Collective, 2018; Stokholm et al., 2021). In the Swedish context, I have worked together with the Asylum Commission to document the conditions for detained and non-deported people during the COVID-19 pandemic (see Häythiö et al., 2020). The knowledge that emerged through these projects comes from non-deported people, and had the explicit aim to support their struggles, by summarising and disseminating it to audiences primarily consisting of non-deported people and solidarity groups, practitioners, and the general public.

Notwithstanding these engagements and the ways in which they have enriched the book, the main bulk of the research has been on the agents of detention and deportation enforcement. The choice of studying state actors raises ethical issues and dilemmas, which I wish to develop here. 'Studying up' seemed, at first, to be an easier way to navigate the complex ethics of the deportation field. Formal ethical requirements were ensured through bureaucratic formalities, including formal access permissions, confidentiality agreements, anonymisation of research sites and participants, and informed and ongoing consent – all of which I did for the research presented in this book.[1] However, studying up also means that we become dependent on and, we may rightly say, complicit with the structures of power we seek to criticise. This was, for instance, manifested in how I was positioned 'on the side of the state' inside the detention camps, where I held similar mobility privileges to those working there – privileges which I did not challenge, for instance by helping someone escape. In these sites of confinement, I was asked to carry the same communication radio and alarm as staff members as a safety measure, and I was not allowed to be left alone with detained people. The keys and alarm radios were material manifestations of how, as a researcher 'of' the state, I became implicated and ordered into its hierarchisation of (im)mobility (see Turnbull, 2015). During fieldwork, I came to witness direct, indirect, and ordinary forms of violence, most of which was legally sanctioned and unproblematised by officials, but also acts, discourses, and practices that were outright abusive and degrading, if not illegal. There were times when my presence during turbulent events made officials uncomfortable, and others where they found it amusing to 'test' and observe my reactions (see Lindberg and Eule, 2020). Sometimes, I reacted to and questioned their practices. At other times, I remained silent. The violence operated on me too and variably manifested itself in discomfort, in anger and frustration, which I found hard to shake off, and periods of exhaustion during and after fieldwork periods. These emotions have been central to my analytical understanding of the field, and of my own positioning within it (see Bosworth and Kellezi, 2016; Wajsberg, 2021). Sitting with those feelings has been important for how I have engaged with issues of participation, representation, and my 'epistemic complicity' (Rozakou, 2019) in the violent processes I was researching. To a great extent, these reflexive exercises have taken place through conversations with friends and colleagues. I would like to share some of them, exchanged between Lisa Borrelli and myself in April 2021.

> From: Annika Lindberg <annika.lindberg@soz.unibe.ch>
> Sent: 2021–04–29 20:18 PM
> Subject: Street level bureaucrats
>
> Hej Lisa, thanks again for talking through this with me. I attach two vignettes that I think I have shared with you before. I would like to talk to you about what makes the different forms of state violence … different. And what difference it makes how we describe it and what difference the street level bureaucrats make. If any of this makes any sense. When you have time, let's talk about it.
>
> / A

> From: Lisa Marie Borrelli <lisa.borrelli@hevs.ch>
> Sent: Friday, April 30, 2021 3:36 PM
> Subject: Re: Street level bureaucrats
>
> Hej! Thanks, I have read it. Some notes from my side …
>
> Both vignettes make me angry. I would describe it as hot and cold anger. On the one hand, the direct violence the prison officers use against the man, the humiliation, and degradation, which makes you furious. On the other hand, we have a Weberian cold bureaucratic apparatus, where violence is made to sound so reasonable, so rational. It gives you a numb feeling reading it, or a kind of cold anger. You can't make up your emotions. You are sort of lured into believing it sounds reasonable, and you are waiting for the twist … in a way, it's more difficult to contest. In both cases, it's the same machine that produces precarious lives; it's the same violence. I have more things to say, but let's talk about it.
>
> /Lisa

The reader will find the two vignettes that Lisa reacted to in Chapter 3 ('hot' anger) and Chapter 4 ('cold' anger), respectively. Lisa first reacts to a scene of abuse with what she calls 'hot anger', an 'ugly feeling' (Ngai, 2005: 3) evoked in response to a matter of urgency, a 'spectacularly' violent aesthetic (Rozakou, 2019: 76). These feelings mirror my own, and they were, and still are, deeply disturbing. But as Lisa also notes, the anger we feel in such confrontations with violence and abuse is also strangely relieving in its immediacy and clarity. Lisa captures it well in her description of a 'numb' reaction to the second vignette, where the violence is implicit and might 'lure' us to accept its logic. Lisa's and my conversation continued the next day.

Annika: I recognise what you say. That description the numbing, the pacifying, the confused emotions. And that there is relief in anger but also shame. Complicity, I guess.

Lisa: Why do we need this anger? And what would happen to it, if we expect to find violence but find kind of nice people? Do we then lose the urge to write about it?

Annika: True. But are we allowed to be 'shocked'? There was something I read the other day, by Ann Stoler, on how exposing shock or moral outrage is a way to assert innocence, whereas in fact, this ignorance is chosen.

Lisa: I think we cannot deny anyone their feelings of being 'shocked'. It's also important to remain startled, to allow for surprise. But we must ask ourselves what that shock means. Are we shocked because we were not aware? Or because the system was designed to shock us? On the one hand, there is a risk that we normalise the exceptional. How many times will you stand up when you see racial profiling on the train? How much violence do you normalise? On the other, the mundane practices, the not-so-shocking moments, the less obvious violence, which includes that of normalisation. Those are the ones we must try to write about.

Lisa underlines the importance of contextualising our shock, anger, shame – in other words, our 'hot' emotions. We need these emotions to respond and react to injustices, to identify and call out violence perpetrated by states, organisations, or individuals, while also ensuring that we stay attuned to the more hidden, systemic forms of violence. If we only focus on the moments of 'shocking', explicit violence, we risk reproducing crisis-pornographic accounts of violence and suffering (see Rozakou, 2019), which add to the dehumanisation of those exposed to it, as well as the viewer. Such a gaze also risks reproducing the notion that violence is exceptional rather than endemic to the border regime. Therefore, we must go beyond our 'numb feelings' to capture the continuum of violence – legal and extra-legal, overt, and indirect, interpersonal, and systemic. Finally, we must consider how our knowledge practices maintain or challenge epistemic violence when we consider and (re)present certain voices, while silencing others. In this book, I have sought to describe different forms of violence along this continuum.

I can only hope that the reader finishes it feeling – not shocked – but engagingly enraged.

Note

1 Research participants and sites have been anonymised to the extent possible. Excepted are people who have asked not to be anonymous, whose names are generally known, or who are public figures within their communities and fields. These are Niels, Aya, and Steve. In Denmark, there is only one deportation prison and three very differently configured deportation camps, which is why I have chosen to name them. In Sweden, it was possible to anonymise the field sites, and I have therefore not named the sites and lent research participants the option of plausible deniability.

References

Abdelhady, D., Gren, N., and Joormann, M. (eds) (2020). *Refugees and the Violence of European Welfare Bureaucracies*. Manchester: Manchester University Press.

Abrams, P. (1988). 'Notes on the Difficulty of Studying the State', *Journal of Historical Sociology*, 1(1): 58–89.

Almend modstand. (n.d.). http://almenmodstand.dk/ (accessed 9 August 2022).

Amit, I. and Lindberg, A. (2020). 'Performing States of Crisis: Exploring Migration Detention in Israel and Denmark', *Patterns of Prejudice*, 54(3): 238–257.

Amnesty International. (n.d.). 'Spørgsmål & svar om Ellebæk', amnesty.dk/vores-arbejde/diskrimination-racisme/udrejsecentret-ellebaek/spoergsmaal-svar-om-ellebaek/ (accessed 4 June 2021).

Andersen, A. C. et al. (2021). '3241 forskere i opråb til regeringen: Tag klart afstand fra angrebet på forskningsfriheden. Det kan føre til selvensur', *Politiken*, 8 June 2021.

Andersen, D. R. (2017). 'Burnout among Danish Prison Personnel: A Question of Quantitative and Emotional Demands', *Scandinavian Journal of Public Health*, 45(8): 824–830.

Anderson, B. (2011). 'Migration: Controlling the Unsettled Poor'. *OpenDemocracy*. www.opendemocracy.net/en/5050/migration-controlling-unsettled-poor/ (accessed 21 May 2021).

———. (2013). *Us and Them? The Dangerous Politics of Immigration Control*. Oxford: Oxford University Press.

———. (2019). 'New Directions in Migration Studies: Towards Methodological De-Nationalism', *Comparative Migration Studies*, 7(1): 36.

———. (2020). 'No More "Back to Normal" – "Normal" Was the Problem: Thoughts on Coronavirus'. *COMPAS blog*. www.compas.ox.ac.uk/2020/no-more-back-to-normal-normal-was-the-problem-thoughts-on-coronavirus/ (accessed 11 August 2022).

Anderson, B., Gibney, M. and Paoletti, E. (2011). 'Citizenship, Deportation and the Boundaries of Belonging', *Citizenship Studies*, 15(5): 547–563.

Anderson, B., Sharma, N., and Wright, C. (2009). 'Editorial: Why No Borders?', *Refuge: Canada's Journal on Refugees*, 26(2): 5–18.

Andersson, R. (2016). 'Europe's Failed 'Fight' against Irregular Migration: Ethnographic Notes on a Counterproductive Industry', *Journal of Ethnic and Migration Studies*, 42(7): 1055–1075.

Andreassen, R. and Myong, L. (2017). 'Race, Gender, and Researcher Positionality Analysed through Memory Work', *Nordic Journal of Migration Research*, 7(2): 97–104.

Andrijasevic, R. and Walters, W. (2010). 'The International Organization for Migration and the International Government of Borders', *Environment and Planning D: Society and Space*, 28(10): 977–999.

Ansems de Vries, A. and Guild, E. (2018). 'Seeking Refuge in Europe: Spaces of Transit and the Violence of Migration Management', *Journal of Ethnic and Migration Studies*, 45(12): 2156–2166.

Anzaldúa, G. (1987). *Borderlands/La Frontera: The New Mestiza*. San Francisco: aunt lute books.

Arbogast, L. (2016). *Migrant Detention in the European Union: A Thriving Business*. Paris: Migreurope.

Arce, J. and Suárez-Krabbe, J. (2019). 'Racism, Global Apartheid and Disobedient Mobilities: The Politics of Deportation in Europe and Denmark', *KULT: Racism in Denmark*, 15: 107–127.

Arce, J., Suárez-Krabbe, J., and Lindberg, A. (2018). 'Contesting Danish Deportation Camps', *OpenMigration*. https://openmigration.org/en/op-ed/against-the-politics-of-killing-slowly-contesting-danish-deportation-camps/ (accessed 11 August 2022).

Arendt, H. (1963). *Eichmann in Jerusalem: A Report on the Banality of Evil*. New York: Viking Press.

Aretxaga, B. (2000). 'A Fictional Reality: Paramilitary Death Squads and the Construction of State Terror in Spain', in Sluka, J. A. (ed.), *Death Squad: The Anthropology of State Terror*. Philadelphia, PA: University of Pennsylvania Press, pp. 46–69.

Armenta, A. (2017). 'Racializing Crimmigration: Structural Racism, Colorblindness, and the Institutional Production of Immigrant Criminality', *Sociology of Race and Ethnicity*, 3(1): 82–95.

Asylum Commission (n.d.). liu.se/en/research/asylum-commission (accessed 20 May 2021).

Ataç, I. (2019). 'Deserving Shelter: Conditional Access to Accommodation for Rejected Asylum Seekers in Austria, the Netherlands, and Sweden', *Journal of Immigrant & Refugee Studies*, 17(1): 44–60.

Ataç, I. and Rosenberger, S. (2019). 'Social Policies as a Tool of Migration Control', *Journal of Immigrant & Refugee Studies*, 17(1): 1–10.

Ataç, I., Rygiel, K., and Stierl, M. (2016). 'The Contentious Politics of Refugee and Migrant Protest and Solidarity Movements'. *Citizenship Studies*, 20(5): 527–54.

Baeten, G., Berg, L. D., and Lund Hansen, A. (2015). 'Introduction: Neoliberalism and Post-Welfare Nordic States in Transition', *Geografiska Annaler: Series B, Human Geography*, 97(3): 209–212.

Balibar, E. (2004). *We, the People of Europe? Reflections on Transnational Citizenship*. Princeton, NJ: Princeton University Press.

Barker, V. (2013). 'Nordic Exceptionalism Revisited: Explaining the Paradox of a Janus-Faced Penal Regime', *Theoretical Criminology*, 17(1): 5–25.

Bauman, Z. (2013). *Modernity and the Holocaust*. Cambridge: Polity Press.

Bejarano, C. A., López Juárez, L., Mijangos, M. A., and Goldstein, D. M. (2019). *Decolonizing Ethnography: Undocumented Immigrants and New Directions in Social Science*. Durham, NC: Duke University Press.

Bendixsen, S. (2020). 'The Care/Security Nexus of the Humanitarian Border: Assisted Return in Norway', *International Migration*, 58(6): 108–122.

Bendixsen, S. and Hylland Eriksen, T. (2018). 'Time and the Other: Waiting and Hope among Irregular Migrants', in Janeja, M. K. and Bandak, A., *Ethnographies of Waiting: Doubt, Hope and Uncertainty*. New York: Bloomsbury.

Berlingske (2020). 'Over 40.000 gange harbeboere på udrejsecenter brudt reglerne'. www.berlingske.dk/samfund/over-40.000-gange-har-beboere-paa-udrejsecenter-brudt-reglerne (accessed 4 June 2021).

Besteman, C. (2020). *Militarized Global Apartheid*. Durham, NC: Duke University Press.

Bhatia, M., and Bruce-Jones, E. (2021). 'Time, Torture and Manus Island: An Interview with Behrouz Boochani and Omid Tofighian', *Race & Class*, 62(3): 77–87.

Bhatia, M., and Canning, V. (2021). *Stealing Time: Migration, Temporality and Necropolitics*. London: Palgrave Macmillan.

Bigo, D. (2006). 'Globalized-In-Security: The Field and the Ban-Opticon', in Sakai, N. and Solomon, J. (eds), *Translation, Biopolitics, Colonial Difference*. Hong Kong: University of Hong Kong Press, 109–156.

———. (2014). 'The (In)Securitization Practices of the Three Universes of EU Border Control: Military/Navy – Border Guards/Police – Database Analysts', *Security Dialogue*, 45(3): 209–225.

Bjerkestrand, S. F. (2021). 'Syrian Refugees Protest Denmark's Attempt to Return Them', *AlJazeera*, 2 June 2021.

Björngren Cuadra, C. and Staaf, A. (2014). 'Public Social Services' Encounters with Irregular Migrants in Sweden: Amid Values of Social Work and Control of Migration', *European Journal of Social Work*, 17(1): 88–103.

Black, R., Collyer, M., and Somerville, W. (2011). 'Pay-to-Go Schemes and Other Noncoercive Return Programs: Is Scale Possible?'. www.migrationpolicy.org/research/pay-go-schemes-and-other-noncoercive-return-programs-scale-possible (accessed 11 August 2022).

Bloch, A. and Schuster, L. (2005). 'At the Extremes of Exclusion: Deportation, Detention and Dispersal', *Ethnic and Racial Studies*, 28(3): 491–512.

Bommes, M. and Geddes, A. (2011). *Immigration and Welfare: Challenging the Borders of the Welfare State*. Boca Raton, FL: CRC Press.

Bonilla-Silva, E. (2003). *Racism without Racists: Color-Blind Racism and the Persistence of Racial Inequality in the United States*. Lanham, MD: Rowman & Littlefield.

———. (2019). 'Feeling Race: Theorizing the Racial Economy of Emotions', *American Sociological Review*, 84(1): 1–25.

Boochani, B. (2018). *No Friend but the Mountains*. London: Picador/Pan Macmillan.

Border Violence Monitoring Network. (2020). *The Black Box of Pushbacks*. www.statewatch.org/media/1661/eu-bvmn-black-book-pushbacks-vol2.pdf (accessed 24 May 2021).

Borevi, K. (2015). 'Family Migration Policies and Politics: Understanding the Swedish Exception', *Journal of Family Issues*, 36(11): 1490–1508.

Borrelli, L. M. (2021). '"They Know the Procedure; They Just Don't Know When We Will Come": Uncovering the Practice of Unannounced Deportations', *Journal of Ethnic and Migration Studies*, 47(15): 3473–3491.

Borrelli, L. M. and Lindberg, A. (2018). 'The Creativity of Coping: Alternative Tales of Moral Dilemmas among Migration Control Officers', *International Journal of Migration and Border Studies*, 4(3): 163–178.

———. (2019). 'Paperwork Performances: Legitimating State Violence in the Swedish Deportation Regime', *Journal of Legal Anthropology*, 3(2): 50–69.

Borrelli, L. M. and Trasciani, G. (2019). '"I Like to Work with People" – Everyday Stories and Reflections from Street-Level Workers in the Migration Regime on What Motivates Their Tasks', *Politiche Sociali*, 3: 407–426.

Bosworth, M. (2014). *Inside Immigration Detention*. Oxford: Oxford University Press.

———. (2016). 'Paperwork and Administrative Power in Detention', *Oxford Law Faculty Blog*. https://blogs.law.ox.ac.uk/research-subject-groups/centre-criminology/centreborder-criminologies/blog/2016/06/paperwork-and (accessed 4 May 2021).

———. (2018). 'Affect and Authority in Immigration Detention', *Punishment & Society*, 21(5): 542–559.

Bosworth, M., and Kellezi, B. (2016). 'Doing Research in Immigration Removal Centres: Ethics, Emotions and Impact', *Criminology & Criminal Justice*, 17(2): 121–137.

Brekke, J.P. and Brochmann, G. (2015). 'Stuck in Transit: Secondary Migration of Asylum Seekers in Europe, National Differences, and the Dublin Regulation', *Journal of Refugee Studies*, 28(2): 145–162.

Brekke, J. P., Vedsted-Hansen, J., and Stern, R. (2020). 'Temporary Asylum and Cessation of Refugee Status in Scandinavia: Policies, Practices and Dilemmas'. *EMN Norway Occasional Papers*.

Brochmann, G. and Dølvik, J. (2018). 'The Welfare State and International Migration: The European Challenge', in Greve, B. (ed.), *Routledge Handbook of the Welfare State*, 2nd Edition. London: Routledge.

Brochmann, G. and Hagelund, A. (2011). 'Migrants in the Scandinavian Welfare State: The Emergence of a Social Policy Problem', *Nordic Journal of Migration Research*, 1(1): 13–24.

Brun, C. (2015). 'Active Waiting and Changing Hopes: Toward a Time Perspective on Protracted Displacement', *ResearchGate*, 59(1): 19–37.

Brygger, R. (2021). 'Få udlændinge ra flygtningeproducerande lande bliver udsendt', videnscenterforintegration.dk/index.php/2021/04/03/faa-udlaendinge-fra-flygtningelande-bliver-udsendt/ (accessed 5 April 2021).

Buckel, S. (2016). 'Welcome Management: Making Sense of the "Summer of Migration", Interview by William Callison'. *Near Futures Online 1: Europe at a Crossroads*. http://nearfuturesonline.org/welcome-management-making-sense-of-the-summer-of-migration/ (accessed 10 August 2022).

Cabot, H. (2012). 'The Governance of Things: Documenting Limbo in the Greek Asylum Procedure', *PoLAR: Political and Legal Anthropology Review*, 35(1): 11–29.

———. (2016). '"Refugee Voices": Tragedy, Ghosts, and the Anthropology of Not Knowing', *Journal of Contemporary Ethnography*, 45, 6(1): 645–672.

———. (2019). 'The Business of Anthropology and the European Refugee Regime', *American Ethnologist*, 46(3): 261–275.

Calavita, K. (2005). 'Law, Citizenship, and the Construction of (Some) Immigrant Others', *Law & Social Inquiry*, 30(2): 401–420.

Canning, V. (2017). *Gendered Harm and Structural Violence in the British Asylum System*. New York: Routledge.

———. (2019a). 'Keeping Up with the Kladdkaka: Kindness and Coercion in Swedish Immigration Detention Centres', *European Journal of Criminology*, 17(6): 723–743.

———. (2019b). *Supporting Sanctuary: Addressing Harms in British, Danish and Swedish Asylum Systems*. London: Calverts Co-operative.

Canning, V. and Bhatia, M. (2021). *Stealing Time: Migration, Temporalities and State Violence*. London: Palgrave Macmillan.

Casas-Cortes, M. et al. (2015). 'New Keywords: Migration and Borders', *Cultural Studies*, 29(1): 55–87.

Cassarino, J. P. (2020). 'Readmission, Visa Policy and the "Return Sponsorship" Puzzle in the New Pact on Migration and Asylum'. *ADiM Blog, Analyses & Opinions*. www.adimblog.com/2020/11/30/readmission-visa-policy-and-the-return-sponsorship-puzzle-in-the-new-pact-on-migration-and-asylum/ (accessed 10 August 2022).

Castaway Souls of Sjælsmark. (2016). *Asylum Seekers in Denmark: Manifesto – For the Right to Have Rights*. alice.ces.uc.pt/news-old/?p=5492 (accessed 30 July 2019).

Césaire, A. (1972 [1955]). *Discourse on Colonialism*. New York: Monthly Review Press.

Chak, T. (2016). 'MLC 2015 Keynote: Undocumented: The Architecture of Migrant Detention', *Migration, Mobility, & Displacement*, 2(1): 6–29.

Clante Bendixen, M. (2011). *Asylcenter Limbo. En rapport om udsendelseshindringer*. Copenhagen: Refugees Welcome.

———. (2017). 'En barndom i ingenmansland', *Refugees Welcome DK*. refugees.dk/fokus/2017/oktober/en-barndom-i-ingenmandsland/ (accessed 21 May 2021).

———. (2020). 'Udelukkelsesgrunde, udvisningsdom og tålt ophold'. *Refugees Welcome DK*. refugees.dk/fakta/lovgivning-og-definitioner/udelukkelsesgrunde-udvisningsdom-og-taalt-ophold/ (accessed 21 May 2021).

———. (2021). 'Kærshovedgård Makes Life as Intolerable as It Can Be in Denmark', *Refugees Welcome DK*. http://refugees.dk/en/focus/2021/april/kaershovedgaard-makes-life-as-intolerable-as-it-can-be-in-denmark/ (accessed 10 August 2022).

Cohen, S. (2002). *States of Denial*. Cambridge: Polity.

———. (2011). *Folk Devils and Moral Panics: The Creation of the Mods and Rockers*. Abingdon and New York: Routledge.

Collyer, M. (2016). 'Geopolitics as a Migration Governance Strategy: European Union Bilateral Relations with Southern Mediterranean Countries', *Journal of Ethnic and Migration Studies*, 42(4): 606–624.

Conlon, D. (2011). 'Waiting: Feminist Perspectives on the Spacings/Timings of Migrant (Im)Mobility', *Gender, Place & Culture*, 18(3): 353–360.

Council of Europe's Committee for the Prevention of Torture and Inhuman or Degrading Treatment or Punishment (CPT). 2019. *Report on Visit to Denmark*. www.coe.int/en/web/cpt/-/council-of-europe-anti-torture-committee-publishes-a-response-of-the-danish-authorities-to-the-report-on-the-2019-visit (accessed 15 March 2020).

Coutin, S. (2010). 'Confined Within: National Territories as Zones of Confinement', *Political Geography*, 29(4): 200–208.

———. (2015). 'Deportation Studies: Origins, Themes and Directions', *Journal of Ethnic and Migration Studies*, 41(4): 671–681.

Cowan, L. (2021). *Border Nation: A Story of Migration*. London: Pluto Press.

Danbolt, M. and Myong, L. (2018). 'Racial Turns and Returns: Recalibrations of Racial Exceptionalism in Danish Public Debates on Racism', in Hervik, P. (ed.). *Racialization, Racism, and Anti-Racism in the Nordic Countries*. Basingstoke: Palgrave Macmillan, 39–61.

Danish Government. (2018). 'Aftale om Finansloven for 2019'. www.regeringen.dk/aktuelt/publikationer-og-aftaletekster/aftale-om-finansloven-for-2019/ (accessed 10 August 2022).

———. (2020). *Response of the Danish Government to Paragraph 117 of the Report of the European Committee for the Prevention of Torture and Inhuman or Degrading Treatment or Punishment (CPT) on Its Visit to Denmark*. rm.coe.int/16809ccbaf (accessed 15 March 2020).

Danish Helsinki Committee. (2017). *Udlændinge- og udrejsecenter i Danmark*, Udlændinge- og integrationsudvalget 2016–17. UUI Amd.del Bilag 218.

Danish Immigration Agency. (2020). 'Tal og fakta på udlændingeområdet 2020'. https://uim.dk/media/9337/1011715-tal-og-fakta-paa-udlaendingeomraadet-2020-final-a.pdf (accessed 10 August 2022).

Danish Institute for Human Rights. (2016). 'Udvisning og udlevering – status 2015–16'. Copenhagen: Institut for Menneskerettigheder.

Danish Ministry of Immigration and Integration. (2019). 'L 140 Forslag til lov om ændring af udlændingeloven, integrationsloven, repatrieringsloven og forskellige andre love'. *Folketinget Samling 2018–19 lovforslag*.

———. (2021). 'L 230 Forslag til lov om ændring af lov om dansk indfødsret'. *Folketinget Samling 2020–21 lovforslag*.

Danish Ministry of Justice. (2013). 'Udrejsecenter skal få fler asylansøgere til at rejse hjem'. www.justitsministeriet.dk/pressemeddelelse/udrejsecenter-skal-faa-flere-asylansoegere-til-at-rejse-hjem/ (accessed 30 September 2022).

Danish Refugee Council. (2020). 'Bliver afviste asylansøgere sendt tilbage?' https://drc.ngo/da/vores-arbejde/viden-og-fakta/25-sporgsmal-og-svar-om-flygtninge/7/ (accessed 11 August 2022).

Das, V. (2004). 'The Signature of the State: The Paradox of Illegibility', in Das, V. and Poole, D. (eds), *Anthropology in the Margins of the State*. Oxford: Oxford University Press, 225–252.

Das, V. and Poole, D. (eds) (2004). *Anthropology in the Margins of the State*. Oxford: Oxford University Press.

Davies, T. and Isakjee, A. (2015). 'Geography, Migration and Abandonment in the Calais Refugee Camp', *Political Geography*, 49: 93–95.

———. (2019). 'Ruins of Empire: Refugees, Race, and the Postcolonial Geographies of European Migrant Camps', *Geoforum*, 102: 214–217.

Davies, T., Isakjee, A., and Dhesi, S. (2017). 'Violent Inaction: The Necropolitical Experience of Refugees in Europe', *Antipode*, 49(5): 1263–1284.

Davis, A. and Dent, G. (2001). 'Prison as a Border: On Gender, Globalization, and Punishment, *Signs*, 26(4): 1235–1241.

Davis, A., Dent, G., Meiners, E., and Richie, B. (2021). *Abolition. Feminism. Now.* London: Haymarket Books.

DeBono, D., Rönnqvist, R., and Magnusson, K. (2015). *Humane and Dignified?: Migrants' Experiences of Living in a 'State of Deportability' in Sweden*. Malmö Institute for Studies of Migration, Diversity and Welfare, Malmo University.

De Coulon, G. (2015). '"L'Illégalité régulière" au cœur du paradoxe de l'état-nation ethnographie de l'interface en tension entre requérant.e.s d'asile débouté.e.s et autorités suisses'. PhD dissertation. Maison d'Analyse des Processus Sociaux (MAPS), Université de Neuchâtel.

De Genova, N. (2002). 'Migrant "Illegality" and Deportability in Everyday Life', *Annual Review of Anthropology*, 31: 419–447.

———. (2016). 'Detention, Deportation, and Waiting: Toward a Theory of Migrant Detainability: GDP Working Paper No. 18'. *Global Detention Project*.

———. (2017). 'Afterword. Deportation: The Last Word?', in Khosravi, S. (ed.). *After Deportation: Ethnographic Perspectives*. London: Palgrave Macmillan.

De Genova, N. and Peutz, N. (eds) (2010). *The Deportation Regime: Sovereignty, Space, and the Freedom of Movement*. Durham, NC: Duke University Press.

De León, J. (2015). *The Land of Open Graves: Living and Dying on the Migrant Trail*. Oakland, CA: University of California Press.

De Noronha, L. (2019). 'Deportation, Racism and Multi-Status Britain: Immigration Control and the Production of Race in the Present', *Ethnic and Racial Studies*, 42(14): 2413–2430.

Dignity and Amnesty International. (2021). 'Brev til justitsministeren vedrørende Udlændingecenter Ellebæk'. www.ft.dk/samling/20201/almdel/reu/bilag/203/2337429.pdf (accessed 20 April 2021).

Djampour, P. (2018). *Borders Crossing Bodies: The Stories of Eight Youth with Experience of Migrating*. Fakulteten för hälsa och samhälle (HS), Institutionen för socialt arbete Malmö universitet, Malmö, Sweden.

Drake, D., Earle, H., and Sloan, J. (2016). *The Palgrave Handbook of Prison Ethnography*. London: Springer.

Drotbohm, H. and Hasselberg, I. (2015). 'Deportation, Anxiety, Justice: New Ethnographic Perspectives', *Journal of Ethnic and Migration Studies*, 41(4): 551–562.

Drotbohm, H. and Lems, A. (2018). 'Introduction: Displacement and New Sociabilities'. *Allegralab*. https://allegralaboratory.net/introduction-displacement-and-new-sociabilities/ (accessed 11 August 2022).

Dubois, V. (2010). *The Bureaucrat and the Poor: Encounters in French Welfare Offices*. Farnham: Ashgate.

ECRE (European Council on Refugees and Exile). (2018). 'European Commission Releases Proposal to Recast Return Directive'. www.ecre.org/european-commission-releases-proposal-to-recast-return-directive/ (accessed 10 August 2022).

———. (2019). 'Asylum Statistics 2018: Changing Arrivals, Same Concerns'. www.ecre.org/asylum-statistics-2018-changing-arrivals-same-concerns/ (accessed 10 August 2022).

———. (2020). 'Return as "Nonessential Travel" in the Time of Pandemic'. *Policy note no. 26*.

———. (2021). 'Denmark: Experts Contributing to COI Reports Condemn Decision to Deem Damascus Safe for Return as UNHCR Reconfirms Its Position on Returns to Syria'. https://ecre.org/denmark-experts-contributing-to-coi-reports-condemn-decision-to-deem-damascus-safe-for-return-as-unhcr-reconfirms-its-position-on-returns-to-syria/ (accessed 10 August 2022).

Edward, S., Elsted, T., and Hansen, N. (2019). *Cast Away Souls*. Copenhagen: Cph:Dox.

Egaa Jørgensen, R. and Shapiro, D. (2019). 'Vi kan ikke tænke nu' – flygtningessociale navigationer i et bevægeligt integrationslandskab', *Udenfor*, 39: 42–51.

Eika, J. et al. (2019). 'Derfor handler deportationslejrene og ghettoplanen om kolonialisme og racisme', *Eftertrykket*.

Ellebæk Contact Network. (2020). 'Letter to the Legal Affairs Committee'. https://xn--ellebkkontaktnetvrk-pxbm.dk/letter.pdf (accessed 8 August 2022).

Ellermann, A. (2010). 'Undocumented Migrants and Resistance in the Liberal State', *Politics & Society*, 38(3): 408–429.

El Qadim, N. (2014). 'Postcolonial Challenges to Migration Control: French–Moroccan Cooperation Practices on Forced Returns', *Security Dialogue*, 45(3): 242–261.

Elsrud, T. (2020). 'Resisting Social Death with Dignity. The Strategy of Re-Escaping among Young Asylum-Seekers in the Wake of Sweden's Sharpened Asylum Laws', *European Journal of Social Work*, 23(3): 500–513.

Elsrud, T., Gruber, S., and Lundberg, A. (eds) (2021). *Rättssäkerheten och solidariteten – vad hände? En antologi om människor på flykt*. Linköpings Universitet.

Esposito, F., Matos, R., and Bosworth, M. (2020). 'Gender, Vulnerability and Everyday Resistance in Immigration Detention: Women's Experiences of Confinement in a Portuguese Detention Facility', *International Journal for Crime, Justice and Social Democracy*, 9(3): 5–20.

Eule, T. G. et al. (2019). *Migrants Before the Law: Contested Migration Control in Europe*. London: Palgrave Macmillan.

Eule, T. G., Loher, D., and Wyss, A. (2018). 'Contested Control at the Margins of the State', *Journal of Ethnic and Migration Studies*, 44(16): 2717–2729.

European Commission. (2019). 'Progress Report on the Implementation of the European Agenda on Migration'. eur-lex.europa.eu/LexUriServ/LexUriServ.do?uri=COM:2019:0481:FIN:EN:PDF (accessed 13 May 2020).

———. (2020). 'New Pact on Migration and Asylum'. https://ec.europa.eu/info/strategy/priorities-2019-2024/promoting-our-european-way-life/new-pact-migration-and-asylum_en (accessed 13 March 2022).

European Commissioner for Human Rights. (2018). *Report by Nils Muiznieks Commissioner for Human Rights of the Council of Europe Following His Visit to Sweden from 2 to 6 October 2017*. https://rm.coe.int/commdh-2018-4-report-on-the-visit-to-sweden-from-2-to-6-october-2017-b/16807893f8 (accessed 1 April 2022).

———. (2020). 'Commissioner Calls for Release of Immigration Detainees while Covid-19 Crisis Continues'. www.coe.int/en/web/commissioner/-/commissioner-calls-for-release-of-immigration-detainees-while-covid-19-crisis-continues?fbclid=IwAR0mbTTlApz0mIwUF4H6nQhqSvwrdXaEkO5W2dsu2p1gknt30I7bbNshpsA (accessed 23 December 2020).

European Migration Network. (2016). 'EMN Synthesis Report on the Return of Rejected Asylum Seekers: Challenges and Good Practices'. Migratpol EMN Doc 000. https://emn.gov.hr/UserDocsImages/EMN_studije/06-The-Return-of-Rejected-Asylum-Seekers-Challenges-and-Good-Practices.pdf (accessed 11 August 2022).

———. (2017). 'EMN Annual Report on Migration and Asylum 2017 Sweden'. European Parliament Research Initiative (2019). 'Data on Returns of Irregular Migrants'. www.europarl.europa.eu/RegData/etudes/BRIE/2019/637907/EPRS_BRI(2019)637907_EN.pdf (accessed 3 July 2019).

European Parliamentary Research Service. (2019). 'The Proposed Return Directive (Recast) – Substitute Impact Assessment'. www.europarl.europa.eu/thinktank/en/document/EPRS_STU(2019)631727 (accessed 10 August 2022).

Eurostat. (2019). 'Enforcement of Immigration Legislation Statistics'. ec.europa.eu/eurostat/statistics-explained/index.php?title=Enforcement_of_immigration_legislation_statistics#Latest_trends_in_enforcement_statistics (accessed 20 May 2021).

———. (2020). 'Immigration Law Enforcement in the EU'. ec.europa.eu/eurostat/web/products-eurostat-news/-/ddn-20200722-1 (accessed 5 June 2021).

FARR. (2016). 'Uppdaterad Info Om LMA-Lagen'. *Asylnytt*.

Fassin, D. (2014). *Enforcing Order: An Ethnography of Urban Policing*. Cambridge: Polity.

———. (2017). *Writing the World of Policing: The Difference Ethnography Makes*. Chicago, IL: University of Chicago Press.

Fekete, L. (2005). 'The Deportation Machine: Europe, Asylum and Human Rights', *Race & Class*, 47(1): 64–78.

Fiddian-Qasmiyeh, E. (2020). 'Introduction: Recentering the South in Studies of Migration', *Migration and Society*, 3(1): 1–18.

Fili, A. (2016). 'The Continuum of Detention in Greece'. *Oxford Criminologies Blog*. https://blogs.law.ox.ac.uk/research-subject-groups/centre-criminology/centreborder-criminologies/blog/2016/05/continuum (accessed 11 August 2022).

Finnsdottir, M., and Hallgrimsdottir, H. K. (2019). 'Welfare State Chauvinists? Gender, Citizenship, and Anti-Democratic Politics in the Welfare State Paradise', *Frontiers in Sociology*, 3(46): 1–12.

Fischer, Nicolas (2015), 'The Management of Anxiety: An Ethnographical Outlook on Self-Mutilations in a French Immigration Detention Centre', *Journal of Ethnic and Migration Studies*, 41(4): 599–616.

Floros, K., and Jørgensen, M. B. (2020). 'Tracing the Future of Migrants' Labour Relations. Experiences of Institutionalised Migrant Precarity in Denmark and Greece', *Political Geography*, 77: 102–120.

Folkebevægelsen for asylbørns fremtid. (n.d). www.asylboernsfremtid.dk (accessed 20 January 2021).

Folketingets Ombudsmand. (2019). *Tilsynsbesøg i Udlændingecenter Ellebæk.* www.ombudsmanden.dk/find/inspektioner/alle_inspektioner/udlaendingecenter _ellebaek/pdf/ (accessed 10 August 2022).

Franko, K. (2014). 'Bordered Penality: Precarious Membership and Abnormal Justice', *Punishment & Society*, 16(5): 520–541.

———. (2020). *The Crimmigrant Other: Migration and Penal Power*. London: Routledge.

Frederiksen, F. (2009). *Fra Sandholm til Ellebæk*. Nyborg: De Grafiske Fag – Statsfængslet i Nyborg.

Freedom of Movements Research Collective (2018). *Stop Killing Us Slowly: A Research Report on the Criminalization of Rejected Asylum Seekers in Denmark.* Roskilde: Roskilde University.

Galtung, J. (1969). 'Violence, Peace, and Peace Research', *Journal of Peace Research*, 6(3): 167–191.

Gammeltoft-Hansen, T. and Whyte, Z. (2011). 'Dansk asylpolitik 1983–2010', in Vitus, K. and Nielsen, S. S. (eds), *Asylbørn i Danmark: En barndom i undtagelsestilstand*. København: Hans Reitzel, 152–172.

Ghezelbash, D. and Feith Tan, N. (2021). 'The End of the Right to Seek Asylum? COVID-19 and the Future of Refugee Protection', *International Journal of Refugee Law*, 32(4): 668–679.

Gibney, M. J. (2008). 'Asylum and the Expansion of Deportation in the United Kingdom', *Government and Opposition*, 43(2): 146–167.

———. (2013). 'Is Deportation a Form of Forced Migration?', *Refugee Survey Quarterly*, 32(2): 116–129.

Gill, N. (2009). 'Longing for Stillness: The Forced Movement of Asylum Seekers', *M/C Journal*, 12(1). https://doi.org/10.5204/mcj.123

———. (2016). *Carceral Spaces: Mobility and Agency in Imprisonment and Migrant Detention*. London: Routledge.

Gilmore, R. (2007). *Golden Gulag. Prisons, Surplus, Crisis and Opposition in Globalizing California*. Los Angeles, CA: University of California Press.

———. (2020). 'COVID-19, Decarceration, and Abolition', *HaymarketBooks*, 17 April 2020.

Glick Schiller, N. and Çağlar, A. (2016). 'Displacement, Emplacement and Migrant Newcomers: Rethinking Urban Sociabilities within Multiscalar Power', *Identities*, 23(1): 17–34.

Global Detention Project. (2018). 'Denmark Immigration Detention Profile'.

Golash-Boza, T. (2015). *Deported: Immigrant Policing, Disposable Labor and Global Capitalism*. New York: NYU Press.

Goldberg, D. T. (2006). 'Racial Europeanization', *Ethnic and Racial Studies*, 29(2): 331–364.

———. (2009). 'Racial Comparisons, Relational Racisms: Some Thoughts on Method', *Ethnic and Racial Studies*, 32(7), 1271–1282.

Goos, S. (2021). 'På Langeland frygter de nyt udrejsecenter – sådan er det gået i Midtjylland', *TV2 Nyheder*. https://nyheder.tv2.dk/samfund/2021-05-20-paa-langeland-frygter-de-nyt-udrejsecenter-saadan-er-det-gaaet-i-midtjylland (accessed 4 April 2021).

Gordon, A. (2008). *Ghostly Matters: Haunting and the Sociological Imagination*. Minneapolis, MN: University of Minnesota Press.

Graeber, D. (2012). 'Dead Zones of the Imagination: On Violence, Bureaucracy, and Interpretive Labor: The Malinowski Memorial Lecture, 2006', *HAU: Journal of Ethnographic Theory*, 2(2): 105–128.

Green-Pedersen, C. and Krogstrup, J. (2008). 'Immigration as a Political Issue in Denmark and Sweden', *European Journal of Political Research*, 47(5): 610–634.

Griffiths, M. (2013). 'Living with Uncertainty: Indefinite Immigration Detention', *Journal of Legal Anthropology*, 1 (3): 263–286.

———. (2017). 'The Changing Politics of Time in the UK's Immigration System', in Mavroudi, E., Pageb B., and Christou, A. (eds), *Timespace and International Migration*. Cheltenham: Edward Elgar Publishing, 48–60.

Griffiths, M., Rogers, A., and Anderson, B. (2013). 'Migration, Time and Temporalities: Review and Prospect', *COMPAS Research Resources Paper*.

Grosfoguel, R., Oso, L., and A. Christou. (2015). '"Racism"', Intersectionality and Migration Studies: Framing Some Theoretical Reflections', *Identities*, 22(6): 635–652.

Gullestad, M. (2002). 'Invisible Fences: Egalitarianism, Nationalism and Racism', *Journal of the Royal Anthropological Institute*, 8(1): 45–63.

Günel, G., Varma, S., and Watanabe, C. (2020). 'A Manifesto for Patchwork Ethnography', *Society for Cultural Anthropology*. https://culanth.org/fieldsights/a-manifesto-for-patchwork-ethnography (accessed 11 August 2022).

Gupta, A. (2012). *Red Tape: Bureaucracy, Structural Violence, and Poverty in India*. Durham, NC: Duke University Press.

Hage, G. (2009). 'Waiting Out the Crisis: On Stuckedness and Governmentality', in Hage, G. (ed.), *Waiting*. Melbourne: Melbourne University Press, 97–106.

———. (2015). *Alter-Politics: Critical Anthropology and the Radical Imagination*. Melbourne: Melbourne University Press.

Hall, A. (2010). '"These People Could Be Anyone": Fear, Contempt (and Empathy) in a British Immigration Removal Centre', *Journal of Ethnic and Migration Studies*, 36(6): 881–898.

———. (2016). 'The Pleasures of Security? Visual Practice and Immigration Detention', in Conlon, D. and Hiemstra, N. (eds), *Intimate Economies of Immmigration Detention*. London: Routledge.

Hammar, T. (1964) *Sverige åt svenskarna – Invandringspolitik, utlänningskontroll och asylrätt 1900–1932*. Stockholm: Caslon press boktryckeri AB.

———. (1999) 'Closing the Doors to the Swedish Welfare State', in Brochmann, G. and Hammar, T. (eds), *Mechanisms of Immigration Control: a Comparative Analysis of European Regulation Politics*. Oxford: Berg.

Hasselberg, I. (2016). *Enduring Uncertainty: Deportation, Punishment and Everyday Life*. New York: Berghahn Books.

Häythiö, S. et al. (2020). *Frihetsberövade människor i Coronakrisen*. Norrköping: Linköpings universitet.

Heegaard Bausager, M., Köpfli, M. J., and Ardittis, S. (2013). *Study on the Situation of Third-Country Nationals Pending Return/Removal in the EU Member States and the Schengen Associated Countries*. Brussels: European Commission.

Heller, C. (2021). 'De-Confining Borders: Towards a Politics of Freedom of Movement in the Time of the Pandemic', *Mobilities*, 16(1): 113–133.

Heller, C. and Kasparek, B. (2020). 'The EU's Pact against Migration, Part One', *OpenDemocracy*. www.opendemocracy.net/en/can-europe-make-it/the-eus-pact-against-migration-part-one/ (accessed 11 August 2022).

Hernández, C. C. G. (2017). 'Abolishing Immigration Prisons', *Boston University Law Review*, 97: 245–300.

Herschend, S. (2019). 'Afviste sidder indespærret I Ellebæk I op til halvandet år: – Det her havde jeg aldrig troet om Danmark', Nyheder TV2, 10 March 2019.

Herzfeld, M. (1992). *The Social Production of Indifference*. Chicago, IL: University of Chicago Press.

Hiemstra, N. (2014). 'Performing Homeland Security within the US Immigrant Detention System', *Environment and Planning D: Society and Space*, 32(4): 571–588.

———. (2020). *Detain and Deport: The Chaotic U.S. Immigration Enforcement Regime*. Athens, GA: University of Georgia Press.

Holm Vohnsen, N. (2017). *The Absurdity of Bureaucracy*. Manchester: Manchester University Press.

hooks, b. (1990). 'Marginality as a Site of Resistance', in Ferguson, R. et al. (eds), *Out There: Marginalization and Contemporary Cultures*. Cambridge, MA: Massachusetts Institute of Technology, 241–243.

Hørkilde, M. (2021). 'S-ordfører om udvisninger til Syrien: En bombe kan falde ned i dit hus. Det er ikke nødvendigvis noget personligt mellem dig og regimet', *Politiken*. https://politiken.dk/indland/art8163613/%C2%BBEn-bombe-kan-falde-ned-i-dit-hus.-Det-er-ikke-n%C3%B8dvendigvis-noget-personligt-mellem-dig-og-regimet%C2%AB (accessed 11 August 2022).

Hörnqvist, M. (2018). 'Enrolment and Exclusion: Juggling with the Paradoxes of the Welfare State', *Border Criminologies Blog*. https://blogs.law.ox.ac.uk/research-subject-groups/centre-criminology/centreborder-criminologies/blog/2018/01/enrolment-and (accessed 11 August 2022).

Hughes, S. (2017). 'Rethinking Resistance: Creativity and Potentiality within the UK Asylum System'. PhD thesis. Department of Geography, Durham University, UK.

Ibfelt, J. and Skov-Jensen, M. (2019). 'Asylansøgere forsvinder ud i det blå: Mange rejser videre til andre EU-lande', *DR Nyheder*.

Iliadou, E. (2019). 'Border Harms and Everyday Violence. The Lived Experiences of Border Crossers in Lesvos Island, Greece'. PhD thesis. The Open University.

Inci, Z., Kullberg, E and Al Akrawi, A. (2020). 'Vart ska de unga hemlösa ta vägen när de blir coronasmittade?', *ETC*, 15 December 2020. www.etc.se/debatt/vart-ska-unga-hemlosa-ta-vagen-nar-de-blir-coronasmittade (accessed 11 August 2022).

Infantino, F. (2021). 'How Does Policy Change at the Street Level? Local Knowledge, a Community of Practice and EU Visa Policy Implementation in Morocco', *Journal of Ethnic and Migration Studies*, 47(5): 1028–1046.

Isin, E. F. (2009). 'Citizenship in Flux: The Figure of the Activist Citizen', *Subjectivity*, 29(1): 367–388.

Jansson-Keshavarz, S. (2016). 'Sveriges historiska produktion av förvarstagbarhet', in Holgersson, H, Sager, M. and Öberg, K. (eds), *Irreguljär migration: Statliga kategoriseringar, politiskt motstånd, vardagserfarenheter*. Göteborg: Daidalos.

Jansson-Keshavarz, S., Lundberg, A., and Obenius, H. (2021). 'Förskjutningar av värlfärdsrättigheter och ansvar', in Elsrud, T., Gruber, S., and A. Lundberg (eds), *Rättssäkerheten och solidariteten – vad hände?* s. 319–334.

Jefferson, A., Turner, S., and Jensen, S. (2019). 'Introduction: On Stuckness and Sites of Confinement', *Ethnos*, 84(1): 1–13.

Johannesson, L. (2017). 'In Courts We Trust: Administrative Justice in Swedish Migration Courts'. PhD dissertation. Department of Political Science, Stockholm University.

Johansen, N. (2013). 'Governing the Funnel of Expulsion: Agamben, the Dynamic of Force, and Minimalist Biopolitics', in Aas, K. F. and Bosworth, M. (eds), *The Borders of Punishment: Migration, Citizenship, and Social Exclusion*. Oxford, New York: Oxford University Press.

Johansson, C. (2005). *Välkomna till Sverige*. Malmö: Bokbox förlag.

Jørgensen, M. B. and Thomsen, T. L. (2016). 'Deservingness in the Danish Context: Welfare Chauvinism in Times of Crisis', *Critical Social Policy*, 36(3): 330–351.

Juárez, S. P. et al. (2019). 'Effects of Non-Health-Targeted Policies on Migrant Health: A Systematic Review and Meta-Analysis', *The Lancet Global Health*, 7(4): 420–435.

Justitieombudsmannen. 2018. *JO Förvar*. www.jo.se/PageFiles/31889/277-2018.pdf (accessed 11 August 2022).

Kalir, B. (2017). 'State Desertion and "Out-of-Procedure" Asylum Seekers in the Netherlands', *Focaal*, 77: 63–75.

Kalir, B. and van Schendel, W. (2017). 'Introduction: Nonrecording States between Legibility and Looking Away', *Focaal*, 77: 1–7.

Kalir, B. and Wissink, L. (2016). 'The Deportation Continuum: Convergences between State Agents and NGO Workers in the Dutch Deportation Field', *Citizenship Studies*, 20(1): 34–49.

Kalir, B., Achermann, C., and Rosset, D. (2019). 'Re-searching Access: What do Attempts at Studying Migration Control Tell Us About the State?', *Social Anthropology*, 7(S1): 1–99.

Kapoor, N. and Narkowicz, K. (2019). 'Characterising Citizenship: Race, Criminalisation and the Extension of Internal Borders', *Sociology*, 53(4): 652–670.

Kasparek, B. (2016). 'Complementing Schengen: The Dublin System and the European Border and Migration Regime', in Bauder, H. and Matheis, C. (eds), *Migration Policy and Practice*. London: Palgrave Macmillan, 59–78.

Kazemi, B. (2021). 'Unaccompanied Minors (Un-)Made in Sweden: Ungrievable Lives and Access to Rights Produced Through Policy'. PhD dissertation. Department of Social Work, University of Gothenburg.

Keshavarz, M. (2018). 'The Violence of Humanitarian Design', in Willis, A.-M. (ed.), *The Design Philosophy Reader*. London: Bloomsbury Academic, 120–127.
Keskinen, S., Mulinari, D., Tuori, S. et al. (eds) (2009). *Complying with Colonialism: Gender, Race and Ethnicity in the Nordic Region*. Aldershot: Ashgate.
Keskinen, S., Norocel, O. C., and Jørgensen, M. B. (2016). 'The politics and policies of welfare chauvinism under the economic crisis', *Critical Social Policy*, 36(3): 321–329.
Keskinen, S., Skaptadóttir, U. D., and Toivanen, M. (2019). *Undoing Homogeneity in the Nordic Region: Migration, Difference, and the Politics of Solidarity*. Abingdon: Routledge.
Khavari, F. (2018). 'Hur länge ska barnen våndas i väntrummet?', *Aftonbladet*.
Khosravi, S. (2009). 'Detention and Deportation of Asylum Seekers in Sweden', *Race and Class*, 50(4): 30–56.
——. (2010). 'An Ethnography of Migrant "Illegality" in Sweden: Included Yet Excepted?', *Journal of International Political Theory*, 6(1): 95–116.
——. (2016). 'Deportation as a Way of Life', in Furman, R. (ed.), *Detaining the Immigrant Other: Global and Transnational Issues*. Oxford: Oxford University Press, 169–181.
—— (ed.) (2017a). *After Deportation: Ethnographic Perspectives*. London: Palgrave Macmillan.
——. (2017b). 'Why Deportation to Afghanistan Is Wrong', *Allegralab*. https://allegralaboratory.net/deportation-afghanistan-wrong/ (accessed 10 August 2022).
——. (2018). 'Stolen Time', *Radical Philosophy*, 2(3): 38–41.
——. (2019). 'What Do We See If We Look at the Border from the Other Side?', *Social Anthropology*, 27(3): 409–424.
——. (2020). 'Afterword. Experiences and Stories Along the Way', *Geoforum*, 116: 292–295.
Kjær, K. (2003). 'Asyllovgivningen: Retssikkerheden under afvikling?', in Seidenfaden, T. et al. (eds), *Når du strammer garnet*. Aarhus: Aarhus Universitetsforlag, 137–160.
Kjellbom, P. and Lundberg, A. (2018). 'Olika rättsliga rum för en skälig levnadsnivå?: En rättskartografisk analys av SoL och LMA i domstolspraktiken', *Nordisk socialrättslig tidskrift*, 17–18: 39–71.
Kobelinsky, C. (2008). '" Faire sortir les déboutés". Gestion, contrôle et expulsion dans les centres pour demandeurs d'asile en France', *Cultures & Conflits*, 3(71): 113–130.
Koch, A. (2014). 'The Politics and Discourse of Migrant Return: The Role of UNHCR and IOM in the Governance of Return', *Journal of Ethnic and Migration Studies*, 40(6): 905–923.
Kotef, H. (2020). *The Colonizing Self: Home and Homelessness in Israel/Palestine*. Durham, NC: Duke University Press.
Kyrkans tidning. (2017). 'Fler Asylsökande Och Mindre Personal Oroar i Paris', *Kyrkans Tidning*.
Lagen. (1914). *angående förbud för visa utlänningar att här i riket vistas*, 196.

———. (2016). *om tillfälliga begränsningar i möjligheten att få uppehållstillstånd i Sverige*, 752.

Landscapes of Border Control. (n.d.) https://borderlandscapes.law.ox.ac.uk (accessed 24 May 2021).

Laszczkowski, M. and Reeves, M. (eds) (2017). *Affective States: Entanglements, Suspensions, Suspicions.* 1st edn. New York: Berghahn Books.

Lecadet, C. (2018). 'Deportation, Nation State, Capital: Between Legitimisation and Violence', *Radical Philosophy*, 2(3): 28–31.

Leerkes, A. (2016). 'Back to the Poorhouse? Social Protection and Social Control of Unauthorised Immigrants in the Shadow of the Welfare State', *Journal of European Social Policy*, 26(2): 140–154.

Leerkes, A., and Houte, M. V. (2020). 'Beyond the Deportation Regime: Differential State Interests and Capacities in Dealing with (Non-)Deportability in Europe', *Citizenship Studies*, 24(3): 319–338.

Leets Hansen, N. and Suárez-Krabbe, J. (2019). 'Introduction: Taking Racism Seriously', *KULT: Racism in Denmark*, 15: 1–10.

Lentin, R. and Moreo, E. (2015). 'Migrant Deportability: Israel and Ireland as Case Studies', *Ethnic and Racial Studies*, 38(6): 894–910.

Lietaert, I., Broekaert, E., and Derluyn, I. (2017). 'From Social Instrument to Migration Management Tool: Assisted Voluntary Return Programmes – The Case of Belgium', *Social Policy & Administration*, 51(7): 961–980.

Lindberg, A. (2020a). 'Minimum Rights Policies Targeting People Seeking Protection in Denmark and Sweden', in Abdelhady, D., Gren, N., and Joormann, M. (eds), *Refugees and the Violence of European Welfare Bureaucracies.* Manchester: Manchester University Press.

———. (2020b). 'In the Best Interest of Whom? Professional Humanitarians and Selfie Samaritans in the Danish Asylum Industry', in McGuirk, S. and Pine, A. (eds), *Profit, Protest, and the Asylum Industry.* San Francisco, CA: PM Press.

———. (2022). 'Feeling Difference: Race, Migration, and the Affective Infrastructure of a Danish Detention Camp', *Incarceration*, 3(1): 1–18.

Lindberg, A. and Borrelli, L. M. (2019). 'Let the Right One In? On European Migration Authorities' Resistance to Research', *Social Anthropology*, 27(S1): 17–32.

Lindberg, A. and Edward, S. (2021). 'Contested Dreams, Stolen Futures: Struggles over Hope in the European Deportation Regime', in Bhatia, M. and Canning, V. (eds), *Stealing Time: Migration, Temporality and Necropolitics.* London: Palgrave Macmillan, 83–104.

Lindberg, A. and Eule, T. G. (2020). 'Organisational Ethnography as a Project of Unease', *Journal of Organizational Ethnography*, 9(2): 237–247.

Lindberg, A. et al. (2017). 'Reclaiming the Right to Llife: Hunger Strikes and Protests in Denmark's Deportation Centres'. *OpenDemocracy.* www.opendemocracy.net/en/can-europe-make-it/reclaimi/ (accessed 11 August 2022).

Lindberg, A. et al. (2020). 'Detained and Disregarded: How COVID-19 has Affected Detained and Deportable Migrants in Sweden', *Border Criminologies Blog.* https://blogs.law.ox.ac.uk/research-subject-groups/centre-criminology/centreborder-criminologies/blog/2020/07/detained-and (accessed 11 August 2022).

Linddahl, M. (2019). 'Beboer på Kærshovedgård: Systemet gør mig kriminel', TV Midtvest.
Lipsky, M. (1980). *Street-Level Bureaucracy: Dilemmas of the Individual in Public Services*. New York: Russell Sage Foundation.
Loftsdóttir, K. and Jensen, L. (eds) (2012). *Whiteness and Postcolonialism in the Nordic Region: Exceptionalism, Migrant Others and National Identities*. Farnham: Ashgate.
Loyd, J., Mitchelson, M., and Burridge, A. (2012). *Beyond Walls and Cages: Geographies of Justice and Social Transformation*. Athens, GA: University of Georgia Press.
Lugones, M. (1994). 'Purity, Impurity, and Separation', *Signs*, 19(2): 458–479.
Luibhéid, E. (2013). *Pregnant on Arrival: Making the Illegal Immigrant*. Minneapolis, MN: University of Minnesota Press.
Lundberg, A. (2017). 'En kommentar till Sveriges krispolitik mot människor på flykt', *Tirsskrift for velferdsforskninge*, 4(20): 349–356.
Lundberg, A. et al. (2017). 'Anmälan mot Malmö stad och Polismyndigheten, Gränspolissektionen Syd avseende begäran och utlämnande av upptifter om personer med utvisningsbeslut november 2016 med stöd av 17 kap 1 § UlL och 10 kap 20 § OSL', *Malmö Högskola Blog*. https://blogg.mah.se/undocumentedmigrants/2017/04/28/jo-utlatande-som-delvis-stodjer-vart-argument/ (accessed 10 August 2022).
Macklin, A. (2018), 'The Return of Banishment: Do the New Denationalisation Policies Weaken Citizenship?', in Bauböck, R. (ed.), *Debating Transformations of National Citizenship*. IMISCOE Research Series, Cham: Springer International Publishing, 163–172.
Magnusson, E. and Mikkelsen, J. (2017). 'Elvaåring i Migrationsverkets förvar vädjar: Snälla, ta oss inte tillbaka till vårt land', *HD*, 29 August 2017.
Maillet, P., Mountz, A., and Williams, K. (2017). 'Researching Migration and Enforcement in Obscured Places: Practical, Ethical and Methodological Challenges to Fieldwork', *Social & Cultural Geography*, 18 (7): 927–950.
Mainwaring, C. and Silverman, S. (2017). 'Detention-as-Spectacle', *International Political Sociology*, 11(1): 21–38.
Majidi, N. (2017). *From Forced Migration to Forced Returns in Afghanistan: Policy and Program Implications*. Washington, DC: Migration Policy Institute.
Makaremi, C. (2018). 'Deportation and the Technification of Force: Violence in Democracy', *Technosphere Magazine*, 15 January 2018.
Malkki, L. H. (1995). 'Refugees and Exile: From "Refugee Studies" to the National Order of Things', *Annual Review of Anthropology*, 24: 495–523.
Malm Lindberg, H. (2020). *De som inte får stanna – Att implementera återvändandepolitik*, DELMI rapport 2020:1.
Marcus, G. (2000), 'Introduction', in Marcus, G. (ed.), *Para-Sites: A Casebook Against Cynical Reason*. Chicago, IL: University of Chicago Press, 1–15.
Martin, L. (2015). 'Deportation and the Dispossession of Time'. *darkmatter: in the ruins of imperial culture* 12(3).
Mayblin, L. (2019). 'Imagining Asylum, Governing Asylum Seekers: Complexity Reduction and Policy Making in the UK Home Office', *Migration Studies*, 7(1): 1–20.

Mayblin, L., Wake, M., and Kazemi, M. (2019). 'Necropolitics and the Slow Violence of the Everyday: Asylum Seeker Welfare in the Postcolonial Present', *Sociology*, 54(1): 107–123.

Mbembe, A. (2003). 'Necropolitics', *Public Culture*, 15(1): 11–40.

Menjívar, C. (2006). 'Liminal Legality: Salvadoran and Guatemalan Immigrants' Lives in the United States', *American Journal of Sociology*, 111(4): 999–1037.

Menjívar, C. and Abrego, L. J. (2012). 'Legal Violence: Immigration Law and the Lives of Central American Immigrants', *American Journal of Sociology*, 117(5): 1380–1421.

Meret, S. and Gregersen, A. B. (2019). 'Islam as "Floating Signifier": Right-Wing Populism and Perceptions of Muslims in Denmark', *The Brookings Institution*. www.brookings.edu/research/islam-as-a-floating-signifier-right-wing-populism-and-perceptions-of-muslims-in-denmark/ (accessed 11 August 2022).

Mezzadra, S. and Neilson, B. (2013). *Border as Method*. Durham, NC: Duke University Press.

Migrationsinfo. (2019). 'Hur många utvisades 2018?'. www.migrationsinfo.se/fragor-och-svar/hur-manga-kommer-utvisas-2017/#fnref-4058-1 (accessed 10 August 2022).

Migrationsverket. (2016). 'Rättsligt ställningstagande angående innebörden av rekvisitet "uppenbart oskäligt" i' 11 § i lagen (1994:137) om mottagande av asylsökande m.fl.' *SR 13/2016*.

———. (2020). 'Årsredovisning 2020'. Migrationsverket.

———. (2021). 'Årsredovisning 2021'. Migrationsverket.

Minor Keywords Collective. (2021). 'Minor Keywords of Political Theory: Migration as a Critical Standpoint', *Environment and Planning C: Politics and Space*, 40(4): 761–875.

Mongia, R. (2018). *Indian Migration and Empire: A Colonial Genealogy of the Modern State*. Durham, NC: Duke University Press.

Moraru, M. (2021). 'The New Design of the EU's Return System under the Pact on Asylum and Migration', *EU Immigration and Asylum Law and Policy*. https://eumigrationlawblog.eu/the-new-design-of-the-eus-return-system-under-the-pact-on-asylum-and-migration/ (accessed 10 August 2022).

Mountz, A. (2011). 'Where Asylum-Seekers Wait: Feminist Counter-Topographies of Sites between States', *Gender, Place & Culture*, 18(3): 381–399.

———. (2020). *The Death of Asylum: Hidden Geographies of the Enforcement Archipelago*. Minneapolis, MN: University of Minnesota Press.

Mountz, A., and Hiemstra, N. (2014). 'Chaos and Crisis: Dissecting the Spatiotemporal Logics of Contemporary Migrations and State Practices', *Annals of the Association of American Geographers*, 104(2), 382–390.

Mountz, A. et al. (2013). 'Conceptualizing Detention: Mobility, Containment, Bordering, and Exclusion', *Progress in Human Geography*, 37(4): 522–541.

Mulinari, D. and Neergaard, A. (2017). 'Theorising Racism: Exploring the Swedish Racial Regime', *Nordic Journal of Migration Research*, 7(2): 88–96.

Mulinari, L. S. and Keskinen, S. (2020). 'Racial Profiling in the Racial Welfare State: Examining the Order of Policing in the Nordic Region', *Theoretical Criminology*, 26(3): 337–395.

Mutsaers, P. (2015). *A Public Anthropology of Policing: Law Enforcement and Migrants in the Netherlands*. Netherlands: Politie.
Nader, L. (1972). 'Up the Anthropologist: Perspectives Gained from Studying Up', in Hymns, D. (ed.), *Reinventing Anthropology*. New York: Random House, 284–311.
Nafstad, I. and Parsa, A. (2020). 'Alternativet till dagens rasistiska polisarbete: nedmontera polisen!' *Sydsvenskan*. www.sydsvenskan.se/2020-07-18/alternativet-till-dagens-rasistiska-polisarbete-nedmontera-polisen (accessed 9 August 2022).
Nationalt Udlændingecenter. (2018). 'Status på udsendelse af udlændinge af Danmark'.
Ngai, S. (2005). *Ugly Feelings*. London and Cambridge, MA: Harvard University Press.
Nordjyske. (2018). 'Udrejsecenter sender flere ud i samfundet end ud af landet', *Nordjyske Nyheder*.
Nordling, V. (2017). *Destabilising Citizenship Practices? Social Work and Undocumented Migrants in Sweden*. Lund: Lund University.
Nordling, V. and Persdotter, M (2021). 'Bordering Through Destitution: The Case of Social Assistance to Irregularised Migrants in Malmö, Sweden', *Nordic Social Work Research*, 11(2): 155–168.
Nyers, P. (2003). 'Abject Cosmopolitanism: The Politics of Protection in the Anti-Deportation Movement', *Third World Quarterly*, 24(6): 1069–1093.
———. (2019) *Irregular Citizenship, Immigration, and Deportation*. London: Routledge.
Olivarius, L. (2013). 'Sultestrejkens år', *VisAvis*, 8: 84–89.
Paik, N. (2021). 'Create a Different Language: Behrouz Boochani and Omid Tofighian', *Public Books*. www.publicbooks.org/create-a-different-language-behrouz-boochani-omid-tofighian/ (accessed 11 August 2022).
Paoletti, E. (2010). 'Deportation, Non-Deportability and Ideas of Membership', *Refugees Studies Centre*, Working Paper Series, (65): 1–28.
Parmar, A. (2019). 'Policing Migration and Racial Technologies', *The British Journal of Criminology*, 59(4): 938–957.
Parusel, B. (2016). 'Sweden's U-Turn on Asylum', *Forced Migration Review*.
Peutz, N. (2006). 'Embarking on an Anthropology of Removal', *Current Anthropology*, 47(2): 217–241.
Peutz, N. and De Genova, N. (2010), 'Introduction', in De Genova, N. and Peutz, N. (eds), *The Deportation Regime: Sovereignty, Space, and the Freedom of Movement*. Durham, NC: Duke University Press.
Polisen. (2019). *Polisens årsredovisning 2018*. https://polisen.se/aktuellt/publikationer/?requestId=0&lpfm.cat=454 (accessed 11 August 2022).
Povinelli, E. (2011). *Economies of Abandonment: Social Belonging and Endurance in Late Liberalism*. Durham, NC: Duke University Press.
Prop. 1996/97:147 Ändring I utlänningslagens förvarsbestämmelser.
Prop. 2010/11:1 Utgiftsområde 8 Migration.
Prop. 2015/16:146 Extra ändringsbudget för 2016 – Ändring av rätten till bistånd för vissa utlänningar.
Prop. 2017/18:1 Utgiftsområde Migration.

Prop. 2018/19:1 Utgiftsområde Migration.
Prop. 2019/20:10 Ett socialt hållbart eget boende för asylsökande.
Pugliese, J. (2008). 'The Tutelary Architecture of Immigration Detention Prisons and the Spectacle of "Necessary Suffering"', *Architectural Theory Review*, 13(2): 206–221.
Puthoopparambil, S. J., Ahlberg, B., and Bjerneld, M. (2015). '"It Is a Thin Line to Walk On": Challenges of Staff Working at Swedish Immigration Detention Centres', *International Journal of Qualitative Studies on Health and Well-Being*, 10: 251–296.
Rajaram, P. K. and Grundy-Warr, C. (eds) (2007). *Borderscapes: Hidden Geographies and Politics at Territory Edge*. New edn. Minneapolis, MN: University of Minnesota Press.
Ramsay, G. (2019). 'Humanitarian Exploits: Ordinary Displacement and the Political Economy of the Global Refugee Regime', *Critique of Anthropology*, 39(4): 3–27.
Red Cross. (2018). 'Rapporten Barn i förvar'. *Svenska Röda Korset*.
———. (2019). 'Trivsel hos børn på Udrejsecenter Sjælsmark'. *Danske Røde Kors*.
Reguera, E., and Mahmoud, A. (2020). 'Nya regler kan sätta stop för asyldrömmarna', *Dagens Nyheter*, 23 September 2020. www.dn.se/varlden/nya-regler-kan-satta-stopp-for-asyldrommarna/ (accessed 20 May 2021).
Return Agency. (n.d.). 'About Us'. www.eng.hjemst.dk/about-us/ (accessed 30 September 2022).
Rigo, E. (2005). 'Citizenship at Europe's Borders: Some Reflections on the Post-Colonial Condition of Europe in the Context of EU Enlargement', *Citizenship Studies*, 9(1): 3–22.
———. (2018). 'Migration, Knowledge Production and the Humanitarian Agenda in Times of Crisis', *Journal of Modern Italian Studies*, 23(4): 507–521.
Robbins, J. (2013). 'Beyond the Suffering Subject: Toward an Anthropology of the Good', *Journal of the Royal Anthropological Institute*, 19(3): 447–462.
Rodríguez, E.G. (2018). 'The Coloniality of Migration and the "Refugee Crisis": On the Asylum-Migration Nexus, the Transatlantic White European Settler Colonialism-Migration and Racial Capitalism', *Refuge: Canada's Journal on Refugees*, 34(1): 16–28.
Rosenberger, S. and Koppes, R. (2018). 'Claiming Control: Cooperation with Return as a Condition for Social Benefits in Austria and the Netherlands', *Comparative Migration Studies*, 6(26): 1–18.
Rosenberger, S. and Küffner, C. (2016). 'After the Deportation Gap: Non-Removed Persons and Their Pathways to Social Rights', in Hsu, R. and Reinprecht, C. (eds), *Migration and Integration. New Models for Mobility and Coexistence*. Vienna: Vienna University Press, 9–28.
Rozakou, K. (2012). 'The Biopolitics of Hospitality in Greece: Humanitarianism and the Management of Refugees', *American Ethnologist*, 39(3): 562–577.
———. (2019). '"How Did You Get In?" Research Access and Sovereign Power During the "Migration Crisis" in Greece', *Social Anthropology*, 27(S1), 68–83.
Rygiel, K. (2011). 'Bordering Solidarities: Migrant Activism and the Politics of Movement and Camps at Calais', *Citizenship Studies*, 15(1): 1–19.

Rytter, M. (2018) 'Writing Against Integration: Danish Imaginaries of Culture, Race and Belonging', *Ethnos*, 84(4): 678–697.
Rytter, M. and N. Ghandchi. (2019). 'Integration via arbejde: Prekær inklusion o gudvidet usikkerhed blandt afghanske flygtninge', *Social Kritik*, 160: 4–17.
Sager, M. (2011). *Everyday Clandestinity: Experiences on the Margins of Citizenship and Migration Policies*. Lund: Lund University.
———. (2016). 'Constructions of Deportability in Sweden. Refused Asylum Seekers' Experiences in Relation to Gender, Family Life, and Reproduction', *NORA – Nordic Journal of Feminist and Gender Research*, 24(1): 30–44.
Sager, M. and Öberg, K. (2017). 'Articulations of Deportability. Changing Migration Policies in Sweden 2015/16', *Refugee Review*, 3: 2–14.
Samaddar, R. (2020). *The Postcolonial Age of Migration*. New Delhi: Routledge.
Sanchez Boe, C. (forthcoming). *The Undeported: The Making of a Floating Population of Exiles in France and Europe*. Lanham, MD: Rowman & Littlefield.
Sassen, S. (1996). *Losing Control: Sovereignty in an Age of Globalization*. University seminars/Leonard Hastings Schnoff memorial lectures. New York: Columbia University Press.
Scheper-Hughes, N. and Bourgeois, P. (eds) (2003). *Violence in War and Peace: An Anthology*. Malden, MA: Wiley-Blackwell.
Schibbye, M. (2019). 'Flykten från Sverige'. *Blankspot*. https://blankspot.se/flykten-fran-sverige/ (accessed 10 August 2022).
Schierup, C. U. and Ålund, A. (2011). 'The End of Swedish Exceptionalism? Citizenship, Neoliberalism and the Politics of Exclusion', *Race & Class*, 53(1): 45–64.
Schierup, C. U., Ålund, A., and Neergaard, A. (2018). '"Race" and the Upsurge of Antagonistic Popular Movements in Sweden', *Ethnic and Racial Studies*, 41(10): 1837–1854.
Schmidt, G. (2021). 'Boundary Work: Investigating the Expert Role of Danish Migration Researcher', *Identities*, 28(5): 543–560.
Schmid-Scott, A. (2018). 'Thresholds to Precarity: Reporting Practices at Patchway', *Society & Space*.
Schultz, J. (2020). 'The End of Protection? Cessation and the "Return Turn" in Refugee Law', *Norwegian Centre for Humanitarian Studies Blog*. www.cmi.no/publications/7097-the-end-of-protection-cessation-and-the-return-turn-in-refugee-law (accessed 10 August 2022).
Schuster, L. (2005). 'A Sledgehammer to Crack a Nut: Deportation, Detention and Dispersal in Europe', *Social Policy & Administration*, 39(6): 606–621.
———. (2011). 'Dublin II and Eurodac: Examining the (Un)Intended(?) Consequences', *Gender, Place and Culture*, 18: 401–416.
Schuster, L. and Majidi, N. (2015). 'Deportation Stigma and Re-Migration', *Journal of Ethnic and Migration Studies*, 41(4): 635–652.
Sellin, B. (2018). 'Migrationsverket: "Syftet har inte uppnåtts"'. *SVT Nyheter*. www.svt.se/nyheter/lokalt/vasternorrland/migrationsverket-syftet-har-inte-uppnatts (accessed 31 March 2022).

SFS 2017:578. Lag om ändring I lagen (1994:137). om mottagande av asylsökande m.fl.

Sharma, N. (2021). 'States and Human Immobilization: Bridging the Conceptual Separation of Slavery, Immigration Controls, and Mass Incarceration', *Citizenship Studies*, 25(2): 166–187.

Sigona, N. (2012). 'Deportation, Non-Deportation and Precarious Lives: The Everyday Lives of Undocumented Migrant Children in Britain', *Anthropology Today*, 28(5): 22–23.

Simpson, A. (2008). 'On Ethnographic Refusal: Indigeneity, "Voice", and Colonial Citizenship', *Junctures*, 9: 67–80.

Skærbæk, M. (2016). 'Derfor vil Støjberg gøre livet utåleligt for folk på tålt ophold', *Politiken*. https://politiken.dk/indland/politik/art5624990/Derfor-vil-St%C3%B8jberg-g%C3%B8re-livet-ut%C3%A5leligt-for-folk-p%C3%A5-t%C3%A5lt-ophold (accessed 11 August 2022).

Skodo, A. (2020). 'Lesson for the Future or Threat to Sovereignty? Contesting the Meaning of the 2015 Refugee Crisis in Sweden', in Abdelhady, D., Gren, N., and Joormann, M. (eds), *Refugees and the Violence of Welfare Bureaucracies in Northern Europe*. Manchester: Manchester University Press, 50–67.

Sliva, S. M. and Samimi, C. (2018). 'Social Work and Prison Labor: A Restorative Model, *Social Work*, 63(2): 153–160.

Slominski, P. and Trauner, F. (2018). 'How Do Member States Return Unwanted Migrants? The Strategic (Non-)Use of "Europe" during the Migration Crisis', *JCMS: Journal of Common Market Studies*, 56(1): 101–118.

Social Services Act 2001:453. www.ilo.org/dyn/natlex/natlex4.detail?p_isn=60673#:~:text=Provides%20for%20regulations%20regarding%20the,and%20active%20participation%20in%20society (accessed 30 September 2022).

SOU 2017:84. *Uppehållstillstånd på grund av praktiska verkställighetshinder och preskription*.

SOU 2018:22. *Ett ordnat mottagande – gemensamt ansvar för snabb etablering eller återvändande*.

Spencer, S. (2016). 'Postcode Lottery for Europe's Undocumented Children: Unravelling an Uneven Geography of Entitlements in the European Union', *American Behavioral Scientist*, 60(13): 1613–1628.

Spivak, G. C. (1988). 'Can the Subaltern Speak?', in Nelson, C. and Grossberg, L. (eds), *Marxism and the Interpretation of Culture*. Champaign, IL: University of Illinois Press, 21–78.

Squire, V. (2017). 'Unauthorised Migration beyond Structure/Agency? Acts, Interventions, Effects', *Politics*, 37(3): 254–272.

Statewatch. (2020). *Deportation Union: Rights, Accountability and the EU's Push to Increase Forced Removals*. www.statewatch.org/deportation-union-rights-accountability-and-the-eu-s-push-to-increase-forced-removals/ (accessed 10 August 2022).

———. (2022). *Building the Biometric State: Police Powers and Discrimination*. Statewatch. www.statewatch.org/publications/reports-and-books/building-the-biometric-state-police-powers-and-discrimination/ (accessed 10 August 2022).

Stel, N. (2020). *Hybrid Political Order and the Politics of Uncertainty: Refugee Governance in Lebanon*. New York: Routledge.

Stern, R. (2014). '"Our Refugee Policy Is Generous": Reflections on the Importance of a State's Self-Image', *Refugee Survey Quarterly*, 33(1): 25–43.

———. (2017). *'We Have Reached Our Limit': On Sweden's Response to the 2015 'Refugee Crisis' and Its Parallels with Recent History*. Rochester, NY: Social Science Research Network. SSRN Scholarly Paper. https://papers.ssrn.com/abstract=3025545 (accessed 10 August 2022).

Stokholm, J. et al. (2021). 'Restoring the Right to Breathe: Migration Detention Must End', *AlJazeera Opinion*. www.aljazeera.com/opinions/2021/3/22/restoring-the-right-to-breathe-migration-detention-must-end (accessed 10 August 2022).

Stoler, A. L. (2004). 'Affective States', in Nugent, D. and Vincent, J. (eds), *A Companion to the Anthropology of Politics*. Oxford: Blackwell, 4–29.

Strange, M., Squire, V., and Lundberg, A. (2017). 'Irregular Migration Struggles and Active Subjects of Trans-Border Politics: New Research Strategies for Interrogating the Agency of the Marginalised', *Politics*, 37(3): 243–253.

Stumpf, J. (2006). 'The Crimmigration Crisis: Immigrants, Crime, & Sovereign Power', *bepress Legal Series*. Working Paper 1635.

Suárez-Krabbe, J. (2022). 'Relinking as Healing: On Crisis, Whiteness and the Existential Dimensions of Decolonization', *Globalizations*. DOI: 10.1080/14747731.2021.2025293.

Suárez-Krabbe, J. and Lindberg, A. (2019). 'Enforcing Apartheid? The Politics of 'Intolerability' in the Danish Migration and Integration Regimes', *Migration and Society*, 2(1): 90–97.

Sutton, R. and Vigneswaran, D. (2011). 'A Kafkaesque State: Deportation and Detention in South Africa', *Citizenship Studies*, 15(5): 627–642.

Sveriges Riksdag. (2017). Interpellation 2017/18:239 om Förändring av EBO-lagen.

SVT Nyheter. (2016). 'Ygeman: Uppemot 80.000 asylsökande kan utvisas'. svt.se/nyheter/inrikes/tiotusentals-asylsokande-ska-avvisas (accessed 21 May 2020).

Swedish Government. (2015). 'Regeringen föreslår åtgärder för att skapa andrum för svenskt flyktingmottagande'. www.regeringen.se/artiklar/2015/11/regeringen-foreslar-atgarder-for-att-skapa-andrum-for-svenskt-flyktingmottagande/ (accessed 20 May 2021).

Syppli-Kohl, K. (2015). 'Asylaktivering og Ambivalens: Forvaltningen af asylansøgere på asylcentre', PhD-afhandling, Det Samfundsvidenskabelige Fakultet, Københavns Universitet.

Taussig, M. (1997). *The Magic of the State*. New York: Routledge.

Tazzioli, M. (2019). 'Governing Migrant Mobility through Mobility: Containment and Dispersal at the Internal Frontiers of Europe', *Environment and Planning C: Politics and Space*, 38(1): 3–19.

———. (2020). 'Disjointed Knowledges, Obfuscated Visibility. Border Controls at the French-Italian Alpine Border', *Political Geography*, 79. https://doi.org/10.1016/j.polgeo.2020.102155.

Tazzioli, M. and Garelli, G. (2018). 'Containment beyond Detention: The Hotspot System and Disrupted Migration Movements across Europe', *Environment and Planning D: Society and Space*, 38(6): 1009–1027. https://doi.org/10.1177/0263775818759335.

Tazzioli, M. and Stierl, M. (2021). 'Europe's Unsafe Environment: Migrant Confinement under Covid-19', *Critical Studies on Security*, 9(1): 76–80. https://doi.org/10.1080/21624887.2021.1904365.

Tervonen, M., Pellander, S., and Yuval-Davis, N. (2018). 'Everyday Bordering in the Nordic Countries', *Nordic Journal of Migration Research*, 8(3): 139–142.

Thompson, D. F. (1980). 'Moral Responsibility of Public Officials: The Problem of Many Hands', *American Political Science Review*, 74(4): 905–916.

Ticktin, M. (2015). 'The Problem with Humanitarian Borders: Toward a New Framework for Justice'. *Public Seminar*. https://publicseminar.org/2015/09/the-problem-with-humanitarian-borders/ (accessed 10 August 2022).

Torbenfeldt Bengtsson, T. (2012). 'Boredom and Action – Experiences from Youth Confinement', *Journal of Contemporray Ethnography*, 41(5): 526–553.

Triandafyllidou, A. and Ambrosini, M. (2011). 'Irregular Immigration Control in Italy and Greece: Strong Fencing and Weak Gate-Keeping Serving the Labour Market', *European Journal of Migration and Law*, 13(3): 251–273.

Trouillot, M. R. (2001). 'Anthropology of the State in the Age of Globalization: Close Encounters of the Deceptive Kind, *Current Anthropology*, 42(1): 125–138.

Tsianos, V. and Karakayali, S. (2010). 'Transnational Migration and the Emergence of the European Border Regime: An Ethnographic Analysis', *European Journal of Social Theory*, 13 (3): 373–387.

Tuck, E. and Yang, K. W. (2014). 'R-Words: Refusing Research', in Paris, D. and Winn, M. T. (eds), *Humanizing Research: Decolonizing Qualitative Inquiry with youth and Communities*. Thousand Oaks, CA: Sage Publications.

Tudor, A. (2017). 'Cross-Fadings of Racialisation and Migrantisation: The Postcolonial Turn in Western European Gender and Migration Studies', *Gender, Place and Culture*, 25(7): 1057–1072.

Turnbull, S. (2015). 'Is It Ethical to Carry Keys for Research in Immigration Detention Centres?'. *Border Criminologies Blog*. https://blogs.law.ox.ac.uk/research-subject-groups/centre-criminology/centreborder-criminologies/blog/2015/02/it-ethical-carry (accessed 10 August 2022).

———. (2018). 'Living the Spectre of Forced Return: Negotiating Deportability in British Immigration Detention', *Migration Studies*, 7(4): 513–532.

UNAMA. (2019). 'The Situation in Afghanistan and Its Implications for International Peace and Security'. 26 February 2019.

United Nations Committee Against Torture. (2016). 'Convention against Torture and Other Cruel, Inhuman or Degrading Treatment or Punishment: Concluding Observations on the Combined Sixth and Seventh Periodic Reports of Denmark'. https://digitallibrary.un.org/record/857890?ln=en (accessed 10 August 2022).

United Nations High Commissioner for Human Rights. (2020). 'Covid-19 Guidance'. www.ohchr.org/en/covid-19/covid-19-guidance (accessed 8 April 2022).

UN News. (2020). 'UN Rights Chief Urges Quick Action by Governments to Prevent Devastating Impact of COVID-19 in Places of Detention'. *UN News*. https://news.un.org/en/story/2020/03/1060252 (accessed 11 August 2022).

Valenta, M. and Thorshaug, K. (2011). 'Failed Asylum-Seekers' Responses to Arrangements Promoting Return: Experiences from Norway', *Refugee Survey Quarterly*, 30(2): 1–23.

Van der Leun, J. and Bouter, H. (2015). 'Gimme Shelter: Inclusion and Exclusion of Irregular Immigrants in Dutch Civil Society', *Journal of Immigrant & Refugee Studies*, 13(2): 135–155.

Van der Woude, M. and van der Leun, J. (2017). 'Crimmigration Checks in the Internal Border Areas of the EU: Finding the Discretion That Matters', *European Journal of Criminology*, 14(1): 27–45.

Van Liempt, I. et al. (2018). 'Evidence-Based Assessment of Migration Deals: The Case of the EU-Turkey Statement'. Utrecht University.

Vanyoro, K., Hadj-Abdou, L., and Dempster, H. (2019). 'Migration Studies: From Dehumanising to Decolonising'. *LSE Blog*. https://blogs.lse.ac.uk/highereducation/2019/07/19/migration-studies-from-dehumanising-to-decolonising/ (accessed 11 August 2022).

Vedsted-Hansen, J. (2017). 'Udlændingerettens grundbegreber, retskilder og myndighedsstruktur', in Dilou Jacobsen, B. et al. (eds), *Udlændingeret: Indrejse, Visum, Asyl, Familiesammenføring* (Vol. 1). Copenhagen: Jurist- og Økonomforbundets Forlag, 17–38.

VisAvis. (2020). 'Avnstrup on strike: Eight problems and demands'. www.visavis.dk/2020/10/avnstrup-on-strike/ (accessed 20 September 2022).

Vistårinteut. (n.d.). vistarinteut.org (accessed 20 April 2021).

Von Werthern, M. et al. (2018). 'The Impact of Immigration Detention on Mental Health: A Systematic Review', *BMC Psychiatry*, 18(1): 382.

Vrăbiescu, I. (2019). 'The State Riddle: Working through Messiness alongside a Shared Deportation Apparatus in France and Romania', *Social Anthropology*, 27(S1): 33–48.

Vuorela, U. (2009). 'Colonial Complicity: The "Postcolonial" in a Nordic Context', in Keskinen, S. (ed.), *Complying with Colonialism: Gender, Race and Ethnicity in the Nordic Region*. London: Routledge, 19–33.

Wagner, I. and Finkielsztein, M. (2021). 'Strategic Boredom: The Experience and Dynamics of Boredom in Refugee Camp. A Mediterranean Case', *Journal of Contemporary Ethnography*, 50(5): 649–682. https://doi.org/10.1177/08912416211008525.

Wajsberg, M. (2021). 'Following Fatigue, Feeling Fatigue: A Reflexive Ethnography of Emotion', *Social Inclusion*, 8(4): 126–135.

Walia, H. (2021). *Border and Rule: Global Migration, Capitalism, and the Rise of Racist Nationalism*. Chico, CA: AK Press.

Walters, W. (2002). 'Deportation, Expulsion, and the International Police of Aliens', *Citizenship Studies*, 6(3): 265–292.

———. (2015). 'Expulsion, Power, Mobilisation', *Radical Philosophy*. www.radicalphilosophy.com/article/expulsion-power-mobilisation (accessed 11 August 2022).

———. (2016). 'The Flight of the Deported: Aircraft, Deportation, and Politics', *Geopolitics*, 21(2): 435–458.

———. (2019). *The Microphysics of Deportation: A Critical Reading of Return Flight Monitoring Reports*. Proceedings of the 2018 ZiF Workshop 'Studying Migration Policies at the Interface Between Empirical Research and Normative Analysis'. PhilArchive copy v1: https://philarchive.org/archive/WALTMO-41v1 (accessed 11 August 2022).

Webber, F. (2011). 'How Voluntary Are Voluntary Returns?', *Race & Class*, 52(4): 98–107.

Weber, L. et al. (2019). 'Beyond Deportation: Researching the Control of Outward Mobility Using a Space of Flows Logic', *Global Networks*, 20(1): 65–84. https://doi.org/10.1111/glob.12226.

Weil, S. (1939). 'l'Illiade, ou le poème de la force', in *Œuvres*. Paris: Quarto Gallimard, 1999, 529–530; 'The "Iliad", or the Poem of Force', trans. Mary McCarthy, first published in English in *Politics*, 1945.

Wekker, G. (2016). *White Innocence: Paradoxes of Colonialism and Race*. Durham: Duke University Press.

———. (2021). 'White Innocence: Race and Cherished Self-Narratives in the Netherlands', Keynote Delivered at the Nordic Migration Research Conference, 12 January 2021.

Wernesjö, U. (2019). 'Across the Threshold: Negotiations of Deservingness among Unaccompanied Young Refugees in Sweden', *Journal of Ethnic and Migration Studies*, 46(2): 389–404.

Wettergren, Å. (2010). 'Managing Unlawful Feelings: The Emotional Regime of the Swedish Migration Board', *International Journal of Work Organisation and Emotion*, 3(4): 400.

Whyte, Z. (2011). 'Enter the Myopticon: Uncertain Surveillance in the Danish Asylum System', *Anthropology Today*, 27(3): 18–21.

Whyte, Z., Campbell, R., and Overgaard, H. (2020). 'Paradoxical Infrastructures of Asylum: Notes on the Rise and Fall of Tent Camps in Denmark', *Migration Studies*, 8(2): 143–160.

Williams, J. M. (2015). 'From Humanitarian Exceptionalism to Contingent Care: Care and Enforcement at the Humanitarian Border', *Political Geography*, 47: 11–20.

Wimmer, A. and Glick Schiller, N. (2002). 'Methodological Nationalism and Beyond: Nation-state Building, Migration and the Social Sciences', *Global Networks*, 2(4): 113–133, 301–334.

Wyss, A. (2019). 'Stuck in Mobility? The Interrupted Journeys of Migrants with Precarious Legal Status in Europe', *Journal of Immigrant and Refugee Studies*, 16(1): 77–93.

———. (forthcoming). *Interrupted Journeys, Disrupted Control: Male Migrants in Europe*. Bristol: Bristol University Press.

Zhang, C. (2020). 'The Epistemic Production of "Non-Western Immigrants" in Denmark', *The Disorder of Things*. https://thedisorderofthings.com/2020/09/30/the-epistemic-production-of-non-western-immigrants-in-denmark/ (accessed 9 August 2022).

Index

abandonment 5, 10, 14–15, 23, 36, 95, 118, 127, 129, 132, 138, 142
  see also destitution; exhaustion, politics of exhaustion
abolitionist(s) 16, 42, 149
absurdity
  absurd 9, 51, 128, 140, 146
Act (1994: 137) *on the reception of asylum seekers and others* 117
  LMA 119, 122, 124–131, 139
  see also asylum, asylum reception
activation 52–53, 105, 116
activist(s) 7, 9, 14–15, 44, 64, 82, 90, 94, 108, 109, 111, 136
  see also Castaway Souls; struggle(s) against deportations; Young in Sweden
activities 2, 39, 43, 48, 52, 77–78, 97, 101, 104–106, 109, 113, 116
Afghanistan 43, 75, 132–139, 143
  Afghan citizens 132–136
  Afghan government 12
Arendt, H. 63, 82–84, 90
  see also banality of evil
asylum
  asylum application(s) 1, 2, 8, 10, 17, 25, 31, 36, 39, 94, 96, 100, 107, 117–119, 124–125, 128, 130, 131, 134–135, 138
  rejected asylum application 8, 39, 100, 125
  asylum camp(s) 3, 30, 31, 39, 65, 96, 98, 105–106, 111
  asylum case(s) 3, 32, 37, 58, 67, 69, 96–97, 100, 110, 113, 129

asylum caseworker 17, 120
asylum law(s) 10, 31, 34, 38, 96, 113, 134, 136, 139
asylum (and migration) policy 27, 29, 33–35, 114
asylum reception 27, 31, 35, 117
  see also Act (1994: 137) *on the reception of asylum seekers and others*, LMA
people seeking asylum 29, 30, 94, 124, 142
  see also liminal legality
Asylum Reception Directive 95
Avnstrup 9, 96–98, 100, 104, 106, 108–109, 112–113, 154

banality of evil 82–84
  see also Arendt, H.
Boochani, B. 5, 10, 45, 58, 89, 110, 149, 152
border(s)
  border controls 5, 35–36, 46
  border crosser(s) 11, 16, 18, 19, 41, 64
  border enforcement 99, 147
  border guard(s) 50, 53, 63
  border industrial complex 10
  border police 13, 67, 123, 131, 139, 154
  border regime(s) 16, 18, 27, 37, 41, 81, 84, 105, 129, 141, 148–149, 151, 158
  border (and migration) research 18, 144–149
  border violence 16, 89, 148

Index

border zones 10, 143
internal bordering 18, 30, 40–41, 129, 144
boredom 58–59
see also waiting
Borrelli, L. M. 5, 6, 18, 22, 38, 58, 77, 80, 118, 153, 157–158
bureaucracy
bureaucratic inscription 38–39, 127, 132
bureaucratic violence 63, 90
'many hands' of bureaucracy 82
street-level bureaucrats 18, 157
see also frontline workers

care
care and compassion 69, 72, 87
care and control 21, 95, 126
see also seeing
cruel care 110
Castaway Souls 11, 15, 21, 94, 111
see also activist(s); struggle(s) against deportations
citizenship
anti-citizen 34
non-citizen(s) 5, 16, 26
racialised citizen(s) 26, 144–145
technology/ies of citizenship 6, 141, 144
civil society 107, 112, 117, 126–127, 131–134, 138
colonialism 19, 26, 140
colonial complicities 37
coloniality
of knowledge 19
modernity/coloniality 145–146
colour-blindness 39, 42, 57
see also Nordic exceptionalism
confinement
architecture(s) of confinement 72
de facto confinement 94, 97
see also Kærshovedgård
solitary confinement 57, 61–62, 65, 79, 86, 89, 92
violence of confinement 57, 81, 89
contestation(s) 1, 5, 8, 10, 69, 94, 113, 138, 142
continuum of (state) violence 13–16, 23, 140, 158
see also violence
Coutin, S. 4–8, 140, 148
COVID-19 11–13, 15, 48, 91, 126, 156

sanitary mobility apartheid 12
criminalisation 9, 23, 27, 31, 44, 49, 64, 98, 100, 108–111, 141, 145

Danish immigration authorities 25, 28, 29, 47, 96
Danish Immigration Agency/Service 48, 154
Refugee Appeals Board 29, 32
Return Agency 31, 51, 96, 104, 153
De Genova, N. 6, 8–10, 29, 118
dehumanisation 5, 16, 17, 19, 45, 53, 57, 62–64, 84, 90, 98–99, 111, 147, 158
deportability 5, 8, 29, 32, 111, 113, 124, 132
deportable 7, 12, 14, 20, 32, 34, 39, 49, 63, 123, 132, 143, 147
non-deportability 9, 11, 124, 127
non-deportable 12, 98, 118
deportation
deportation gap 4, 8
deportation order 3, 8, 17, 33, 39, 47, 67, 88, 91, 97, 105, 107, 110, 113, 117, 118, 120–122, 125, 139
deportation process 8, 13–14, 44, 51, 65, 69, 73–75, 77, 78, 91, 97, 102, 116, 118–119, 122, 123, 125, 133, 154
deportation regime(s) 6, 7, 9, 14, 18, 21, 23, 46, 51, 62, 70, 82, 104, 106, 112, 113, 115, 123, 133, 136, 151
deportation studies 6, 148
deportation turn 7, 26
see also expulsion; voluntary return
deportspora 5, 143
derecording 23, 118, 125, 127, 132, 137
deservingness 129, 131, 133, 137, 144
see also vulnerability
destitution 4, 9, 10, 16, 117, 124, 126, 127, 129, 139, 146
see also abandonment; exhaustion, politics of exhaustion
deterrence 31, 32, 100, 124, 126–127, 134, 137–138, 142
see also motivation enhancement measures

Index

displacement 4, 6, 8, 34, 46, 73, 145
  in law and policy 34, 131, 137
Dublin Regulation 7, 24, 27, 51, 75, 96, 125, 134–136

egalitarianism 5, 17, 26, 34, 38, 40–41
Ellebæk deportation prison 43, 46, 63, 64, 69, 154
  see also incarceration; migration, migration-related detention
emotions 78, 82, 156–158
  racial emotions 56
epistemology
  epistemic complicity 157
  epistemic violence 18, 158
ethics 18, 66, 151, 156
ethnography
  patchwork ethnography 20–21
  political ethnography 5, 17–19, 142
Europe 5, 7, 8, 12, 23–25, 27, 30, 33, 40, 107, 108, 114–115, 129, 134, 136, 137, 142, 145
  European Union 24
    European Commission 6, 7, 24
    New Pact on Asylum and Migration 7
  European Commissioner for Human Rights 12, 126, 131
  European Convention of Human Rights (ECHR) 24, 95, 139
exclusion 25–26, 34–38, 84, 99, 100, 113, 131, 138, 141–142
  bureaucratic exclusion 38–40
  exclusion from welfare 125–127
  inclusive exclusion 39
exhaustion 118, 127, 137, 156
  politics of exhaustion 127, 136
  see also abandonment; destitution
expulsion 4, 9, 41, 44, 58, 64, 73, 84, 88, 118, 142, 146
  see also deportation

fantasy/fantasies 4, 7–10, 19, 32, 56, 74, 75, 99, 102, 140, 142, 150
force
  coercive force 36, 75, 81, 95, 122, 123
  force of law 120–121
frontline workers 5, 18, 20
  caseworker(s) 17, 74–76, 117, 122
    return caseworker 126, 131, 140, 148

migration official(s) 5, 23, 122–123, 130–131, 134–136, 154
police officer(s) 5, 13, 20–21, 26, 51, 59, 62, 91, 123, 131, 154
social worker(s) 5, 20–21, 102, 129, 130–131, 137, 154
  see also bureaucracy; street-level bureaucrats
future(s) 29, 31, 74, 108–110, 113–114, 132–133, 135, 152

gatekeeping 40
gender 8, 20–21, 53, 131, 141
  gender studies 42
Gilmore, R. W. 5, 16, 41, 145, 149
Goldberg, D. T. 26, 37, 41, 84
Gordon, A. 113, 146

harmonisation 7, 27, 136
healthcare
  access to healthcare 10, 39
  emergency healthcare 104, 110
hope(s) 74, 105, 109–110, 114, 120, 133–134, 136
hostile hospitality 72
humanitarianism 17, 26, 35, 37, 69, 89, 123
  humane and dignified 69–70
  humanitarian actors 21, 104
    see also Red Cross
  humanitarian minimum 106, 126
  humanitarian values 36
  see also Nordic exceptionalism
human rights 8, 31–33, 35, 39, 70, 73, 127, 146
  human rights conventions 29, 95, 108
  human rights organisations 15, 100
  Universal Declaration of Human Rights 138

ignorance 146, 158
illegalisation 19, 145
  illegalised 5, 8, 88, 136
incarceration 5, 9, 15, 16, 38, 45, 47, 48, 58–59, 69, 71, 75, 80, 87–89, 95, 96, 129, 142, 145–146
  see also Ellebæk deportation prison; migration, migration-related detention
indifference 17, 63, 118
individualisation 63, 90

Index

infrastructure(s)
   infrastructures of deterrence 32
   infrastructures of intolerability 95
   infrastructures of racism 6, 16, 64
integration 29–30, 33, 37–38
interview(s) 20–21, 39, 94, 131, 154–155
   asylum interview 17, 134
intolerability
   intolerability regime 104, 107, 109–111, 113
   intolerable 1, 5, 32, 39, 95, 102, 104, 106, 108, 110, 151

Kærshovedgård 93, 96–100, 110, 112, 113, 116, 154
   see also confinement, *de facto* confinement; Sjælsmark deportation camp
Khosravi, S. 5, 6, 11, 16, 19, 22, 26, 33–34, 38–40, 64, 70, 72–73, 114, 129, 133, 137, 143–144, 148
knowledge 6, 19–21, 23, 37, 90, 147–149, 156, 158
   source of knowledge 55–56

labour
   exploitable labour 9, 144
   labour market 32–33, 39, 88, 144
   prison labour 52–53
   welfare and labour rights 6, 25, 30, 39
law
   deportation law 31, 34
   (im)migration law(s) 9, 16, 30, 35, 42, 50, 65, 82, 100, 136
   law enforcement 39, 51, 139
   Law 'on temporary restrictions in the possibility to obtain residency in Sweden' 33
lawyer(s) 17, 20, 21, 32, 44, 54, 68, 71, 73, 81
legal status 25, 53, 143–144
   see also liminal legality
legibility, illegibility 52, 56, 136
legitimacy 56, 64, 83, 87, 113
liminal legality 9–10, 142
   see also asylum; legal status

Mbembe, A. 110, 127
   see also necropolitics

migrants
   migrants' advocacy groups 12, 15, 20
   racialised migrants 34, 38, 40
migration
   (im)migration control regime(s) 7, 25, 29, 33, 35, 136
   migration-related detention 18, 19, 23, 58, 71, 80, 90
   see also Ellebæk deportation prison; incarceration
motivation enhancement measures 2, 94, 105–106, 110
   see also deterrence; Sjælsmark deportation camp

nationalism
   national identity 35
   national order of things 8–9, 19, 64
necropolitics 126–127
   see also Mbembe, A.; violence, slow violence
non-governmental organisations (NGOs) 6, 39, 105, 123, 126, 131, 137, 148, 155
non-*refoulement* 8
non-Western 30–31, 38, 42, 53, 56
Nordic exceptionalism 22, 40
   see also colour-blindness; humanitarianism

Parliamentary Ombudsman 49, 139
penal code 42, 48
police 11, 13, 19, 29, 32, 50, 59–62, 65, 70, 75, 81, 85–87, 91, 98, 101, 103, 17, 119, 128–129, 131, 133
   Danish police 49, 153
   Swedish police 36, 51, 67–68, 74, 121–123, 139
politics of presence 111, 113, 133
precarity
   precarious condition 131, 136
   precarious legal status 12, 25, 144
premature death 5, 15, 16, 22, 41, 58, 108, 114, 140, 152
   see also vulnerability, distribution of vulnerability
Prison and Probation Service 1, 36, 43, 45–46, 50, 73, 98, 103, 153–155
punishment 6, 23, 64, 69, 100, 107
punitive measures 49, 62, 65

race 8, 13, 16–17, 53, 64, 73, 141, 145
  see also racism
racialisation 24, 64, 89
  racial exceptionalism 36–37
  racial homogeneity 22, 35, 37
  racial inequality 16, 34, 37, 41, 53
  racial matrices 53–54, 64, 144
  racial order 81, 145, 147
  racial slurs 54, 57, 65
  see also race; racism; whiteness
racism 16, 30, 34, 37–38, 40–41,
    44, 57, 63–64, 73, 86–87, 145
  see also race; racialisation; whiteness
rationality 90–91
readmission agreement(s) 7, 29, 32,
    122–123, 142
Red Cross 32, 39, 96, 98, 104–106,
    110, 112, 153
  see also humanitarianism,
    humanitarian actors
relational analysis 26
research industry/industries 19, 141,
    147–148
responsibilisation 23, 111, 127, 137
Return Directive 27, 95

Schengen 23–24, 36, 43
  Schengen Regulation 27
seeing 76–77, 88, 131
  unseeing 88
  see also care, care and control
Sjælsmark deportation camp 1, 11,
    22–25, 94, 96, 114, 154
  see also Kærshovedgård; motivation
    enhancement measures
Social Democracy
  Social Democratic government
    (Danish) 30, 31, 93, 98–99, 112
  Social Democratic prime minister
    (Swedish) 33
social services 128–130, 139, 153
  Social Service Act (2001: 453) 130
solidarity 37, 98, 143
  solidarity networks 112
solitary confinement 57, 61–62, 65, 79,
    86, 89, 92
spectacle 51, 75, 98
Stanley, S. N. 11, 22, 93–95, 98, 100,
    114–115, 140–141, 146, 151,
    159
struggle(s) against deportations 6, 21, 23
  struggles by non-deported people 112

  see also activist(s); Castaway Souls;
    Young in Sweden
stuckedness 10, 143
Suárez-Krabbe, J. 22, 26, 30, 37–38,
    41, 42, 90–91, 111–112, 145,
    147
suicide 58, 62, 79–80, 87, 89, 152
surveillance 7, 20, 30, 31, 36, 46, 103,
    119, 129, 142
Swedish Aliens Act 34, 72, 119
Swedish border police 67, 75, 139
Swedish Migration Agency 17, 81, 85,
    91, 117–121, 123, 125, 127–
    128, 130, 133, 136, 138–139,
    140, 148, 153–154
  accommodation units 117, 124,
    131
Syria 28–29, 32, 115, 143

temporary law 33, 133
time
  temporal indeterminacy 11, 100
  temporal violence 58, 109

unaccompanied minors 35, 131–133

violence
  anticipation of violence 58–59, 102
  everyday violence 57, 62
  slow violence 14–15, 21, 23, 95,
    110–111, 114–115, 127, 151
  see also necropolitics
  structural violence 14–15, 40, 59,
    81, 137
  symbolic violence 15
  see also continuum of (state) violence
voluntary return 35, 36, 96, 104, 106,
    118–121, 137
  see also deportation
vulnerability 125, 127, 144
  distribution of vulnerability 13
  see also premature death
  see also deservingness

waiting 9–11, 58–59, 94, 104, 108,
    113, 128, 134–135, 143, 148
  awaiting deportation 43, 46, 51, 77,
    91, 96
  see also boredom
welfare
  access to welfare 12, 25, 30, 118,
    129, 130, 137

(minimum) welfare provisions 23, 40, 95, 104, 117–118, 125, 129
social welfare 19, 39, 117, 118, 124, 131
welfare policy 131
welfare state(s) 5, 22–23, 25–26, 30, 34–42, 76, 83–84, 88, 127, 129, 131–132, 137–138, 140–141, 146
whiteness 20, 56, 81, 90
  see also racialisation; racism

Young in Sweden 132–133
  see also activist(s); struggle(s) against deportations

www.ingramcontent.com/pod-product-compliance
Ingram Content Group UK Ltd.
Pitfield, Milton Keynes, MK11 3LW, UK
UKHW042119180825
461986UK00009B/740

EU authorised representative for GPSR:
Easy Access System Europe, Mustamäe tee 50,
10621 Tallinn, Estonia
gpsr.requests@easproject.com